George Miksch Sutton

George Miksch Sutton

ARTIST, SCIENTIST, AND TEACHER

Jerome A. Jackson

University of Oklahoma Press : Norman

ALSO BY JEROME A. JACKSON

In Search of the Ivory-Billed Woodpecker (Washington, D.C., 2004; New York, 2006)

Nature's Habitats (Washington, D.C., 1991)

This book is published with the generous assistance of William R. Johnson and the Wallace C. Thompson Endowment Fund, University of Oklahoma Foundation.

Library of Congress Cataloging-in-Publication Data

Jackson, Jerome A.
    George Miksch Sutton : artist, scientist, and teacher / Jerome A. Jackson.
        p. cm.
    Includes bibliographical references.
    ISBN-13: 978-0-8061-3745-2 (alk. paper) 1. Sutton, George Miksch, 1898–1982. 2. Ornithologists—United States—Biography. 3. Wildlife artists—United States—Biography. I. Title.
QL31.S96J33 2007
598.092—dc22
[B]   2006027676

The paper in this book meets the guidelines for permanence and durability of the Committee on Production Guidelines for Book Longevity of the Council on Library Resources. ∞

1 2 3 4 5 6 7 8 9 10

*To Bette, Brent, and Matt, who endured years of
my following the "trails" of George Miksch Sutton*

Contents

Illustrations

FIGURES

Preface

One of the nightmares of any biographer is to find the kind of letter I found in the archives of the Western History Collection at the University of Oklahoma. In September 1974, George Miksch Sutton wrote to Robert Storer, a longtime friend at the University of Michigan: "These days I am having some not altogether pleasant hours going through a lifetime's correspondence and destroying most of it." Two months later he wrote similarly to Andrew J. Berger, another friend and former student at Michigan: "For weeks I have been utterly ruthless in destroying old correspondence. Friends argue that I should not do this, that I should put all of this in the archives of one institution or another, but I can't bear the thought of various and sundry Philistines pawing through my letters, deciding what's juicy, etc., etc."[1]

Without doubt, George Miksch Sutton anticipated a biographer. In a 1947 letter to Fred Haecker, he wrote comments about the political nature of the American Ornithologists' Union and added: "What I have just said is not for the record. In fact, I'd appreciate your tearing this letter up rather than having it round for various possible biographers to read."[2]

Although he himself destroyed considerable correspondence, the recipients of his letters often did not. For example, Sutton had a thirty-year friendship with Josselyn Van Tyne at the University of Michigan but then had a bitter falling out. George destroyed all his correspondence with Van Tyne; Van Tyne kept carbon copies of his own letters and all of George's—a treasure to find. Certainly Sutton's efforts made finding his correspondence infinitely more difficult.[3]

George often spoke of writing an autobiography and pondered the kinds of material he would like to have in it. In a letter to John and Eleanor Kirkpatrick he quotes a passage from Pierre Teilhard de Chardin's *The Phenomenon of Man*: "A rocket rising in the wake of time's arrow, that only bursts to be extinguished; an eddy rising on the bosom of a descending current--such then must be our picture of the world."[4] Then, with characteristic enthusiasm, he wrote: "Now isn't this amazing language? I seem to get the same thrill out of it that I get out of parts of the Psalms of David. One of the continuously rewarding by-products of reading is 'surprise passages' of this sort. Were I ever to do an autobiography I'd want to refer to such passages as part of my life--for that's (in a sense) what they are."

George Miksch Sutton was in many ways a Victorian gentleman. He was trained in science but equally versed in art, music, and literature. He was at home before a garden club or in a classroom, in the High Arctic or in the tropics. He wrote as he spoke. I knew George for the last eighteen years of his life and I can still never read his books or articles without hearing him say the words. The exceptions are a few works for hire, in which editors have so curtailed individual style characteristics that the chapters could have been written by anyone; the Sutton voice simply is not there.

George was a wonderful raconteur. He was not a good autobiographer. Certainly we learn a great deal about him from his popular and scientific writings—especially his autobiography, *Bird Student*. But as with the autobiography of his lifelong friend Sewall Pettingill, the "life" ends with completion of his doctorate—in George's case, only the first thirty-four years of a long and productive life.[5]

In 1970 George wrote to his friend Robert W. Storer, then president of the American Ornithologists' Union: "Work on the autobiography (that keeps showing its ugly head) takes too much time, so I probably shall abandon the whole idea. . . . Digging up facts about the past simply takes too much time for a perfectionist or near-perfectionist." His autobiography was not to appear for another decade.[6]

To read any of George's books is to share his life, to see what he saw, hear what he heard, feel what he felt. But the stories he told were often entertaining stories about his observations of human behavior or about birds rather than about George Miksch Sutton. Most frustrating to me, I discovered as I began researching George's life that his wonderfully written autobiography was essentially done from memory. Many of the early dates in *Bird Student* are in error, and crucial details are missing. Where I have found such variances, I have corrected and noted them in this biography.

Finally, George Miksch Sutton is perhaps best known for his drawings and paintings of birds and for the many books and scientific papers he illustrated. In preparing this biography, I was fully aware that most of his finest art has already been published, and I saw little point in providing a sampler of art from his own books. Instead I have assembled a diversity of Sutton art representing various periods of his life and focusing on art that either has not been published or was published long ago or in obscure places. Many of those most familiar with the name George Miksch Sutton will be astounded to see the mushrooms he painted, his drawing of a weasel, a lizard, hunters with a dog, and a decorative border around the prayer of St. Francis of Assisi. Enjoy these. Then return to the beauty we know so well in his masterful portrayal of birds.

Acknowledgments

I am especially grateful to George Miksch Sutton for giving me bird-skinning lessons, sharing his home with me when I came to examine specimens in his care, sharing his perspective on ornithology and bird art in the twentieth century, and offering his friendship. George's wonderful sister Dorothy Miksch Sutton Fuller and cousin Greta Nordstrom and her daughter Shirley Beck opened their hearts, homes, and family to me. Andrew J. Berger, Olin Sewall Pettingill, Jr., Phillips B. Street, and Kenneth C. Parkes followed my journey, suggested avenues worth investigating, and shared details of long friendship with George.

I thank many colleagues and friends of George Sutton's who shared personal anecdotes, correspondence, artwork, and other materials and many of my friends and colleagues who assisted me in gaining access to materials. These include Richard Banks, Pat Bergey, Charles and Mary Brown, Albert Buckelew, Paul and Francine Buckley, Gifford and Grace Bull, Tom J. Cade, Ben and Lula Coffey, George Lynn Cross, Brenda Dale, Ernest P. Edwards, Bruce G. Elliott, John T. Emlen, Robert H. and Mary Frances Furman, George Hall, Karl Haller, Warren D. Harden, Byron and Joyce Harrell, Harry C. House, Douglas James, John Janovy, Jr., William R. Johnson, John E. Kirkpatrick, Henry C. Kyllingstad, David Ligon, Harold F. Mayfield, Frank McCamey, Robert and Marion Mengel, John and Emma Messerly, Linda Minde, John O'Neil, David N. Nettleship, Lew and Kay Oring, Kenneth C. Parkes, David Parmelee, George Lynn Paul, Aevar Petersen, Roger Tory Peterson, Olin Sewall Pettingill, Jr., James A. Pittman, Don Radovich, Amadeo Rea, Orville Rice, C. Richard Robins, Edward Shafter, Steve K. Sherrod, Kristina L. Southwell, Stanley C. Stahl, Peter Stettenheim, Robert W. Storer, Phillips B. Street, John S. Tomer, Jack D. Tyler, Doris Watt, John Weske, and John Wiens.

Others to whom I am indebted for assistance with materials in their care include John Lovett and colleagues at the Western History Collection at the University of Oklahoma; Therese M. Matthews and Gary D. Schnell, Sam Noble Oklahoma Museum of Natural History; R. Jeanne Cobb, Bethany College, Bethany, West Virginia; Bill Cox, Smithsonian Archives; David D. Danneberger, pastor of the Moravian

Church in Gnadenhutten, Ohio; J. B. Milam, McFarlin Library, University of Tulsa; Janet Hinshaw of the Van Tyne Library, University of Michigan Museum of Zoology; the registrar's office, University of Pittsburgh; Dan Smith, art director for the National Wildlife Federation; Marcia Theel and Jane Weinke, Leigh Yawkey Woodson Art Museum; Byron Webster, James Ford Bell Museum of Natural History, Minneapolis; and archivists at the Carnegie Museum of Natural History, Cornell University, Disciples of Christ Historical Society, Oberlin Conservatory of Oberlin, Ohio; Nebraska State Historical Society, Smithsonian Institution, and University of Nebraska.

I am most grateful to William R. Johnson for assistance and generous support that facilitated inclusion of so much of Sutton's art in the biography. My son, Jerome A. Jackson, Jr., assisted with photography and with editing some of the art—and taught me a great deal along the way. My parents, Wayne and Phyllis Jackson; brother and sister-in-law, Mike and Barb Jackson; and sister, Donna Schuff, opened their homes to me on my many trips to Oklahoma.

I thank Sally Antrobus for her superb skills as a copyeditor.

Finally, I especially thank Karen Wieder, Charles Rankin, Eddie Gonzalez, and other editors and staff at the University of Oklahoma Press for their patience and hard work in seeing this book to fruition.

George Miksch Sutton

CHAPTER 1

Family Ties

This is the story of George Miksch Sutton, ornithologist, artist, teacher, raconteur, philanthropist, brother, son, and friend. It is not merely a travelogue of his journey through life, for George himself has provided a wonderful travelogue in his many books and papers. My goal is to provide a view looking over George's shoulder—both from behind him and from in front of him: what did he face, what did he leave behind. And why? And how? What influenced George's life? What and who did George's life influence? What was his art all about? Where did his artistic talent come from? And where did it take him? What was it that set George Miksch Sutton apart from his contemporaries and from ornithologists and bird artists today?

This is an adventure story about a lifelong journey taking a man from the tropics to the tundra on his quest for birds, some of them the rarest of the rare, such as the Ivory-billed Woodpecker. The journey is also a quest for understanding of the relationships between birds and humans, birds and their habitats, light and line, poetry and life. It is a story of lost love between a man and a woman, a story of a deep love for humanity, for birds, and for the natural world.

To understand George Miksch Sutton better, I traced his roots back two generations on each side of his family. My own journey in search of Suttons and Mikschs was literary, electronic, and literal. I traveled to Florida, Ohio, Minnesota, Nebraska, Illinois, Texas, West Virginia, Pennsylvania, New York, Michigan, and Oklahoma, seeking relatives, friends, and clues. A bit here, a bit there, the puzzle of George's family and the fullness of George's life began coming together. Near the end of my journey I found several new leads via the Internet and discovered artwork I had not known about—advertised on E-bay!

George's paternal great grandfather, Samuel Sutton, married Margaret Critton in Virginia on January 24, 1824. Although the family had settled and become established in the South, growing social problems as well as hope for a better job and brighter future for their children led Samuel and Margaret and most of their seven children to leave Virginia in 1841 for central Illinois to take advantage of new land and opportunities. In Peoria, Illinois, Samuel found two job options that seemed viable: work in the coal mines or work in the lumber industry. He chose fresh air and the rigors of being a lumberjack. His choice turned out to be unfortunate. Shortly after he became established in his job, a tree fell on him. He died on December 21, 1841, of a broken back.[1]

The family was destitute. For Samuel's sons this meant no money for continued schooling. Young Critton Sutton (1837–1911), George's grandfather, was then four years old.[2] He grew to know the value of an education, however, and continued to further his education on his own. He became a farmer and married Polly Ann Stowell (1843–1921), who had come from New York. They later moved to El Paso, Illinois, thirty-two miles to the east, where their first son, Frank Eugene Sutton, was born December 23, 1865. A second son, Harry Trumbull Sutton, was born on September 20, 1867. The family grew to include another two children, Elsie arriving in 1869 and Montie in 1879 (fig. 1.1). In 1890 Critton Sutton and his family moved to a farm west of Winnebago, Minnesota. All of Critton Sutton's children were brought up to value education, and at some point each gained employment as a teacher.

Harry Trumbull Sutton, George Miksch Sutton's father, seemed a perpetual student. Frank's daughter Greta Nordstrom, born in 1913 and the only first cousin George ever had, told me that her father could go to school only in winter, attending "normal" school at Valparaiso, Indiana, after the crops were in. Harry, on the other hand, "went to school everywhere and all the time," she said. Greta considered Harry Trumbull Sutton "one of those whose idea of a good time was sitting down and studying the dictionary. He loved words and loved a good conversation, regularly asking: 'What'll we talk about today?' of anyone at hand."[3]

Through the Disciples of Christ Historical Society I learned a good deal more about Harry Trumbull Sutton. He began his career as a pastor in the Church of Christ in Milford, Indiana, serving there from October 1889 to February 1890. From February through July 1890 he was pastor at a church in Decatur, Indiana. Then he studied as a student preacher at Nevada Christian University in Nevada, Missouri, serving for the 1890–91 academic year. (The town and school are pronounced "Nevayda.") Harry

1.1 *The family of Critton and Polly Sutton, George Miksch Sutton's paternal grandparents. (Back row, from left) Harry Trumbull Sutton (George's father) and Frank; (second row, from left) Elsie, Polly, and Critton; (front) Montie. Courtesy of Dorothy Miksch Sutton Fuller.*

continued his studies as a student preacher at Northwestern Christian College at Excelsior, Minnesota, from October 1891 through June 1893.[4]

Following his schooling at Northwestern Christian College, Harry took a position as pastor of a church in Marcus, Iowa, serving from September 1894 through September 1895. During the early 1890s, in addition to his pastoral duties, he traveled from town to town in the upper Midwest with the summer Chautauqua movement, entertaining listeners with his renditions of the classics as well as enlightening them with the gospels. Greta Nordstrom believes that it was while traveling with Chautauqua in the early 1890s that Harry met and fell in love with a young lady who played the piano and guitar and led singing for the group—Lola Anna Mix. While he was a pastor at Marcus, on May 15, 1895, Harry Trumbull Sutton and Lola Anna Mix were married. After their marriage Harry again enrolled in school, this time at Drake University in Des Moines, Iowa, from September 1895 through June 1896.

In July 1896 the Suttons moved to Bethany, Nebraska, where Harry took a position as head of the Department of Eloquence at Cotner College (fig. 1.2). Harry was to teach at Cotner for 11 years, the longest tenure of any job he was to hold.

George's father was also a poet, writing volumes of poetry but rarely getting it published. George commented in *Bird Student* on his father's poetry: "Occasionally Father read us verses he had composed in explanation or dramatization of the [Bible] lessons. The poems bored me dreadfully. I felt they were a waste of time. But Father was dedicated to writing them, and his ability to concentrate while at work on them won my admiration. Mother listened to them faithfully, whether she liked them or not."[5]

One particularly long poem, *The Temptation of the Man Unpurchasable* was published in book form.[6] George was right; it is dreadful. Harry also

1.2. Harry Trumbull Sutton, George's father, during his tenure on the faculty of Cotner College in Nebraska and his campaign as the Prohibition Party candidate for governor of Nebraska. Courtesy of the Nebraska State Historical Society and Dorothy Miksch Sutton Fuller.

published at least one additional small anthology of poetry and left many poems in the files of the Disciples of Christ Historical Society. He was successful in getting other poems published in the *Overland Monthly* and *Christian Century*. While generally spiritual in quality, some did lean toward a "nature" theme. I include one here because I think it contributes to an understanding of Harry's influence on George.

"From My Window" was published in the *Overland Monthly* in 1909, when George was eleven:

> The day is done;
> Soft glows the west;
> The clouds fly by;
> Earth sinks to rest.
>
> Yon distant dome
> Strikes 'gainst the sky;
> The glow meets gloom;
> Stars climb on high.
>
> The hush to hush
> Calls even' song;
> The day is done—
> Night comes along.[7]

Lola Anna Mix had not always been Lola Anna Mix—and she was not happy with her last name. Lola Mix was of Moravian ancestry, and she had been born Lola Anna Miksch. The Miksch family had been in the United States for a long time. George mentions finding the year 1743 carved on the gravestone of Benjamin Miksch in the Moravian cemetery in Bethlehem, Pennsylvania.[8] When the name Miksch had been carved, it was misspelled, then corrected by adding a missing letter above the place where it should have been, providing George with an illustration of the "frugality" of his ancestors. The Mikschs had settled in the Moravian communities in Winston-Salem, North Carolina, and Bethlehem, Pennsylvania. Sometime before 1843 George's great grandfather, George Frederick Miksch, moved to Gnadenhutten (pronounced "Jinaydin-huttin," meaning "tents of grace") in Ohio, with other Moravians attempting to reestablish a settlement at the site of a Moravian Indian mission where a terrible massacre of Christian Indians had occurred in 1782.[9]

It is not certain when the Miksch family arrived in the area, but it was probably about 1824 when Gnadenhutten was platted as a town. In tracing

Lola's roots I found Gnadenhutten a sleepy, well-kept little town that prides itself on its Moravian ancestry. A museum tells the history of the Moravian settlement, and displays include a receipt for piano lessons given by a Miksch. Lola taught piano much of her life. The cemetery reveals that the Miksch name was prominent in Gnadenhutten in the mid-1800s. Many settlers lived near the town, especially just across the river. The attractions of the area included a gristmill that allowed farmers to grind their grain, the wells that had been dug in the center of town, and the Moravian Church.

George Frederick Miksch died in Gnadenhutten in the summer of 1843, three months before his son, also named George Frederick Miksch, was born. This son was Lola's father, George Sutton's maternal grandfather. Sometime in the 1860s George Frederick Miksch married a young woman named Elizabeth, George's maternal grandmother; no last name is given for her in the records. The extended Miksch family, which must have included brothers of the elder George Miksch, seemed to prosper. In 1853 sixteen lots known as the Miksch subdivision were added to the town of Gnadenhutten. George Sutton's mother, Lola Anna Miksch, was born in Gnadenhutten in 1868 to George Frederick and Elizabeth Miksch.[10]

Sometime prior to 1880, responding to the news of richer and less expensive farmland, George Frederick Miksch and his family moved to southern Minnesota. It was hard work, preparing the new land and fitting into a new community that was not dominated by Moravians. Neighbors who could not pronounce their last name forever frustrated the Miksch family. Wanting to fit in, George Frederick Miksch changed the family name to its phonetic spelling: Mix. Lola, then a teenager, did not like the name change.[11]

Nonetheless when Lola enrolled at the Oberlin Conservatory of Music in Oberlin, Ohio, it was as Lola Mix, and she used Mix as a middle name after she married. In 1906 she was listed on the program of the thirty-ninth Annual Convention of the Nebraska Christian Missionary Society, held at Bethany, Nebraska, as "Mrs. Lola Mix Sutton, Song Leader." Although she accepted her father's name change for herself, she perpetuated her Moravian family name by bestowing it as the middle name for each of her children.

A visit to the Oberlin Conservatory revealed that Lola left there after only one year. George's assertion in *Bird Student* notwithstanding, she did not graduate from the conservatory. On her return to Minnesota, she found employment in what she loved--music. She played and taught piano, then joined the Chautauqua movement, serving as pianist and song leader. It was apparently through the Chautauqua movement that Lola met Harry, ultimately returning with him to the church he served from fall to spring and traveling with him on the Chautauqua circuit in summer.

Those must have been happy, exciting days, traveling with a group of other idealistic young people who shared their love of music and culture. Life on the Chautauqua circuit, however, was not conducive to raising a family. Lola and Harry lost their first child, and when they found they were expecting again, they sought the security of a permanent position in a fixed location. Chautauqua had given them the advantage of meeting many people and getting to know numerous cities and towns in the region.

Harry found a seemingly secure and appropriate position at Cotner College, a Christian Church school founded in 1888 in Bethany, Nebraska, a suburb of Lincoln. From their vagabond summer life, the Suttons settled into academia. Born in Bethany, Nebraska, on May 16, 1898, George Miksch Sutton was the oldest surviving child and only son of Lola Anna Mix and Harry Trumbull Sutton (fig. 1.3).

As head of the splendidly named Department of Eloquence at Cotner College, Harry was highly praised in 1906 in the *Cotner Collegian*, the commencement yearbook: "The School of Eloquence under the master hand of Prof. H. T. Sutton has just closed the most glorious year's work in the history of Cotner University. In this one man, we have preacher, teacher, missionary, poet, orator and leader, and we do not blush to say so. He does not blow a big brass horn, nor tell of his ability with flashy handbills, but he has said as much in his students."[12]

Certainly the spring semester of 1906 was a good and busy one for the Sutton family. Young George was in school, his two sisters were still at home, their mother Lola taught piano to a few students, and Harry— Harry was on top of the world. He was well thought of at Cotner and was becoming well known as a speaker at churches around the state and in neighboring states. Buoyed by this popularity, Harry Trumbull Sutton tossed his hat into the ring as the Prohibition Party candidate for governor of Nebraska. The summer and fall of 1906 were filled with campaigning. When election day came, however, Harry placed a distant third in the governor's race, garnering 5,106 votes and beating only the Socialist Party candidate.[13]

Perhaps it was this political failure that led the Suttons to move on. In June 1907 for reasons not known, the Sutton family moved to Ashland,

1.3 Lola Anna Mix Sutton holding her son George on his first birthday, May 1899. Courtesy of Dorothy Miksch Sutton Fuller.

Oregon, where Harry taught at State Normal College. A year later they moved to Eugene, Oregon, where he had obtained a job at Eugene Bible University for the 1908–9 academic year. His salary there was eight hundred dollars per year—down from the thousand a year he had been making at Cotner.[14]

George thought of himself as having "grown up" in Eugene, "almost in the shadow of the University of Oregon buildings." He remembered the town's hills, noting that he used to ride "licketty-split down from the campus" to the level on which his family's house stood.[15]

The Suttons moved again when Texas Christian University in Fort Worth offered Harry a position at one thousand dollars per year. That position lasted from summer 1911 through June 1914, when he was offered twelve hundred dollars a year to teach at Bethany College in Bethany, West Virginia. The pattern of frequent moves and changing jobs was hard on the family, but Harry noted in a letter to the editor of the *State Journal* in Lincoln, Nebraska, that the "changes in geography have had an important effect—they have made a good American of me. That is, I have found much to love and praise in many parts of my native country. North, south, east, west—all are nourishing soils for human rootage."[16]

In spite of such praise as he received at Cotner, Harry Trumbull Sutton never seemed to be able to hold a job for long. The Sutton family story is one of constant uprooting and cross-country travel. According to Greta Nordstrom, Harry seemed not to be very practical, and his family was always poor—in part because he sent a sizable portion of his income off to the missions. Family financial difficulties often led Uncle Milton, George's Aunt Montie's husband, to buy shoes for George and his sisters. The rest of Harry's family despaired that he could not take care of his wife and children, yet he did.[17]

George's sister Dorothy was born in July 1901 in Aitkin, Minnesota, where the Suttons were that summer (see chapter 2). A second sister, Pauline, was born in Bethany in 1903, and a third sister, Evangel (Evie), was born in Eugene in 1908. Being the oldest child and only son allowed development of an exceptionally strong bond between George and his mother, and George was imbued with a sense of seniority and responsibility toward his siblings.

Relatives always considered George to be his mother's favorite child.[18] He was also much closer to his sister Dorothy than to his other sisters (fig. 1.4). Pauline died as a child, but George "looked out" for both Dorothy and Evangel all his life, sending checks when needed and offering emotional support. Theirs was an unusual but close-knit family.

Following an extended illness, George's mother died in Bethany on July 23, 1937. On July 28 he wrote to Frederick Gaige at the University of Michigan Museum of Zoology: "You did not know Mother. But whatever gaiety and a good share of the determination I have is hers."[19]

Dorothy Miksch Sutton Fuller was a wonderful person; I met her in 1993 to discuss family history and George's life. She had studied at Johns Hopkins University School of Nursing and worked as a nurse for two decades before returning to school at Washburn University. She completed a bachelor's degree in 1939 and went on to earn a doctorate in psychology at the University of Kansas in 1947 and served there as an assistant professor from 1948 to 1951. From 1951 to 1955 and 1959 to 1975 she was on the staff at the Menninger Clinic in Topeka, Kansas, serving for many years as chief psychologist in the Division of Child Psychiatry. Between 1956 and 1959 she was a psychologist for the Family

1.4. George and his sister Dorothy on New Year's Day, 1911, at their paternal grandparents' home in Winnebago, Minnesota. Courtesy of Dorothy Miksch Sutton Fuller.

Service and Guidance Center in Topeka. She retired from the Menninger in 1975 and lived out her life in Topeka.[20]

Evangel shared George's love of art and writing, and she helped him with some of his popular writing efforts, such as his first book, *An Introduction to the Birds of Pennsylvania*. She also designed Christmas cards featuring their family home in Bethany, West Virginia (see fig. 3.4). In 1937 she illustrated a book of poetry with fanciful rabbits. During the 1940s Evie lived in Greenwich Village in New York, married physician Harry Swartz, and in 1946 had a son, Mark, who died in an automobile accident as a young man. Evie and her husband moved to Mexico, where she died of cancer on March 8, 1980.[21]

George's father, Harry Trumbull Sutton, continued to serve as a replacement preacher in many different churches. In October 1921 he took a job as pastor of a church in Ocean View, Delaware, serving there until April 1923. In June that year he found a pastorate in a Pittsburgh suburb and served until November 1925. After 1925 Harry occasionally held other short-term preaching positions, the last in Elizabeth City, North Carolina, in 1947. He then retired to Penny Farms, Florida, a community dominated by retired preachers.[22] There he met and married his second wife, Anne, who had been widowed by the deaths of her first two husbands—both preachers. Following Harry's death in 1962 at the age of ninety-five, George and Dorothy kept in close touch with Anne. In 1967 she married another minister, J. W. Creighton. On April 6, 1982, George wrote that "Anne (our step-mother), who still lives in Penny Farms, recently broke her hip. . . . She is, I believe, 91 or 92." Anne died in 1990 at the age of 101.[23]

George's continuing involvement with this aged and distant step-mother, although not a significant factor in his life, further reflected the closeness of the Sutton family. Distant relatives were linked by understanding, support, and sharing. Their closeness included round-robin letters, shared and contributed to by all. Each letter started with one individual—more often than not with George—and comments and news were added by the first recipient, sent on to the next, and so on, ultimately being delivered back to the sender while another was already making its rounds. From an early age George was "cruise director and host" for a remarkable family journey through life—the strong cord that held family together through life's trials.

CHAPTER 2

Growing Up

*I was an unprepossessing youth with a big brown
birthmark just below the right side of my mouth, a
penchant for forgetting to have my hair cut, and a
naiveté close to that of an average small-town yokel.*

—GEORGE MIKSCH SUTTON,
unpublished manuscript

There may be no such thing as a "normal" childhood, unless we define it in terms of our own. It is difficult to imagine someone else's childhood, especially from a different era. As children we are captives of our parents' circumstances in life and are forever influenced by those circumstances. We are also molded by the greater world as we grow up, but that world is perceived differently at different ages. Places where one spent hours playing as a child, remembered as a wild creek and cliff a great distance from home, may turn out upon later inspection to be a drainage ditch and a six-foot dirt bank just two blocks away. The perspective of childhood when drawn from memory alone is a narrow, biased, even romantic perspective, but it truly is as we saw that childhood while living it. Both the memory and the reality are important, however, for it is the reality we experience as children that forms our beliefs, our hopes, and our dreams.[1]

George was born in a small house at the edge of Bethany, Nebraska, but his family also spent time at Aitkin, Minnesota, when he was very young. George did not know why they went to Aitkin or what it was that his father did there. This seems to have been a seasonal home, since his father was continuously employed at Cotner from 1896 to 1907. It is possible that Aitkin was just a pleasant summer home, but it is likely that Harry also had summer employment there. At the time Aitkin was primarily a lumbering community; his father may have worked in a mill there for a while or ministered to the lumberjacks at a small church.

Perhaps George remembered the strange matter of a Ruffed Grouse that drummed on the windowsill of their cabin in the woods near Aitkin, or perhaps this was a recollection reinforced by family tales of the bird later in his life. His sister Dorothy was born in that cabin by the lake in 1901. In 1903 the Sutton family grew once more with the birth of Pauline Miksch Sutton.[2]

With three children in the family, Lola had her hands full. George took on important responsibilities looking after his sister Dorothy, and the two became very close. Dorothy looked up to her big brother, following his lead. George viewed Dorothy as his personal charge, as a student to be taught—especially about birds and other wild things.

In 1950 George returned to Nebraska for a meeting and encountered family friends who had known him as a youngster there. He wrote to his family: "These people all but called me Georgie to my face, which amused me a bit. . . . They had tales to tell about what I had said as a child of four or five, I suppose, and some of these yarns out-mothered mother herself. One was about me and my love for 'the bees, the birds and the flowers'; another was about my insistence of using the word 'urination'; another had to do with going naked or something. What a brat I must have been!"[3]

George's first truly remembered encounter with birds may have come in 1904 or 1905, when he was six or seven years old. He had found a Blue Jay's nest, climbed to it, and stolen a nestling. The nestling Blue Jay must have been about half grown, since George describes it in *Birds in the Wilderness* as "very pretty in his 'baseball clothes.'"[4] In the course of this raid one of the adult Blue Jays attacked him, striking him on the head. As he proceeded home with his prize protectively clutched in his hands, he felt the warm trickle of blood on his forehead. He was thrilled. *He* had been *wounded* by a Blue Jay!

Some mothers understand the impulse to bring home a nestling to "raise" as a pet and sense a child's need for such communion with wild things. Part of nurturing the development of the child is allowing the child to nurture. George's jay was dead within a few days, fed an inadequate diet. Baby birds in the hands of children are like balloons: they give joy and excitement at first, but the venture almost always ends with tears as the balloon bursts or the bird dies. Such emotional trips are an important part of growing up.

Was George first an artist or first an ornithologist? Drawing birds was a compulsion he could not deny. But where did he get the inclination to draw anything? George received his first copy of Frank M. Chapman's *Bird Life* in 1903, at the age of five. By the time he left home he had gone through three copies, cutting the illustrations for study of the birds and of artist Ernest Thompson Seton's techniques.[5] His "professional" career (in the sense of being paid for his efforts) began at least by the age of seven, when he found that he could sell his bird drawings for a penny or a few pennies each. One year for Christmas his parents gave him a stuffed Pintail that he hauled around in a wagon. Neighbors would often bring him dead birds they had found, and George marveled at the way feathers overlapped to form a smooth continuous surface.[6]

Although George rarely mentioned art or birds as interests of either of his parents, his sister Dorothy told me that when their mother was pregnant with George, she bought a bird book and often sat studying it. George's fascination with birds did not arise out of thin air; clearly his mother had an interest in birds and an influence on the development of his passion. In the dedication to his first book, *An Introduction to the Birds of Pennsylvania*, George acknowledges some of his mother's influence, noting that she knew enough about birds "to let me bring them, alive, dead, or worse than dead, into her busy household."[7]

George also told me (and recounts in *Bird Student*) that when they lived in Illinois, his father had shown him how to draw a snipe, and his father's snipe had been a good one. Perhaps there was more of a family influence there than we know.[8]

Few of George's early works survive, but more may yet be found. He noted that among his earliest sketches were drawings he made in the margins of hymnals in church. While his father preached, he carefully studied and drew the birds and feathers that adorned the hats of ladies in the congregation.[9] We can hope someone may someday discover one of these "annotated" hymnals (I keep checking the antique malls and used-book stores in Lincoln).

The Sutton family physician in Bethany, Dr. David Clark Hilton, also influenced George. A young man who had graduated from medical school in 1903, Hilton was interested in birds. Later in life he contributed articles to *Nebraska Bird Review*, the journal of the Nebraska Ornithologists' Union. George was only six or seven years old when Dr. Hilton found him sitting on the Sutton doorsteps cradling a Northern Harrier that had been shot by a neighbor boy. The doctor stopped to give George a lecture about the economic value of birds of prey. George noted that one of Dr. Hilton's hands gripped his medical satchel, while the other spread one of the hawk's wings.[10]

Following Harry's defeat in the Nebraska governor's race, the family moved to Ashland, Oregon. There George was baptized into the Christian Church, an event he remembered well because as a baptismal present, one of the church members gave him a spread pair of hawk wings. Obviously George's interests were already well known outside his family.[11]

In less than a year the family moved again, this time to Eugene, Oregon, where his father taught at Eugene Bible University. George told a little of his life in Eugene, and a little more emerges from comments made in letters to friends and from researching the school where his father taught. The Sutton family lived next to and downhill from the university, and George delighted in pulling his wagon up to the college, then riding it back down.

In 1907 or 1908 George watched Violet-green Swallows near his home and delighted in their seeming play in flight as they caught, dropped, and recaught feathers. He had access to *Home and School*, a popular magazine of the time, and read many of the articles on nature that were written by its editor William L. Finley. George wrote to Finley, believing the editor would be interested in his observations; he thought Finley may have commented on his observations, but I have not found reference to them. George had begun reaching out. He was seeing wondrous things and was anxious to share his observations.[12]

In 1908, at the age of ten, George received from his parents a copy of the latest edition of Frank M. Chapman's *Bird Life*. He ventured into the biology building on the nearby University of Oregon campus and met Professor Albert R. Sweetser. This well-read ten-year-old student of birds must have impressed Professor Sweetser, for he took George on as a helper. George was fascinated by Sweetser's small collection of study skins and the professor encouraged George's interest, allowing him to straighten the collection after class use and to study a copy of Florence Merriam Bailey's *Handbook of Birds of the Western United States* (see chapter 4 for more detail about study skins).[13]

Whether it was a result of his encounter with Fuertes's drawings in *Handbook of Birds of the Western United States* or just a natural progression of his interest, George began drawing birds with a passion. He set up his "studio" at a table in his home. There he prepared a series of bird drawings in pencil, pasting them end to end so that he could roll them up. That scroll of drawings from Eugene is now in the Western History Collection at the University of Oklahoma. The drawings are primitive, one showing a bird imbued with an extra joint on each leg.[14]

When the family moved to Eureka, Illinois, early in 1909, George found a new mentor at Eureka College, biology professor James S. Compton. Compton gave George his first real lessons in preparing study skins.[15]

As George entered his teenage years, with an ever-watchful eye on birds, he began to notice other dimensions in his world. He fell "madly, hopelessly, in love with a girl named Lillian Callahan." He "wrote sentimental poems about her and broke school rules sending these to her desk." George did not seem to be a favorite with teachers—indeed, he seemed not to be enthralled with formal education at all. His informal education, however, seemed almost a full-time endeavor.[16]

All was not well in the Sutton household. Pauline was sick, terribly sick. Harry and Lola took her to Battlecreek, Michigan, to see a specialist, but to no avail. Pauline died in the summer of 1909 and was buried in Eureka. The family grieved. Perhaps it was the trauma they had been through that precipitated the next disruption: Lola left the family for several weeks. According to George, she went to Chicago to study music under Fannie Bloomfield-Zeisler. In her absence, he was sent to spend the winter with his grandparents, Critton and Polly Sutton, near Winnebago, Minnesota. Adding to the calamity, Critton died during George's stay. Dorothy went to live with her aunt and uncle, Montie and Milton Fuller, in Albert Lea, Minnesota. Some years later, after Montie's death, Dorothy would marry Uncle Milton. Evie went to live with Uncle Will and Aunt Elsie Lobb on a farm near Huntley, Minnesota. During this period George got taxidermy lessons from his Uncle Frank.[17]

On May 30, 1910, while walking along a stream near Eureka in Woodford County, Illinois, George found and captured a Black Rail. He took the bird home, kept it for two weeks until it died, then prepared a rough study skin of it. The skin was lost, but years later, in response to an article he had read, George pulled out the notes he had made at the age of twelve and published his record of the Black Rail in the *Auk*, the journal of the American Ornithologists' Union.[18]

George's first published drawing was probably one of a Baltimore Oriole that appeared in a statewide Illinois school journal or annual in about 1910 or 1911. Neither the date nor the title of the publication is known; thumbing through numerous such publications has not yielded the drawing.[19]

In the spring of 1911 the family was reunited in Eureka. George, following up on his Uncle Frank's training, began taking mail-order taxidermy lessons from Northwestern School of Taxidermy in Omaha (as thousands of youngsters used to do; I did it in the 1950s). George used the forceps provided for that course for most of his life. Although he and Dorothy had occasionally gotten together at Uncle Milton's during their separation from their parents, they were relieved to have all the family together once more.

Again and again the family moved. In 1911 it was to Fort Worth, Texas, where George's father became a professor at Texas Christian University. There George became acquainted with the characteristic creatures of the Southwest: scorpions, tarantulas, horned lizards, roadrunners, and the Scissor-tailed Flycatcher. There too George had an adventure that would circulate far beyond the confines of ornithology—his encounter with a Turkey Vulture at its nest in a hollow log. Years later he told the tale in *Atlantic Monthly* under the title "Birdnesting under Difficulties" and included it in *Birds in the Wilderness*.[20] Since then, the story has been published repeatedly in a variety of anthologies, often under the title "An Adventure with a Turkey Vulture."[21] Other Fort Worth encounters with Turkey Vultures led, decades later, to George's publication of a note in the *Auk* on their ability to carry food in the beak.[22]

At the age of fifteen while in the eleventh grade, George published his first journal article. The journal was *Bird-Lore*, a semiprofessional periodical bridging the gap between popular and scientific ornithology. Although his article "A Pet Road-Runner" was published in a special section for the works of children, it was of scientific value. So complete were his descriptions that the article has been cited repeatedly in the professional literature. Already we see attention and emphasis placed on details such as flesh colors and textures: "Their mouths were blood-red, and their black-skinned bodies were covered with long white hairs." We can forgive George the reference to "hairs," since these natal feathers are indeed hairlike. The extent of George's reading and knowledge of birds at the age of fifteen is also revealed by his reference to the emerging tail feathers of the roadrunner chick "reminding one of a Mot-mot, with long quills, and small bursted tips."[23]

No doubt George's self-confidence and motivation were enhanced by the comments of Alice Hall Walter, the department editor, at the end of the article: "The foregoing history of a baby Road-runner is quite unique in the columns of this Department, and the information given will be of value to all of our readers. . . . We shall look forward to a continuation of this particular Road-runner's history." That his work was "of value" to others was critical.[24]

In lieu of high school, George attended college preparatory classes for high school students at Texas Christian University in Fort Worth for a year (not university classes, as might be surmised from a 1970–71 *Who's Who in America* account). George's second scientific publication appeared in the July 1914 issue of the *Oologist*, a semipopular journal that focused on egg collecting but had begun branching out into all areas of field ornithology as egg collecting lost favor.. Simply titled "The Interesting Road-Runner," this paper included measurements and status information for several Texas roadrunner nests and observations of the behavior of nestlings he raised.[25] In 1922 George published additional observations he had made of roadrunners at Fort Worth between 1911 and 1914—this time in a more scholarly format in the *Wilson Bulletin* and illustrated by drawings of adult and nestling roadrunners—demonstrating the rapid maturing of both his science and his art.[26]

The same month, July 1914, the Sutton family moved to Bethany, West Virginia, where Harry had taken a job as a professor at Bethany College. Lola was tired of moving. The children needed more stability. She wanted a real home. George noted that he had "frequently been guilty of wishing for a more sedentary childhood." But putting the best spin on things, he also felt that these frequent moves gave him "an admirable first-hand knowledge of the birds of the United States."[27]

How else did the moves affect George and his sisters? They never had the opportunity to establish long-term friendships with other children, thus family ties were probably enhanced. George and his sisters and parents remained close although they later lived far apart. The Sutton children never had a chance, either, to establish themselves in any kind of dominance hierarchy within school groups. In small schools where a single teacher might have the same students for multiple years, George and his sisters were always the newcomers. Perhaps that is why George noted: "I felt that my teachers did not like me: the thought that any of them might learn to love me, or be truly interested in me, never entered my mind."[28]

In contrast to the group activities often typical for youngsters, it seems that George was more self-reliant, focusing his energies on birds and how to draw them. At Fort Worth he had kept a menagerie of animals, including a skunk, roadrunners, and screech-owls, but birds held his focus.

George had grown accustomed to the boxing up and shipping off of

family possessions for frequent moves. He was used to the family board-
ing a train, carrying as much as they could carry. On this move, heading
for the rugged terrain of northern West Virginia, he carried boxes with
his roadrunners and screech-owls in addition to family items. Although
his childhood had been filled with uncertainty and change, he was now
certain that his life would be devoted to birds.

CHAPTER 3

Bethany, West Virginia

It was about as little as a town could be.

GEORGE MIKSCH SUTTON, *Bird Student*

W hen the Suttons arrived in Bethany, West Virginia, in 1914, George was sixteen, ready for his senior year in high school. There was no high school in the small community, only the Bethany College Preparatory School.[1] Bethany College admitted him as a special college-prep student, and he found the transition to college courses easy. At Bethany George quickly became known and involved in several endeavors. He was on campus constantly and seemed to be into everything. He worked part-time that first fall as a janitor at the school and was responsible primarily for cleaning Oglebay Hall, the science building.

At first Bethany was the perfect community for the Suttons. It was small and culturally oriented; everyone was "family." Being the children of faculty gave George and his sisters status, and they all seemed to fit in readily. Being the oldest, George quickly took charge. One of his early endeavors was the establishment of a club known as the "Mu Nus," consisting mostly of the children of Bethany College faculty. The club put on plays, traveled to nearby Wheeling to see movies, and once picked beans to earn money to support the war effort.

One of George's first jobs as an artist—and the one he considered his "very first professional job"—was sketching the heads of Guernsey calves born into the school's prize dairy herd. They were valuable animals, and these sketches of their unique head markings were how the school kept records on them. The sketches were not portraits, by any means, but simple outlines of the calves on which George drew the unique patterns (fig. 3.1).[2]

George also began learning about the birds near his new home. On November 13, 1914, he made a forty-mile trip to Waynesburg, Pennsylvania, to visit Professor Sam Dickey, James Carter, and Warren Jacobs, all avid egg collectors. His observations on the trip resulted in another early publication in the *Oologist*—which on this occasion succeeded in misspelling not the ever-problematic Miksch but his surname, which turned up as Suttard.[3]

Harry taught oratory and English at Bethany in the fall of 1914. In the spring of 1915, Lola also joined the faculty as an assistant instructor to teach English. She was to teach there only through the spring of 1915. As at other schools, Harry's tenure there was to be short—he taught at Bethany only through June of 1918.[4]

Perhaps it was in one of Harry's or Lola's classes, or perhaps in a class taught by George himself, that a certain Ed Miller, then about fourteen, won an essay contest. For his winning essay, "Why the Mallard Duck Is my Favorite Bird," Miller received a watercolor of a Mallard painted by George (plate 1). That painting has remained in the family and now resides with Miller's nephew, ornithologist John Wiens. In spite of his apparent early interest in birds, Ed Miller did not go on to become an ornithologist, but his talents led him to a career as an English professor.[5]

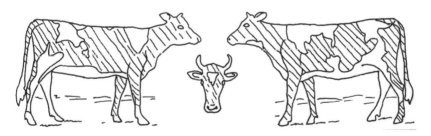

3.1. Schematic drawings of a Guernsey cow from the Bethany College herd during the early twentieth century showing how George drew the pattern of markings to allow individual identification of each animal. Redrawn from records in the archives of Bethany College, Bethany, West Virginia.

In 1915 George published another article in *Bird-Lore*, this time with a drawing illustrating one of the roadrunners he had brought from Texas in a "fright" display (fig. 3.2).[6] The color plate of several juncos in the front of the issue in which his article appeared was by the artist he most admired: Louis Agassiz Fuertes. After considerable discussion with his parents, George wrote to Fuertes, praising the artist's work and seeking help with his own bird art.

Although Fuertes's influence on Sutton is well known and was the subject of Sutton's book *To a Young Bird Artist*, the attention he received from Fuertes was not unique. Fuertes himself had been tutored in similar fashion by Abbott Thayer and felt a lifelong obligation to pass on the tutelage. Fuertes had written to Thayer: "My whole youth was sweetened and deepened, more than any one can know, ever, by the close and lovely contact of those two years under your hospitable roof." No human being, Fuertes wrote, "ever gave me the disinterested and unmeasured affection and priceless help that he so voluntarily gave me."[7]

Fuertes's debt to Thayer could be repaid only by sharing his own skills with other young artists. On January 21, 1916, he invited seventeen-year-

3.2. Sutton drawing of a Roadrunner illustrating its "fright" display, reproduced from Bird-Lore, *where it was published in 1915.*

old George Miksch Sutton to spend a summer with him: "I should consider it a privilege to pass on to you what little of the help and encouragement I could of all that has been so freely lavished on me by my good friends in days and years now past, and if I should seek reward for so poorly doing what was so richly done for me, I should in truth feel like a worse parasite than I hope I shall ever have to feel!"[8]

Summers were sometimes lean; both Harry and George sought summer employment wherever they could find it. Early in the summer of 1916 George worked on a road crew, earning money for his trip to spend the late summer at Sheldrake Springs, New York, with Louis Agassiz Fuertes.

George's time with Fuertes was minimal. At the age of eighteen he spent most of July and perhaps most or all of August 1916 with the Fuertes family, living in a small tent adjacent to their summer cabin at Sheldrake Point on Cayuga Lake. Fuertes's daughter, Mary Fuertes Boynton, recalls the frequent presence of boys aspiring to be artists occupying a tent outside their summer cabin. Wildlife artists Courtenay Brandreth, Conrad Roland, and Keith Shaw Williams were among the others who thus learned from Fuertes.[9]

At Sheldrake Point George marveled at the magic Fuertes wrought with pencil and brush. Standing at the master's elbow he watched as Fuertes showed him how to lay down a wash, how to "sharpen" the point of his brushes by moistening them with his lips, how to correct errors by heavy-handed use of an eraser.

George painted no birds while he was at Sheldrake Point, but he learned how to choose and use the artist's tools, learned the values of light and line, the sequence of jobs in completing a painting, the patience needed to allow paint on paper to dry to prevent muddying, and the rapidity that was sometimes required to achieve brisk transitions between colors. He learned that watercolor has its versatility but that it is a quick medium, with many limitations. Fuertes's letters to George prior to the trip had been like gold to him. The hours he spent studying each were paying dividends as he watched. George left Sheldrake Point with new skills, new faith in his abilities, new motivation, and an old paint box, all gifts from Fuertes that he would carry the rest of his life.

On returning to West Virginia, George continued correspondence with Fuertes, sending him paintings for critique and savoring each return letter, reading and rereading them. The letters provided keys to overcome technique problems and encouragement to continue. George's painting of an Eastern Wood-Pewee is one of the efforts Fuertes praised (plate 2). To

George, Fuertes was proof that one could make a living and a contribution to humanity through bird art. Sutton shared those letters in *To a Young Bird Artist*, and other advice given him by Fuertes occasionally crept into his correspondence and writings. In response to a comment by ornithologist Robert Arbib about the awkward poses of birds in some of Audubon's paintings, George recalled that Fuertes often told him: "Don't try to show all sides of a Wood Duck, even though you know it's beautiful all the way around."[10]

As George's art matured, he sought further advice from Fuertes. How does one go about selling bird art? What is a fair price? What should one look out for in a contract? George was anxious to make a name for himself as an artist—and make a living.

While George was in New York, his family moved to Pughtown, twenty-five miles north of Bethany, where Harry served as a summer replacement preacher. At Pughtown, Harry found himself among fundamentalists and was quite outspoken about their extreme religious views. George suggested to him that he take a less critical approach. During that summer Harry became somewhat of a local legend for his passion for hollyhocks. He is said to have carried seeds with him, planting them wherever he went. He also collected seeds from his flowers, taking them back to Bethany and planting them there the following year.[11] The Bethany area today has a profusion of hollyhocks, and three people told me of the man who loved them so much that he planted them everywhere.

George began studying the birds of the region, building up a collection of study skins and drawings. He held various part-time jobs to support his hobby and his social life. He also joined the Psi Chapter of Beta Theta Pi fraternity and became active in campus politics. The review of the social side of his academic career in the 1919 Bethany College annual, *The Bethanian*, suggests that he was incredibly active in campus life, although in his autobiography George says he was not an athlete and therefore was not a "big man on campus." At Bethany College he was president of the Neotrophian Literary Society (1916), a member of the Science Club (1917), Y.M.C.A. Treasurer (1916–17), secretary of the Oratorical Association (1918), and a member of the Men's Glee Club (1919). From 1917 to 1919 he was on the staff of *The Bethanian* and the college newspaper, the *Bethany Collegian*. He was treasurer of the junior class (1917) and president of the senior class (1919). During 1917 and 1918, he was also an instructor in "Prep. English." The last item on his list of credentials is "Barbarian."[12]

Once at Bethany, George's mother was ready to settle down. She had a nearly grown son and teenage daughters. They needed stability. She needed stability. Following the spring semester of 1918, however, for what George suspected was his father's outspokenness, Harry Trumbull Sutton's contract at Bethany College was not renewed. To make matters worse, Harry had invested the family savings in the Chemical Lime and Sand Company—an investment that paid no returns.[13] To Lola it made no difference. They had moved enough. She was staying put, and he would have to find another job locally. Thus Harry Trumbull Sutton's career as an academic came to an end, and he took a job as a salesman at a mill in a neighboring community and worked as a replacement preacher at various churches between 1918 and 1920. The loss of his job at Bethany College was a frustration from which Harry Trumbull Sutton never seemed to recover.[14]

When Harry got a temporary preaching job near Pittsburgh, George accompanied him and Harry took his son to see the Carnegie Museum. At the museum, as they passed a huge door labeled "Laboratory of Ornithology," George paused and asked if he could go in. Harry offered to accompany him, but George said no. There George met W. E. Clyde Todd, the curator of birds. Amazingly, Todd knew of George, having read his articles in the *Oologist*. In the course of their discussions, George asked for a job—"no matter how small the salary might be." Todd was impressed with this young man and agreed to hire him for the summer. George left, full of excitement. The barbarian was to be an ornithologist affiliated with *the* Carnegie Museum! On the trip home, however, his enthusiasm was overshadowed with fever and illness. The next day he was covered with red spots: an ornithologist with chicken pox![15]

In June 1918 George moved to an apartment in Pittsburgh and began work at the Carnegie. One of his first tasks was to add color to the black-and-white illustrations in the *Catalogue of Birds in the British Museum*, a task that sharpened both his artistic skills and his knowledge of world birds. He also curated the egg collection, learned the technique of relaxing poorly made specimens, honed his skinning techniques, and was given the opportunity to write materials for the public describing the displays.[16]

Although he returned to Bethany College in the fall of 1918, George maintained contact with Todd and others he had met in Pittsburgh and busied himself not only with class work, fraternity life, and campus politics as president of the senior class, but also with birds and finding outlets for his bird art. He bought a life insurance policy from Charles B. Horton of Pittsburgh, paying the premiums for the policy with paintings of common birds instead of with cash. Many of the paintings began as sketches drawn surreptitiously during the droning of class lectures at Bethany. The forty-five paintings done for Horton—each seven inches by twelve inches—were later purchased by Frank Preston of Butler, Pennsylvania, who donated them to the Audubon Society of Western Pennsylvania. George's art was opening possibilities, gaining him recognition, and beginning to pay bills.[17]

In support of the war going on in Europe, Bethany College joined many other schools in sponsoring a Reserve Officer Training Corps (ROTC) program, and at Bethany it was mandatory for all male students. George thus donned a uniform, learned to march, and took part in traditional ROTC activities. He describes his ROTC experience matter-of-factly—almost as if he relished it—in *Bird Student*, choosing not to elaborate on the rather incredible period of turmoil in his life deriving from his ROTC service.

It was in spring 1919, the last semester of his senior year, that ROTC service at Bethany was made mandatory. George was senior class president, active in fraternity life, and convinced that this military organization was inappropriate as a mandatory part of life at a church-sponsored college such as Bethany. He was outspoken, rallied support for opposition to the mandatory ROTC, and was one of the leaders of a strike against the school. All but seven of the 498 students enrolled during the spring semester of 1919 joined in the strike, refusing to enroll in ROTC or to attend classes unless the mandate for enrollment in ROTC was reversed. Newspapers were quick to report on the conflict, and the challenge to authority at Bethany escalated with each news story or editorial. George was at the center of it. The ringleaders of the revolt, including George, were expelled just weeks short of graduation. On June 15, 1919, at the peak of the fracas, Bethany College President Thomas Ellsworth Cramblett, who had instituted the mandatory ROTC service, died. It was a terrible time at Bethany and a terrible time for George. He did not graduate from Bethany in 1919, although his photo appears in the college annual for that year as a graduating senior.[18]

George left Bethany and began full-time work at the Carnegie Museum as an assistant curator, although he recognized the importance of completing his undergraduate degree and sought reinstatement as a student. In late 1922 he worked out an agreement with Bethany College: he would be reinstated as a student and allowed to graduate in the spring of 1923 if he would take a special course in English literature from Anna Ruth Bourne. He bought a car and learned to drive with the patient help of Pittsburgh friends Eloise Anderson and her family. During the week he worked at the Carnegie; on weekends he traveled the sixty miles to Bethany to meet with Mrs. Bourne. George's family had moved to Akron, Ohio, where his father had taken a job at a rubber company. Thus, on those weekends when he returned to Bethany, George stayed with Professor H. Newton Miller and his family. It was Miller's son, Ed, who had won George's Mallard painting in the essay contest. In June 1923 George was awarded a bachelor of science degree from Bethany College, paving the way for graduate school. As a gift for their generous hospitality, George presented Miller and his wife with a painting of a Purple Finch (plate 3).[19]

In spite of the trauma of his senior year, George remained loyal to Bethany College all his life, donating specimens, funds to equip a lab and to support activities of the George Sutton Audubon Society, and maintaining contact with the school on several levels. A biology lab and a chemistry lab at Bethany have been dedicated to him. The Sutton biology room today includes a bronze bust, a portrait of Sutton by Kenneth Washburn, and an original Sutton painting of two Hooded Mergansers, which had appeared on the cover of *Outdoor Life* magazine (plates 6, 16).[20]

In the spring of 1952 Bethany recognized George's accomplishments and loyalty by awarding him an honorary doctorate. It was a grand occasion and, of note, the Bethany College president who conferred the degree was Wilbur Haverfield Cramblett, son of president Thomas E. Cramblett who had died during the student revolt in 1919. Wilbur Cramblett mispronounced George's name miserably during the presentation: George "Miske" Sutton—and the local newspapers dutifully printed it as pronounced.[21]

Once George was gainfully employed full-time, his first investment was a home for his family, who had moved back to Bethany. He bought them a home adjacent to a stream near Bethany College. It came to be known as Pebble Hearths because of the stones that George and his sisters brought up from the stream at the back of the property and cemented into the hearth (fig. 3.3).[22] George worked in Pittsburgh, Harrisburg, and elsewhere, but for years Bethany and Pebble Hearths were truly home to George and his family—roots had taken hold. Pebble Hearths was a refuge, a place where he could work uninterrupted. Most of the illustrations for Todd's *Birds of Western Pennsylvania* were painted in that house.[23] Lola's ashes would in due course be buried on the slope behind the house.[24]

Pebble Hearths remained recognizable in 1990 from family photos and a block print George's sister Evie had done in 1938 as a Christmas card (fig. 3.4). It was rental property in need of attention, likely housing another generation of Bethany students and nurturing other careers. George's skills as an artist grew within its walls and in this small-town setting as he returned again and again, to family and solitude, to work on drawings and paintings that were to contribute to his success at the Carnegie and beyond.

3.3. *Pebble Hearths, the Sutton family home in Bethany, West Virginia, as it appeared in 1990. Photo by Jerome A. Jackson.*

3.4. A block print featuring Pebble Hearths, created by Evangel Miksch Sutton as a family Christmas card in 1938. Courtesy of Dorothy Miksch Sutton Fuller.

CHAPTER 4

Pittsburgh and Carnegie

I never learned to like the city. . . . The trees and grass were real enough, but their being where they were, between walks and pavement, always neat, always carefully trimmed, made them seem part of an evil plan to make captivity tolerable.

GEORGE MIKSCH SUTTON, *Bird Student*

eorge's summer job in 1918 working with W. Clyde Todd at the Carnegie Museum in Pittsburgh had begun what was to be a long association with the museum and an opportunity for professional development and establishment of friendships and other contacts that would further his dual career as an artist and ornithologist. Todd had found an enthusiastic, capable assistant, and George had found a way to pursue a career in ornithology.

With minimal funds and no automobile, George rented an apartment near the museum.[1] He quickly became friends with museum curators, preparators, and artists, assisting them and learning from them, sometimes joining them for concerts, dinner, or birding on weekends. During this period he also made the rounds of churches of different denominations and participated in séances, in part out of curiosity, in part as the social thing to do. Apparently attending the séances was to please Todd.[2]

Contacts with the birding community in the Pittsburgh area came quickly as George became active with the Audubon Society of Western Pennsylvania and a local chapter, the Sewickley Valley Audubon Society.

Among his friends Rudyerd Boulton, an ornithologist and artist colleague from the Carnegie, was one of George's roommates in Pittsburgh.[3] Bayard Christy, who would be a lifelong friend, was a patent lawyer from Sewickley and longtime president of the Sewickley Valley Audubon Society and editor of their journal, the *Cardinal*.[4] Christy persuaded his new young friend to draw a cardinal for the journal cover. It was also at about this time that George painted a male Northern Cardinal for his sister Dorothy. Cardinals were probably George's favorite songbirds, and he painted or drew them many times.

Christy introduced George to John Bonner Semple, an inventor, arms manufacturer, and trustee of both the Carnegie Institute of Technology and the Carnegie Institute, from which he served on the institute's Museum Committee. Sutton and Semple quickly became good friends, and George always referred to him as JB.[5]

During the summer of 1920 George participated in his first major expedition as Todd's assistant, the ninth Carnegie expedition to explore the Labrador Peninsula. Todd, Sutton, and two crew members traveled north along the Labrador coast from Battle Harbour to Port Burwell at the tip of the peninsula from July 7 through August 18. Then they split up, Todd to travel southwest from Port Burwell on another boat, while George traveled southeast on the *Northern Messenger* with the hired crew.

On August 27 the navigation chart on board the *Northern Messenger* blew overboard and sank out of sight just before they were hit by a squall. Although he tried to hire a local pilot to bring him into one of the ports, George was unsuccessful, and they ended up trying it on their own, only to run aground in shallow water. The stranded sailors drew lots, and George stayed with the yawl while his crew took a small boat to find help ashore—fifteen or twenty miles away. George feared that with an incoming tide he might be swept out to sea, but a day later the crew returned with help, and they made it into port. The trip was successful, producing many specimens for the Carnegie, but because of the lateness of their journey's start, ice floes, and fall ice conditions, it was less of a success than they had hoped. It had, however, given George vital experience and begun his love affair with the far north. His accounts of this, his first real expedition, in *Birds in the Wilderness* and *Birds of the Labrador Peninsula*, reveal the excitement and adventure and his inimitable style. It was during this trip that George first grew the moustache that became part of his persona.[6]

Following his return from Labrador in mid-September and before Todd had made it back, George wrote up his notes as a narrative of the trip and in a series of species accounts. He then prepared a large water-color painting of a Glaucous Gull that he had sketched at a nesting colony at Cape Mugford, Labrador. Then he turned to other paintings Todd had requested: a Santa Marta Parakeet and Colombian Chachalaca —birds he had never seen except as specimens. These were used by Todd and Carriker in their monograph on the altitudinal distribution of Colombian birds. He also painted an illustration showing variation in head and neck plumage pattern in crested quails from Colombia, and this was used as color plate illustrating an article by Todd in the *Auk*.[7]

George joined the American Ornithologists' Union (AOU) in 1919 and the Wilson Ornithological Club (now Wilson Ornithological Society) in 1920 and became active in both professional organizations, influenced not only by Todd but by the steady stream of ornithologists who visited the museum to examine specimens. In 1920 he attended his first AOU meeting in Washington, D.C., and was pleased that his painting of the Glaucous Gull was included in a special exhibit of bird art at the Library of Congress. It was an ambitious event that featured works of twenty-four contemporary bird artists and twenty-four bird photographers, in addition to items of historical interest from the library's collections. George reveled in the attention his painting received and also in being able to peruse the art with his mentor, Fuertes, discussing the merits of each work.[8]

Through the Department of Fine Arts at the Carnegie Museum, George became acquainted with other artists, new techniques, and new media. He first tried his hand at oil painting at the suggestion of Remi Santens, chief taxidermist at the museum. In 1921 he painted the background for a habitat group featuring a Great Horned Owl poised to capture a skunk. Pleased with the results, he did additional oil paintings, working after hours at the museum to take advantage of better lighting there. His oil portrait of a Great White Heron was displayed at the Carnegie and then at the Cooper Ornithological Society meeting at the Los Angeles County Museum in 1926. It was later published as a halftone in the *Condor*, journal of the Cooper Ornithological Society. Harry Harris commented on the oil paintings George exhibited in California: "The two oils . . . by their striking contrast and sheer beauty did not fail to arrest the attention and praise of everyone. His superb Great White Heron . . . illustrates admirably the decorative value of the bird, and also shows the great and rapid strides this artist has recently made in the development of his expression."[9]

Just after Christmas in 1921 George traveled to Chicago to attend his first Wilson Ornithological Club meeting, where he also gave his first scientific paper at a professional meeting. It would appear as "Some Remarks on the Facial Expressions of Birds" in the *Wilson Bulletin* in 1922. Clearly George's writing skills were still developing: the paper was wordy, with many long, awkward sentences and flowery prose. Yet the message was a good one that made unique points, blending the benefits of his artistic eye and knowledge of avian anatomy with keen insight into animal behavior. His insight had come from both field observations and having hand-raised many birds. His thesis was that birds *do* show facial expressions but that they are centered on the eyes, especially the positions and movements of the eyelids, and on slight manipulations of facial feathers.[10]

The lead article in the first issue of the *Wilson Bulletin* for 1922 was also George's: "Notes on the Road-Runner at Fort Worth, Texas." Illustrated by two full-page black-and-white plates, the article is an extension of his three earlier notes. It provided additional observations and insight concerning the behavior of both wild and captive roadrunners, the fruit of his careful observation and of keeping a detailed journal even as a child. Another publication initiating a series of leaflets at the Carnegie Museum featured a photograph of the Red-shouldered Hawk diorama at the museum along with George's plea for students to learn about and protect birds. Also in 1922 George began a lengthy correspondence with Harold Bailey about illustrating Bailey's planned book on the birds of Florida.[11]

George's employment at the Carnegie provided him an audience that appreciated his combined knowledge of birds and skill as a bird illustrator, and it provided opportunities to use his art professionally. He reached out to the ornithological community. As an advertisement, George published this full-page notice in *The American Oologists' Exchange Price List of North American Bird Eggs*. The statement is so revealing of his artistic goals that I reproduce it here in its entirety.

Fellow Bird-Men:
To faithfully reproduce the delightful glimpses every Ornithologist has of birds in the field;
To artfully idealize the bird without neglecting its scientific structure and color;
To portray the living bird in its most natural and therefore most charming aspects—to these tasks have I set my hand and brush.
Very truly yours,
George Miksch Sutton
Carnegie Museum, Pittsburgh[12]

Perhaps this advertisement was "in-kind" payment for use in the catalog of George's black-and-white plate of two unidentified eggs showing proper marking of eggs for collections.

With the confidence of a professional and praises from the ornithological community, George became an artist for hire. Jobs came quickly. An early one was local. Pittsburgh businessman and amateur ornithologist T. Walter Weiseman decided he wanted to prepare a field guide for the identification of birds of prey. He asked George to prepare line drawings that could be used to identify hawks in flight as well as perched.

George prepared twenty-five drawings of thirteen species and sent them to Weiseman in October 1922, noting: "Each one has been worked out with the specimen in hand, and they do not in all cases agree with Mr. Ernest Thompson Seton's diagrams, done some years ago. The adult male bird only is considered, although as you know, the real difficulty in identifying hawks in the field, as well as in the laboratory, comes with the females, and particularly immature birds. . . . To me this work has [been] most interesting, and I have learned a great deal. I shall be glad to see your writeups when they appear."[13]

Weiseman's publication apparently never came to fruition. In time the drawings were donated to the Cleveland Museum of Natural History, where they remain today (figs. 4.1, 4.2). Another assignment did appear in print. William Dawson, completing his mammoth *The Birds of California*, included George among his illustrators, though rather late in the game: George and Fuertes are each represented in *The Birds of California* by a single plate. George's contribution was a portrait of a pair of Lawrence's Goldfinches.[14]

In 1923 George began a long association with the National Association of Audubon Societies (later the National Audubon Society), by contributing bird records from southwestern Pennsylvania to the "Seasons" reports in *Bird-Lore*, the predecessor of *Audubon* magazine.[15] He also began painting the seventy-six plates for H. H. Bailey's *The Birds of Florida*.[16] He had never been to Florida and could only imagine the habitats from written descriptions, photos, and the artwork of others. Many of the birds he knew only from the study skins at the Carnegie. He worked on the plates in the "bird range" at the Carnegie, where he had ready access to study skins as well as good light.

A study skin is a bird that has been skinned and stuffed with cotton so that its wings are folded against its body as if at rest, and its legs are crossed and tied together, usually with the string of a specimen label that provides documenting information for the specimen. Study skins lack the

4.1. A perched Osprey. Black-and-white wash drawing commissioned by Pittsburgh businessman T. Walter Weiseman for a guide to hawk identification that apparently was never published. Courtesy of the Cleveland Museum of Natural History.

4.2. View from below of an Osprey in flight. Black-and-white wash drawing commissioned by T. Walter Weiseman for a hawk guide never published. Courtesy of the Cleveland Museum of Natural History.

lifelike pose of a taxidermy mount but allow scientists to take standardized measurements and also allow for ease of storage in minimal space in insect-proof metal cabinets. A bird range, such as George worked in at the Carnegie, Cornell, and in Michigan and Oklahoma, is a room in which there are many such cabinets filled with specimens.

With his bachelor's degree from Bethany firmly in hand, in the fall of 1923 George enrolled in graduate school at the University of Pittsburgh, a part of his life with which he was apparently not happy, since he makes no mention of it in *Bird Student*. When he contemplated applying for graduate school at Cornell University in 1928, he noted: "My school work and publication of papers have been in a singularly disorganized state since taking my B.S. at Bethany; I should have had an M.S. from Pitt a year ago, but there was some confusion as to my registration, apparently."[17]

Records at the University of Pittsburgh indicate only that George took one zoology course in the fall of 1923 and two more in the spring of 1924. A brief biographical sketch in *Audubon* indicated that George had also taught "Ornithology" at the University of Pittsburgh in 1925, although there seem to be no other records of this. It is easy to understand why George might not have been the best of students in classes at Pittsburgh since during this period he went on extended expeditions for much of both semesters.[18]

At the beginning of his first semester as a graduate student at the University of Pittsburgh, he was once again in the far north (fig. 4.3). From August 19 to October 11, 1923, he traveled with Todd to the James Bay region of northern Quebec on a trip funded and led by Semple. The purpose of the James Bay trip was to obtain specimens for a Blue Goose exhibit at the Carnegie. In 1923 the nesting grounds of the Blue Goose were unknown, but it was known that large concentrations of Blue Geese assembled along both shores of Hudson Bay, funneling south toward James Bay and the United States. Traveling by canoe down the Abitibi and Moose rivers, the "Blue Goose Expedition" surveyed the birds of the region and collected many specimens. However, obtaining the Blue Geese that were the main focus of the trip was dependent on arrival of cold weather farther to the north, wherever it was that Blue Geese were nesting, to drive migrant geese southward. Toward the end of the expedition, as the first ice was appearing on local ponds, the party was rewarded with all the geese they needed.[19]

In the spring of 1924, in what might have been an extended "spring break" from George's graduate work, he and JB tied a canoe to JB's car

4.3. George at a camp site near the south end of James Bay in northern Quebec during the 1923 Carnegie Museum Blue Goose expedition. Courtesy of the Carnegie Museum of Natural History.

and headed to Florida. JB had a winter home in Coconut Grove, near Miami. George was anxious to see some of the Florida birds he had been painting, and Todd was anxious to have them bring back specimens for the museum. They were in the field most of the time from March 10 to April 3, much of that deep within the Everglades.[20]

In addition to doing course work at the University of Pittsburgh, George served on the local committee for the annual meeting of the American Ornithologists' Union, held November 10–13, 1924, at the Carnegie Museum. His major role for the meeting was the organization of an exhibit of contemporary bird art. He worked closely with the Department of Fine Arts and was successful in obtaining the works of thirty-one artists. The AOU's report of the meeting referred to the exhibit as exceeding the one that had been held in the Library of Congress two years earlier, hailing it as "the chief feature of the meeting." This success was soon followed by George's appointment as Pennsylvania's first "state ornithologist." He was moving to Harrisburg and on to new challenges.[21]

At the Carnegie George had gained entry to professional ornithology. He had learned about museum work: how to prepare specimens, catalog them, protect them, and use them for scientific research. He had also learned about the logistics of field expeditions to distant, remote areas, how to be self-sufficient, to handle various kinds of boats, and to find his way in poorly known wilderness.

Although he had been incredibly busy with projects for the museum and outside commissions for artwork and truly enjoyed most of his colleagues at the museum, George was feeling uneasy about his relationship with Todd and in 1924 was looking for other opportunities. In *Bird Student* he suggests that Todd was not happy with his taxonomic efforts.[22] Perhaps Todd was also uncomfortable with the extent of George's outside work. Perhaps it was because George wanted to be something more than an assistant curator. Or perhaps it was simply time to "fledge" from the institution that had nurtured his development. But were there other reasons he wanted to leave Pittsburgh? Did it have anything to do with his work as a graduate student at the University of Pittsburgh? Did it have anything to do with more personal matters—such as his relationship with a young woman named Eloise?

CHAPTER 5

Eloise

hrough Sewall Pettingill I learned of an important personal crisis in George's life sometime between 1924 and 1929. Pettingill describes it briefly in his own autobiography but also discussed it with me and in letters to George's sister Dorothy.[1] Perspectives from her and from George's cousin Greta Nordstrom and a few additional mentions in personal correspondence in various archives supply the only other details—though none of the correspondence was with Eloise herself.

Sewall Pettingill first met George in the fall of 1930 when they were both graduate students at Cornell. It was that fall, Sewall said, that George confided to him that prior to going to Southampton Island he had been engaged to be married and that he was to have been married on his return. When he returned from Southampton, to his complete surprise, his fiancée, Eloise, had already married someone else. During his graduate student days at Cornell he spoke repeatedly and with bitterness of this rejection, and Sewall said there were days when George would hardly speak to anyone. He referred to George as being in a "blue funk" at such times.[2]

In October 1934, when Sutton and Eleanor and Sewall Pettingill were driving to the AOU meeting in Chicago, George asked them to stop as they were driving through Batavia, New York. He wanted them to meet Eloise. They visited for about half an hour, after which he said only that he felt "relieved." That was the last time he ever mentioned Eloise to Sewall.

What about this love lost? Who was Eloise? Piecing the story together as best we can is of importance in understanding George.

Eloise was Eloise Anderson of Pittsburgh. George mentions her in his autobiography: "Rud Boulton introduced me to a young lady named

Ruthanna Anderson, who lived with her younger sister Eloise and her widowed mother at 4626 Fifth Avenue, a house that was to become a kind of second home. At 4626 things that mattered were talked about, the music was fine, and meals were celebrations. The Uncle Jared mentioned in conversations was none other than Dr. Jared P. Kirtland, for whom the Kirtland's Warbler had been named."[3] George added in his autobiography: "Had it not been for those three charming Anderson ladies, I might never have learned to drive a car. But I wasn't well enough off to buy one."

What George did not reveal was that in 1922 his roommate Rudyerd Boulton had "fixed" George up with a blind date with Ruthanna.[4] George then became a friend of the family. Their home became his home away from home, and he often traveled with them on weekends. And George did buy a car—he had to have one in order to make the weekly trips to Bethany in the spring of 1923 to complete the requirements for his undergraduate degree. Presumably it was during the fall of 1922 that the Andersons gave him driving lessons. In time he fell in love with the younger sister, Eloise.

In a letter to Pettingill, George's sister Dorothy provided support for Sewall's story and an indication of what we cannot know: "I have been going through George's letters to the family and to me (letters that I have kept since 1935). I am turning them over to the Archives at the University of Oklahoma. I have gone over them very carefully, as you would surmise, deleting what should be deleted."[5]

Among the deleted materials, she said, was a letter from George dated December 17, 1962, referring to a visit from Eloise—Eloise Anderson Ray. Although Dorothy destroyed George's letter, she quoted extensively from it in her own letter to Sewall. George had said: "I was depressed by this visit, so depressed that I gave in and went to bed early. Eloise's husband looked so hopelessly done-in and (I hate to say this) like a victim of gross over indulgence; his very shape made me miserable—fat, flabby, etc. I'm an old meany to say this, but it's the way he impressed me. I felt shamelessly 'young and spry' by comparison and why should that have made me feel guilty? Answer me that!" A pang of jealousy for a love never quite forgotten?

Dorothy went on to say: "Your having told me that George had been engaged to Eloise before he went to Southampton Island helped me to understand why George had reacted as he did to the Rays' visit." *Dorothy had not known of George's engagement.* Both in her letter and in conversations with me, Dorothy indicated that all she knew of the relationship between George and Eloise came from Pettingill; she noted that a biography of George "would certainly not be complete" without it.[6]

Greta Nordstrom knew few details but told a slightly different story. George had told her that Eloise turned down his proposal, after which he told his Uncle Frank, Greta's father, that he was "through with women."[7]

George later made brief reference to Eloise's family in a letter to George E. Gifford, Jr. In discussing Gifford's article about the Kirtland's Warbler, Sutton notes: "The [Kirtland's Warbler] is of great interest to me partly because, when I was living in Pittsburgh many years ago I became acquainted with a Mrs. Hartley Anderson, who must have been related to Jared Kirtland, for they and her children (a son and two daughters) always referred to Dr. Kirtland as 'Uncle Jared.' The Andersons once drove me to Youngstown, Ohio, to visit some of their relatives and we stopped in Poland long enough to look at the Kirtland house."[8]

George left Pittsburgh in 1925 to assume the position of state ornithologist in Harrisburg. He would leave that job in 1929 to spend a year on Southampton Island in the Arctic. Did Eloise remain living in Pittsburgh? If so, how often could he have visited her? Not often, it would seem, busy as his career was. Did she tire of waiting or coming in second in competition with George's career?

As best we can understand what happened, it appears that George was in love with Eloise and that before he left for the Arctic, he may have proposed to her but been turned down. A rejection would explain why nowhere in his diaries of his year in the Arctic does he mention Eloise. He does mention many individuals—fraternity brothers, other friends, and family—and he frequently received messages from them broadcast by the Pittsburgh radio station KDKA (see chapter 7). The only comment in his diary that may be a reference to Eloise is an entry on Wednesday, April 9, 1930, just after he had found the first Snow Buntings that had returned from the south: "I think that never before did I get such reassurance and strength of revival of hope from the return of any spring bird—the winter has seemed so difficult from the human relationship standpoint—whereas it might all have been so pleasant!" I suspect, however, this reference in his diary is to difficult relationships that developed within the Southampton community during the long winter.

One might think that at least some of his family would have known—especially his sister Dorothy, with whom he was always close. Having been rebuffed and then absent for a year, George may have had hopes of rekindling his relationship with Eloise, only to find on his return that there was nothing to be rekindled.

His feelings about losing Eloise may have been behind his words of comfort to an anguished friend years later: "A man's heart can be smashed so flat that there seems no hope of its ever functioning again. It is at times of such a sort that one's friends ought to step in and be what they can be. . . . At any rate, just between ourselves, I can ask God's blessing upon you and offer once more my friendship, for what it is worth. So many of the finest things in the world are to be had, like air and sunshine, for less than the asking. We have only to take them—deep into our systems as we would take a deep, deep breath."[9]

George apparently continued to maintain some contact with Eloise's family long after his return from Southampton Island. For example, in a letter to his own family on March 12, 1950, he noted that he would be giving a talk in Pittsburgh on the way to the Wilson Club meeting and "probably will drop round to see Mrs. Anderson."

And there is one more possibly relevant fragment. In the Western History Collection at the University of Oklahoma is the following undated poem that may have been meant for Eloise, the girl he had left behind. One can imagine George composing it in the darkness of the arctic winter on Southampton Island, in the cold room above the store at the trading post, perhaps looking at a snapshot:

What of the future, my beloved?

What is the future but each moment as it passes,
No sooner mentioned than arrived and gone?
What is sunset or midnight or darkness
But a way of remembering that there is a dawn?
Heaven is not a time or place
Beyond the farthest year, or cloud, or sea;
Heaven is now, this fleeting instant,
Wherein I look at thee.

The poem is signed simply "GMS."

CHAPTER 6

Pennsylvania State Ornithologist

To *the student of the distribution of bird life the rugged mountains, high plateaus, deep, broad valleys, rivers, and lakes of Pennsylvania present a fascinating problem.*

W. E. CLYDE TODD, *Birds of Western Pennsylvania*

Leaving the Carnegie Museum and Pittsburgh may have been a wrench, but at Carnegie, George was not his own man. He was Todd's assistant. Other factors may have been involved in the decision as well, as we have seen. Perhaps George's graduate school experience at the University of Pittsburgh had been a frustration. There was no ornithologist there under whom to work. Perhaps there had been difficulties in his relationship with Eloise Anderson. For certain, however, the position as state ornithologist for Pennsylvania offered a title, status, a better salary, and the independence that George sought. It also offered added opportunity for connections with commercial publishers and the direct charge of work on behalf of the state's birds.[1]

George's new position was officially called "Chief of the Educational Service of the Board of Game Commissioners" for the Commonwealth of Pennsylvania. Seth Gordon, the executive secretary of the board, described the position: "Recently the Board decided to add an Educational Service to its staff and place a trained ornithologist in charge. They assigned to that service not only all ornithological matters but also other activities pertaining to the education of the public on the work of the Board. [This person] is, therefore, in reality the official state ornithologist for Pennsylvania."[2]

Undoubtedly the title "state ornithologist" was preferable to George. But what does a state ornithologist do? He was the first person ever to hold the position in Pennsylvania, and he would in part define it. Clearly it was a political position involving a great deal of interaction with the public and a great deal of work with mammals as well as with birds.

As state ornithologist George had to move to the capital, Harrisburg. There he roomed for awhile with businessman Charles Beck and his family.[3] In performing his duties George was often away, traveling around the state, interacting with hunter groups, studying the problem of growing deer populations, looking at the economic value of birds, and weighing the role of hawks and owls in nature. He met many people who were to be supportive of his many endeavors. Almost immediately he located collections of birds that were no longer wanted and he was able to secure some of these for his recent alma mater, Bethany College.

A curious article in the *Bethany Collegian* on February 4, 1925, announced George's new position as Pennsylvania state ornithologist and mentioned that he had been awarded an honorary doctorate.[4] No details are given as to the nature or source of the doctorate and apparently this was an exaggeration, but it was at this time that George earned the nickname "Doc," by which friends knew him the rest of his life. Another article on the same page of the paper reports on eighty-five mounted birds that George had secured for Bethany College, ten of which he had mounted.[5] Most of these birds were still in the biology department at Bethany in 1996.

In late February 1925, during the transition from Carnegie to Harrisburg, George made one of his many trips to Pymatuning Swamp in northwestern Pennsylvania. It was about as far as he could get from Harrisburg and remain within the state. It was a chance to visit one of the places he had grown to love, and a time to reflect. This time he was accompanied by his sixteen-year-old sister Evie and they had a grand time. George found magic in certain places. Pymatuning was one; the Black Mesa of western Oklahoma and Rancho del Cielo in Mexico were others. All three were transition areas—where birds from north or east mingled with birds from south or west in habitats that were also transitional. George was intrigued by the dynamics of these populations and contributed greatly to our understanding of them.[6]

George's first year as state ornithologist was an incredibly busy one. He had to win the support of hunting clubs and to deal with problems facing game species, but he also wanted to raise awareness and appreciation of songbirds. He traveled extensively in the state, speaking to sportsmen's organizations and civic clubs, championing both hunting and conservation and promoting an appreciation for songbirds as well as game species.

His first major publication for the Game Commission, *A Year's Program for Bird Protection*, appeared in early 1925 and was illustrated with his own artwork and photographs from commission files and from colleagues around the state. George made a case for protecting most hawks, but also strongly endorsed hunting of game birds and killing of some predators, especially feral cats. He addressed all types of bird mortality, making some statements that seemed apropos at the time but that would be viewed as "politically incorrect" today, voicing then prominent ethnic stereotypes: "The foreign element in our population is a serious enemy of birdlife. Chief among these offenders are the Italians. . . . These Italians in America are sometimes difficult to deal with, since they are temperamental in nature, and resent interference."[7]

At the same time George defended "the small boy who goes about with stones, sling-shot, or other weapon," noting that he is "not always a serious enemy of bird-life, and he often later becomes a splendid bird student and ardent conservationist." Well ahead of his time with a refrain often heard today, George acknowledged the contributions of hunters to conservation through their license fees and suggested: "If all bird-lovers each year paid for a license they might be in a better position to criticize methods of enforcement and demand their views on protection of wildlife be heard. . . . Why should not all bird-students join the sportsmen in defraying the expenses of law enforcement, winter feeding, and maintenance of State refuges?"

The pamphlet concluded with information on the economic value of birds and on attracting birds with feeders, housing, and water. George also promoted the idea that birds were worthy of protection for aesthetic reasons alone. Although he said there was very little original in it, the pamphlet was favorably reviewed in the *Auk* and *Wilson Bulletin* as promoting sound conservation.[8]

Ruffed Grouse populations plummeted in 1924, and one of George's first tasks was to attempt to find out why and what could be done about it. He contacted game agents and visited hunters and hunting clubs throughout the state seeking information about the grouse. By late 1925 he was able to report that the likely cause of the decline was the cold, wet spring, which had resulted in nest losses, but that surviving adults were in good health and the population would rebound if protected. He praised hunters for their conservation efforts and rallied them to support a closed season on Ruffed Grouse to facilitate their recovery.[9]

Although employed by the state of Pennsylvania, George continued his illustration efforts for other projects. In 1925 he did a color plate featuring a tightly arranged group of diverse birds—ranging from penguins to ostriches and sparrows and everything in between—for a dictionary published by the John C. Winston Company of Philadelphia. The same publisher also used this plate as a frontispiece for William Atherton DuPuy's *Our Bird Friends and Foes*, published in the same year (plate 4). George later regretted having done the plate and many drawings for the book, feeling that they were among his worst work. He was particularly embarrassed by his drawing of a female Wood Duck carrying a chick from its nest (fig. 6.1); we now know that Wood Duck chicks leave the

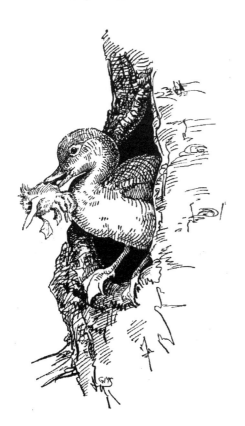

6.1. *Sutton's drawing of a female Wood Duck with a chick in her bill was a product of his imagination; the behavior depicted is now known to be biologically incorrect. George considered this and other drawings in* Our Bird Friends and Foes *to be among his worst.*

nest on their own. His immature American Golden Plover is credible, but its feathers are not (fig. 6.2). Several illustrations involve dramatic behavior, including encounters between species such as a Red-shouldered Hawk and a Great Horned Owl, allowing Sutton to insert a "story" into DuPuy's text (fig. 6.3).[10]

George became increasingly involved with the Wilson Ornithological Club. In 1925 he drew a male Wilson's Warbler for the cover of the *Wilson Bulletin*, which in 1926 replaced the Wilson's Phalarope that had been in use since 1916. The phalarope had been drawn by Karl Plath, former curator of birds at the Chicago Zoo (later known as the Brookfield Zoo). The new cover was used by the society through 1962, when it was replaced by another Wilson's Warbler illustration by Sutton.

6.2. *An immature American Golden Plover drawn by Sutton for* Our Bird Friends and Foes *illustrates his growing ability to capture the essence of a species and to provide the impression of feathers without the detail. Later he was not happy with these efforts. This immature Golden Plover, a species with which he was very familiar, was one of his better drawings in the book.*

6.3. *A dramatic chase is captured in Sutton's drawing of a Great Horned Owl about to steal a squirrel from a Red-shouldered Hawk. It was one of several "action" drawings he included in DuPuy's* Our Bird Friends and Foes. *Such action had rarely been portrayed in bird art.*

The March 1926 issue of the *Wilson Bulletin* also featured a color frontispiece of an American Avocet by Sutton. This seems to be the first color plate to have appeared in one of the major ornithological journals.[11]

In addition to his duties with the state Game Commission and his various ornithological activities, George was also involved in the Harrisburg Community Theatre, following somewhat in his father's tradition. In 1926 he was elected president of the Community Theatre.[12]

Bird banding was still in its infancy as a scientific tool when George obtained his permit. He was never a systematic bander but banded birds opportunistically, or to assist others, especially his students, in specific projects. On May 12, 1926, he banded a Common Loon that had mistaken wet pavement for a stream and had been captured unharmed. It was found dead a year later on the north shore of Lake Ontario.[13]

In the summer of 1926 George took leave from his job for another expedition to James and Hudson bays with Todd and JB. It was another search for Blue Geese, and they were hoping to find nests. Again the party split up, George and JB taking one route, Todd and colleagues another. On this expedition JB fell and severely injured his shoulder. In obvious pain, day after day he grew weaker, and George feared that he might die. No nesting geese were found, but the party collected many specimens for the Carnegie and established new bird records for Labrador; JB survived.[14]

In late August 1927 George was dealt a hard blow: his friend and mentor Louis Agassiz Fuertes had been killed on August 22 when his car was struck by a train in upstate New York. A friend had seen notice of the accident in the newspaper. George was shocked, wounded, suddenly very lost. He locked his office door and sat in silence for a long time, then went to his window. A cardinal fluttered against the glass, and the expression on the bird's face reminded him of Fuertes. Fuertes could have captured that moment on paper, he thought. Fuertes would be remembered for his ability to capture such moments. George wrote in *To a Young Bird Artist* about "human beings who take the time to look, really look, at living birds and at pictures of them. What could be closer than that, I ask, to immortality?"[15]

In some sense Fuertes's death in 1927 elevated his art in the same way that untimely death has altered our views of other great people. Fuertes had been Sutton's mentor, and George rallied to his defense whenever Fuertes's work was criticized (although he would occasionally find fault with specific Fuertes works himself). An article in *Coronet*, for example, compared the art of Fuertes with that of Rex Brasher, who was quoted as suggesting that Fuertes's work would have been better had he not been busy raising a family. Sutton was livid. He wrote to Bob Storer: "The thing makes my blood boil." In fury he labeled the author as "probably the sort who would identify a road-runner as a chicken hawk and a pileated woodpecker as an oddly colored penguin."[16]

Fuertes's death left a void, and it was a good business strategy for George to defend and promote Fuertes, although one doubts whether he thought of it in these terms. Much of Fuertes's art became very public as a result of his illustration of innumerable government publications, and it continues to be used today. But publishers constantly seek new material and Sutton—as Fuertes's student and defender, as the successful illustrator of *The Birds of Florida*, and later as resident bird artist at Cornell—was heir to many of the illustration jobs that came along. With Fuertes's early assistance and promotion, George had established his own clientele, but now many others came knocking.

In 1926, perhaps as a result of contacts made through his position with the Pennsylvania Game Commission, but also because of his link with Fuertes, George began a series of contributions to *Outdoor Life* magazine (plate 5). These included cover paintings of a flock of Gadwall (September 1926), a Wild Turkey (February 1927), Ruffed Grouse (August 1927), a pair of Hooded Mergansers (December 1927), and a pair of Northern Shovelers (December 1928). As he was preparing to leave for the Arctic in 1929, George's paintings of a pair of Prairie-Chickens (January 1929), and a pair of Northern Pintails (April 1929) appeared as color plates in *Outdoor Life*. The original painting for the Hooded Merganser cover (plate 6) hangs today in the Sutton Laboratory at Bethany College, Bethany, West Virginia, where its origin and history had been forgotten.

Another job that was probably "inherited" from Fuertes was that of providing bird illustrations for Thornton W. Burgess's *The Burgess Seashore Book for Children*. For that volume George provided three color plates: Herring Gull and Common Tern (plate 7); Black-bellied, Semi-palmated, and Piping plovers; and Black-crowned Night-Heron and American Bittern.[17] Fuertes had illustrated some of Burgess's earlier books.

Popular belief of the time cast birds of prey in the role of villain, and the shooting of hawks and owls was considered good sport—especially during fall migration, when migrating raptors would pass along north-south ridges by the thousands, riding air currents thrust upward as horizontal winds hit the steep slopes. The Kittatinny Ridge near Philadelphia was one of the favorite shooting sites. Part of George's job was to look at the influence of hawks and owls on game populations, to answer queries from hunters, and to make recommendations relative to providing bounties to encourage the killing of predatory birds. George came to the defense of most hawks and owls, contributing popular articles to newspapers and magazines calling for an understanding of the positive role of these birds in nature. It was quite a balancing act, because his job was a political one and his constituency consisted largely of hunters, who were convinced that hawks and owls were bad.[18]

In 1928 George published his first book, *An Introduction to the Birds of Pennsylvania*. And proud he was of the effort. Following the style used in Audubon's and Wilson's great efforts of a century earlier, the title page provided his professional pedigree: "State Ornithologist of Pennsylvania, Chief of Bureau of Research and Information Pennsylvania State Game Commission, Member of the American Ornithologists' Union, Etc." The dedication in the book was to his mother: "My mother thinks she does not know much about birds; but she knew enough about them to let me bring them alive, dead, or worse than dead, into her busy household, and I think she is a good ornithologist." His sister Evie was also acknowledged for her help.[19]

The book sports a color frontispiece of a pair of Baltimore Orioles on the limb of an apple tree in flower. The plate is not merely a vignette of the birds but a portrait of them in their habitat. Although it is a beautiful portrait of the birds and apple tree, the right foreground seems "muddy" and overworked. The dust jacket features a handsome male Northern Cardinal, head back and mouth open in song, perched on a forsythia branch in full bloom (plate 8). The species accounts are illustrated with 175 small pen-and-ink sketches that are remarkable in providing the key features for species identification. George would doubtless have preferred color illustrations, but he capitalized on the black-and-white, pointing out that it kept the book more reasonably priced and that the black-and-white drawings could become a good teaching tool. He suggested that as one identified a species, the drawings could be carefully colored with crayon or watercolors and that teachers might thus combine artwork with nature study. Good ideas have a way of returning: this is the kind of interdisciplinary effort that some progressive teachers use today.

When *Introduction to the Birds of Pennsylvania* came out, Witmer Stone gave it a mixed review in the *Auk*. On the one hand, he was glowing in his praise of George's line drawings, noting that Sutton was one of the best bird artists in the country. The magic of Sutton's drawings was that "his ability to present an identifiable portrait of a bird without the use of colors is well shown. . . . In every case he has caught a characteristic pose and has brought out the color values in black and white in a remarkable manner." On the other hand, Stone chided Sutton for leaving out the King Eider, several of which had been killed near Harrisburg, and lamented that Sutton had not gotten the assistance of someone who knew the distribution of birds in the eastern part of the state.[20]

George had by now clearly established a reputation for his illustrations. Between 1928 and 1931 he published twelve color plates in *Bird-Lore*, the journal of the National Association of Audubon Societies. Although he had earned his position within American ornithology, no doubt it was to his benefit that the journal was published in Harrisburg, Pennsylvania, where his office as state ornithologist was located. His *Bird-Lore* plates were specifically designed to focus on plumages of males, females, and sometimes juveniles within species or species groups. His efforts included several woodpeckers and cuckoos (plate 9).

From May 20 to July 3, 1928, Sutton, Todd, and JB were again in Labrador, this time accompanied by J. Kenneth Doutt, an undergraduate in mammalogy at the University of Pittsburgh. This was Carnegie's twelfth (Sutton's third) expedition to Labrador. Plagued by dangerous ice floes being blown in near shore, the group had to confine most of their activities to areas along coastal rivers. It was on this trip that George met Sam Ford, a chief trader for the famed Hudson's Bay Company. Sam Ford and George talked of Blue Geese; although this was a commonly hunted bird, its nesting grounds had yet to be discovered. Sam knew Blue Geese well—and he had talked to Eskimos (as the native inhabitants were then called) who had seen Blue Geese nesting at Cape Kendall. Sam promised to help George find the nesting ground if George would spend a year at his trading post at Coral Harbour near the south end of Southampton Island. The Hudson's Bay Company had established the trading post at Coral Harbour in 1926, and a supply ship visited the post once each year.

Sometime between June 5 and 8, while the party was camped near the mouth of the Kegashka River, a most unexpected visitor happened upon their camp: Arthur A. Allen from Cornell University, who was gathering background information and photos for his book *The Book of Bird Life*. This encounter is not mentioned in accounts of the Carnegie expedition, but in an August letter to George, Allen wrote: "I certainly enjoyed my short trip along the Labrador coast immensely and secured some very satisfactory pictures of the birds. It certainly added to the pleasure of the trip to be able to exchange greetings with you in that bleak land. Did you take a photograph of your camp there at the Kagashka River? I am working up a lecture 'June on the Labrador Coast' and it would add considerably to the human interest of the lecture if I could show a picture of your camp and mention the meeting."[21]

George had known Allen through the AOU, had met him at meetings, and had corresponded with him regarding the grouse problems in Pennsylvania. He was well aware of the graduate program in ornithology at Cornell; its potential appealed to him, and his position as state ornithologist was becoming increasingly bureaucratic and political. He was ready to move on and was contemplating simply leaving his job to spend a year on Southampton Island to search for nesting Blue Geese. Graduate school was another possibility. Perhaps his trip to Southampton could result in a dissertation. On August 22, 1928, he wrote to Allen: "I am expecting to spend the year July, 1929–August, 1930 at Southampton Island, Hudson Bay, and want to know whether the authorities at Cornell will let me select the thesis Fauna of Southampton Island for a doctorate degree. . . . I should like to line up with you and Cornell in this Southampton work, and want to get matters in perfect order before going North."[22]

Allen responded positively on August 31, noting that he was having the Cornell graduate school send an announcement and application materials for their program and that three years of residency would be required for a Ph.D. He added that George could register "in absentia," and one or two years away from campus would count as resident time.[23]

George responded forthwith: "I shall not be surprised if I resign from my present position just prior to going to Southampton Island, since a trip of this kind naturally means a considerable hiatus in the work of this bureau. Just what I will do upon my return I cannot say at the present time although there seems to be a considerable demand for bird illustrations and it may be that I will turn my attention toward lecture and illustrative work."[24]

By the end of September George had submitted his application to Allen for approval and it had gone on to the graduate school. In February 1929 he again wrote to Allen, inquiring about costs for graduate school, possibilities for having time to do outside lectures, space for his collections and art, potential problems if he were late to arrive in the fall of 1930, and about potential illustrating jobs.[25] Everything seemed to be falling in place. And then George fell.

In March 1929 he investigated a possible Peregrine Falcon nest (which turned out to be a Common Raven nest) a couple of miles south of McElhattan, Pennsylvania. He had gone to McElhattan to give a lecture to a sportsmen's group, arrived early, and learned of the possible nest. He *had* to know if it was a Peregrine nest. In his business suit he went to the site, climbed fifty feet up a sheer cliff to the nest, and fell, breaking ribs and vertebrae and injuring a collarbone. A woman writing for a Philadelphia newspaper wrote the following tribute to his efforts:

> Doc Sutton once had a cravin'
> for catchin' a Loch Haven raven.
> But stepped off the edge
> of a fifty-foot ledge,
> And the pieces were hardly worth savin'.[26]

George was briefly hospitalized in Lock Haven. On his return to Harrisburg he stayed with his assistant Leo Luttringer and his wife while he healed. In a letter to his sister Dorothy he noted that in spite of his convalescence he was painting and was finishing up several commissioned works: illustrations for *The Burgess Seashore Book for Children*, for *The Birds of Minnesota*, and for a new series being published by the Nebraska Ornithologists' Union. He added: "What fun! It looks as though I were really an established bird-painter at last."[27]

Leo later typed George's letter of resignation for him. Throughout his tenure as state ornithologist George had maintained contact with Todd, making frequent visits to Pittsburgh to deliver specimens recently collected or to examine specimens for one of his many projects. He had discussed the trip to Southampton with Todd and JB. The Carnegie Museum wanted the specimens; JB would pay for them, and that would finance the trip. No ornithologist had yet found the nesting grounds of the Blue Goose, and George was determined to be the first. He was going to Southampton and then to graduate school at Cornell.

CHAPTER 7

Southampton Island

The Eskimos that inhabit this vast heap of rock call it Shugliak: the Island-Pup that is Suckling the Continent Mother Dog. They never call it Southampton Island.

GEORGE MIKSCH SUTTON, *Eskimo Year*

L ying near the western edge of the mouth of Hudson Bay, Southampton Island is just south of the Arctic Circle and is now part of Canada's Nunavut Territory. At sixteen thousand square miles in extent, it is among the three dozen largest islands in the world. It is a rocky tundra landscape during the brief summer. To the north and east, elevations reach nearly two thousand feet; to the south near Coral Harbour there are limestone plains and plateaus that reach less than six hundred feet above the sea.

Coral Harbour on Southampton's southeast coast was George's destination. JB had driven him to Montreal to board the Hudson's Bay Company supply ship, the *Nascopie*, and JB and George's Bethany College Spanish teacher, Pearl Mahaffey, were there to see him off on July 16, 1929. Then it was northeast down the St. Lawrence River to the Atlantic and northwest across the Labrador Sea along the coast of Labrador, through the Hudson Strait to Baffin Island, and finally to Coral Harbour on Southampton.[1] The journey took a month as the ship stopped to unload supplies and drop off passengers at Hudson's Bay Company trading posts all along the way. For some, such as Coral Harbour, it was only once a year that supplies were replenished and furs picked up in exchange.[2]

George's trip to Southampton Island is chronicled in his *Eskimo Year* as well as in multiple scientific papers (some of which served as his Ph.D. dissertation) and popular articles. David Parmelee, who received his own Ph.D. working in the Arctic as Sutton's graduate student, would become imbued with a polar obsession after reading Sutton's *Eskimo Year* as a youngster. In his foreword to the second edition Parmelee described the book as "an unusual blending of a unique people with a unique wildlife."[3]

George had no training as an anthropologist, yet *Eskimo Year* and his popular article "Quaint Folk, the Eskimos" are narratives that provide considerable insight into the Aivilikmiut, the people with whom he lived for a year. The Aivilikmiut were a people described in early narratives more often by missionaries than by scientists. George's article about them appeared in *Atlantic Monthly* and was later reprinted in *Reader's Digest.* Through his contacts with Sam Ford and the Hudson Bay Company, George arranged to stay at the post from mid-August 1929 through mid-August 1930. He would thus be able to greet the Snow Geese when they arrived in spring and to document their nesting.[4]

His departure from Pennsylvania was with great fanfare and with the aid and blessings of dozens of people—friends he had made in Pittsburgh, Harrisburg, and throughout the state. Leo Luttringer and his father gave George a canvas photographic blind. The Scranton Camera Club provided him with photographic equipment. Even the Girl Scouts of Harrisburg helped out, sending along boxes of jewelry for Eskimo children. Francis Coffin and his wife, friends from Scranton, had given him a watch with a radium dial for the long dark winter—they had called it "Sunny Jim," and it served him well.[5]

The *Nascopie* arrived at Coral Harbour on Southampton on August 17. There George was met by Sam Ford, Sam's nineteen-year-old son Jack, two French missionaries, and, as George said, "Eskimos and Eskimos and Eskimos." These were to be his daily companions, his close, *constant* companions, for the next year. Sam Ford spoke English, his son and the missionaries spoke less English, and most of the Aivilikmiut spoke only the Inuit language Inuktitut. During the long trip from Montreal George had had daily lessons in Inuktitut, but his cultural journey was going to be a long one.[6]

By mid-August the Southampton summer was nearly over, and he needed to make the best of what was left. For his first weeks at Coral Harbour he spent three to four hours afield each day and often took extended trips away from the post. Preparing specimens, drawings, and paintings and keeping them all from being destroyed by mice, dogs, or greasy fingers of curious observers were daily challenges. George was given an unheated room over the trading post in which to work, and ice crystals would sometimes form on his brush as he was painting.

Food required significant adjustment. George had packed some potatoes and oranges, but these would not last long. His diet regularly included raw fish and various kinds of blubber, and in *Eskimo Year* he seems to dwell on the matter, giving vivid descriptions that seem designed to disgust squeamish readers. He too was squeamish—indeed revolted by the texture—and the very idea of eating raw fish and blubber, as his journals reveal—but fuel was not available for cooking on extended trips, and the high energy provided by the blubber was essential for survival.[7]

Throughout his year on Southampton, George kept a journal chronicling his daily activities, scientific observations, the precise eye color of this or that specimen as it was being skinned, and his personal feelings. Reviewing his journal entries alongside his recounting of the daily events in *Eskimo Year* is illuminating. To be sure, George's journal is the foundation of *Eskimo Year*, but it was a mere road map for the wonderful tales brought out on the printed page. In places the road map goes to places not touched by *Eskimo Year*; and in places poetic license has *Eskimo Year* differing in details from the journal.

Journal entries paint a routine of feverish fieldwork as long as the weather was good, with specimen preparation, journal writing each day, and drawing and painting as time permitted. Evenings were often spent in storytelling and playing cards, and the French missionaries occasionally joined in. Sam Ford was busy running the trading post, so it was his son Jack who usually assisted George, and they became close friends. The word was put out that animals should be brought to the "doctor" for his work. George was especially thrilled if they were brought in alive so that he could document accurate flesh colors, posture, and facial expressions. Dealing with such captives was often a challenge. On October 18, for example, he wrote in his journal: "It is so stormy to-day that I did not go out; besides, I had a young King Eider which was to be painted, and some skins to finish. The Eider, feet tied and wings wrapped up in a soiled gray shirt, made a nice subject, and I worked on him until I got the desired facial expression. He has extremely strong wings & he got out of his wrappings three times, raising several pads & hurling various objects off the table & down the steps."[8]

Other challenges included getting the Aivilikmiut to understand just what it was he wanted. A woman brought in fresh skins of some puppies she had killed for George; another brought in a whole tray of seal heads with skulls bashed in. George wanted the skulls as specimens, but the provider thought he wanted the brains, eyes, and tongues to eat. As he noted in his journal, "What a queer nut they must think I am, asking for seal heads to eat!"[9]

During George's arctic year he had no way to contact the outside world except for messages he sent back on the supply ship that had taken him to Southampton. Among the last messages he sent was one to Arthur Allen at Cornell, checking one last time on possible living accommodations when he arrived at Cornell.[10]

George could and did receive messages from the outside world, however. They were broadcast on two AM radio stations, WCKY in Cincinnati and KDKA in Pittsburgh. These radio stations broadcast personal messages to explorers and others after the normal broadcast day had ended. WCKY broadcast such messages on Wednesday nights and KDKA on every other Saturday night.[11]

Radio station KDKA surely had one of the most powerful radio transmitters in the world in 1929—perhaps the most powerful. During that year, KDKA broadcast news and messages to George in the Arctic and to Admiral Richard Byrd in the Antarctic. Messages were often long and personal—usually read by the announcer but at times given in person. Recipients could only listen—and listen they certainly did. KDKA was a highlight of George's routine, and he often gathered his Aivilikmiut friends with him around the radio to hear those messages from so far away.[12]

George's mother played the piano for him, and in December the Bethany College Orchestra played for him. His fraternity brothers from the Beta Theta Pi Chapter at Bethany sang for him. Members of the American Ornithologists' Union and the Wilson Ornithological Club were notified in the *Auk* and the *Wilson Bulletin* of George's expedition and his accessibility through KDKA announcements: "Mr. George Miksch Sutton is now on Southampton Island, Canada. The Broadcasting Station KDKA broadcasts to the far north twice a month. Messages for Mr. Sutton may be sent through this station. . . . His friends are invited to send some word to him through the long winter."[13]

The WCKY and KDKA broadcasts were increasingly important to George as the nights and his isolation from friends and family grew longer. Sometimes there were no messages; sometimes the reception was too poor to receive them. On October 20 he struggled to tune in to hear Lewis Kaufman, the usual radio announcer, and later wrote:

> Our three-hour session with the radio last evening was a bitter disappointment. I didn't hear a word from home & it was after hours dialing that we heard Lewis Kaufman's voice at all. He was then in the midst of a letter from Arthur Hen, & I heard most of a long letter from Leo about the Office & Game Commission, but not a word from home. I fear it will seem rather long before November 2, especially with the knowledge that we may not be able to hear decently, even then, what is being said to us from so far away.[14]

On Sunday, December 15, George was ecstatic:

> KDKA's broadcasting of messages to me last night was little short of perfect. We could all hear mother's playing & voice, & it was a wonderful experience to hear her: how impossible the thousand miles of water, ice & rock between here & Pgh. seemed. Many messages surprised me greatly, & I wonder if someone hasn't been carrying on a special campaign in my behalf. Harold Griffen, for instance! I have scarce thought of him for years! And the friends at Lincoln, Nebraska, and the man in Italy, whose name I did not get—and Dorothy Jessup, & the Game Commissioners of Pa., & Sam Church, & Dr. Holler, and so on. It was a great treat for me. And the boys seemed to enjoy it too.[15]

During that broadcast, however, George learned that a party of Canadians led by Dewey Soper had won the race to discover nests of the Blue Goose. While he was en route to Southampton, they had been on their way back from Baffin Island, where they had found the geese. George was surprised by the news and looked forward to finding Blue Geese on Southampton as well. His notes reflected surprise at the color of the eggs: "We were all especially interested in the accounts of Soper & the Blue Goose. From 1 to 5 eggs, & *white*. . . . I expected they'd be pale olive-green, or maybe bluish." George did find nesting Blue Geese on Southampton, including pairs that were mixed. Snow and Blue geese were the same species.[16]

In late November George noted that the missionary priests had been down and that they had had a pleasant time. His journal notes for the day end with a description of "Dick, the cannibal."

> Dick was in last evening. He has long wavy, dirty hair, red-rimmed small eyes, and a rather hunking gait. Sam calls him the cannibal. And of

course a story was forth coming. This man, at point of starvation, shot his daughter in the chest with a shotgun, then told her to fetch ice to thaw for boiling her! The poor girl went & was able to bring back the ice before she died. Dick was dreadfully afraid of the police for a while, but lately he has been less blue about it. Sam says the man would not nowadays, harm a mouse![17]

George's journal for the next day notes that he and John Ell, Sam Ford's right-hand Aivilikmiut at the trading post, started off for East Bay on a caribou hunt at about ten o'clock. He describes the cold and the day's trip and indicates briefly how John Ell made them an igloo. As it was being built Dick appeared, helped John finish the igloo, and decided to spend the night. In *Eskimo Year* George tells the story differently—it was not "Dick, the cannibal" who arrived but "Khagak, the cannibal"; presumably Khagak sounded more authentic.[18]

As the days lengthened and warmed ever so slightly in the spring of 1930, life on Southampton stirred as well. An hour-and-a-half program that came through clearly on KDKA especially warmed April 5. The next day George described it in his journal:

Well, last night's KDKA program was a wonderful surprise & gave both Jack & me a great deal of happiness. Heard every word & note come through clearly and Jack seemed to get almost as much kick as I out of the band, the beautiful . . . songs, & the messages. The whole hour and a half were a succession of . . . thrills. . . . How proud I was of the college orchestra or band & of Dr. Weimer, & the Beta Boys, & Mother. It all seemed a good deal like a happy dream.[19]

Eskimo Year presents a wonderful, positive adventure that introduces the reader to Aivilikmiut life, the creatures of the Arctic, and the harshness of the long winter. In the preface to *Iceland Summer* he refers to his winter on Southampton as "that long, wonderful winter." It did, however, include some troubles and tensions. George endured frostbite and adapted to a diet of raw fish and blubber without complaint. But from his journal it is clear that interpersonal relationships sometimes went awry. By early April they were emerging from the long winter, but there were problems that may have been building all winter. The bout of "cabin fever" came to a head as Easter was approaching. It seemed to result from an accumulation of little things: film lost, cigarettes left burning in a storage shed, and on top of that, nineteen-year-old Jack flexing his need for independence from his father and embarking on a budding relationship with one of the servant girls. George describes it clearly in *Eskimo Year*, but that retrospective does not convey the despair and loneliness of the moment that is evident in his journal:

Tuesday, April 15. . . . I confess I am feeling so low that I can't write much. There isn't such a thing as fair play here.

Thursday, April 17. . . . This weather is awful; no one can get out and we are all so miserable over Jack & that woman that I am half desperate. My sense of humor seems to be leaving me.

Friday, April 18. . . . We found a cigarette stub in the shop [where many of George's specimens and supplies were stored] showing that someone is breaking rules. Things are not, in other words, going too well. I get half crazy, sometimes, worrying about what may happen to the collection, and our own inability to get any early spring trips to the floe under way.

Monday, April 21. . . . Only 10° above this morning and some snow—a rather wet snow which for some time promised to ruin our chances for getting any motion pictures. But with careful sheltering of the lens, etc., I guess I got some scenes—showing the komatik races, the running of men & women, & the very funny scramble for boots. I haven't much heart in the celebrations I must say. Jack stands around like a 'gentleman' doing little or nothing while Sam & I plod along like galley slaves. Well, there's nothing to do but put up with it all. I'm not intending to try to put up with a year like this again without a friend along who knows a little of my language as I understand it. Everything would be all right if Jack wouldn't turn . . . the minute the natives come around. I get along with the natives by themselves fine.

Easter Sunday, April 30. . . . Last night we had a real row. Things were said that hurt me deeply, but they may be true. It is certain that I never wintered this way before in an isolated place & that probably has something to do with it all.[20]

In the end all made amends that Easter Sunday in a renewal of friendship and harmony that provided new resolve and vigor for the long days of exploring, collecting, and painting that followed. The spring was filled with returning birds, and the longer days were crammed with the activity needed to keep up with the specimens, notes, and painting. With the first flowers came a profusion of butterflies, and George shifted his focus to them and to mosses and other life emerging from beneath melting snow (fig. 7.1). The *Nascopie* arrived on schedule in August 1930, and on August 15, with specimens, notes, and paintings carefully packed, George said a brief hello to new visitors to Southampton, bade farewell to friends, and boarded the ship for the long voyage home.[21]

The scientific legacy of George Sutton's year on Southampton Island is a treasure trove of information on the geological, meteorological, and biological characteristics of the area. The scientific report appears in the Memoirs of the Carnegie Museum as volume 12, under the title: *The Exploration of Southampton Island, Hudson Bay* by George Miksch Sutton. The volume is divided into three parts (1932–36): part 1 provides general background information, part 2 focuses on zoology, and part 3 on botany. Parts 2 and 3 include not only *The Birds of Southampton Island* (part 2, section 2, the 275-page treatise that constitutes George's doctoral dissertation) but also an incredible array of other reports authored by George and others using specimens and data he brought back. Part 2, section 1, "The Mammals of Southampton Island," is authored by George Miksch Sutton and William J. Hamilton and includes photographs taken by George and black-and-white reproductions of his paintings of Atlantic walrus.[22]

The remaining sections of part 2 cover fishes, insects, spiders, mollusks, and starfishes. Part 3 covers the fungi, algae, mosses, liverworts,

7.1. With spring snow melt on Southampton Island in 1930, George turned his attention to the profusion of wildflowers emerging on the tundra. This photograph appeared in Eskimo Year.

ferns, higher plants, and lichens that George collected. In addition to the articles he authored, his efforts resulted in fourteen articles written by fourteen other scientists. Among the insects George collected was a crane fly that was named by Charles P. Alexander as a new species—in George's honor: *Tipula suttoni*.[23] Among the plants was a moss named by O. E. Jennings as a new species, also in George's honor: *Pylaisia suttoni*.[24]

One of the personal legacies of George's year on Southampton was his love of fat. Blubber, the fat just under the skin of marine mammals, was one of the mainstays of the Aivilikmiut diet on which George lived that year. It provided high energy and helped build his body fat and defenses against the extreme cold of arctic winters. Upon his return from Southampton, George had a craving for fat that continued. Whenever he had his meals out, he specifically requested that no fat be removed from his meat—he wanted it all; so much for modern medicine and clogged arteries. For George Sutton, a personal high energy level apparently allowed a diet that resulted in neither excess body weight nor overly clogged arteries. Years later ornithologist Andrew J. Berger wrote to Sutton requesting a description of the exotic foods he had eaten while on Southampton. *Eskimo Year* provides a litany of such foods, including raw eggs and raw seal liver as well as blubber and raw fish; afield there was little opportunity to cook food, and survival at constant temperatures well below zero degrees Fahrenheit required eating a lot. Sutton responded:

Are you delving into the mysteries of the cholesterol content of human blood? You must be. I've eaten white whale (beluga; *kellilughak*) blubber many times, but never Greenland whale (*akvik*) blubber. I've eaten lots and lots of *netchek* seal blubber, some *oogjook* seal blubber, and some *kashigiak* seal blubber. Doesn't all this make your mouth water? But I don't recall ever eating a meal that was *all* blubber. The ideal meal in winter on Southampton Island was some raw caribou plus some cooked caribou and cooked seal blubber. Delicious! Another wonderful meal was fried char plus raw caribou plus cooked seal blubber. I didn't like raw seal blubber. It too often had a "weaselly" smell.

I've eaten many kinds of wild duck and goose eggs, of course; tern eggs galore; gull eggs galore; one set of Whistling Swan eggs; and a good many Snowy Owl eggs. All these were good. All were fresh or nearly fresh. I remember being fiercely hungry about the time I was preparing some swan eggs, so I ate raw what I had blown from the shells and it was mighty good.[25]

During George's year on Southampton he found eighty-six species of birds and painted or collected most of them. The plates in *The Birds of Southampton Island* include several photographs George took of birds and their nests, eggs, and young, plus a painting illustrating the downy chicks of thirteen species of water birds (plate 10) and four paintings of birds in their Southampton habitat, including the Blue Goose, the species that had been a stimulus for the expedition (plate 11).

George also collected mammals, fishes, butterflies and other insects, plants, and rocks and made exquisite watercolor paintings of mushrooms (plate 12), some of the mammals, and some fishes. Most of his collections went to the Carnegie, although a few specimens went to specialists at Cornell and elsewhere. The Barren Ground caribou that he collected were ultimately mounted in a habitat group for display at the Carnegie Museum.[26]

On George's return trip, the *Nascopie* continued westward to the trading post at Chesterfield on the west coast of Hudson Bay. There he found an opportunity for a speedier return, left the *Nascopie*, and boarded the motor yacht *Nowyah* for the trip south to Churchill, Manitoba. From Churchill he was able to take a train to Winnipeg and civilization. En route by train to New York, he stopped in Minneapolis to visit friends at the University of Minnesota. He would soon be a part of academia—a student at Cornell.[27]

CHAPTER 8

Cornell

Life was bewilderingly full.

GEORGE MIKSCH SUTTON, *Bird Student*

George's return from the Arctic was without fanfare but into a new setting and role as a graduate student at Cornell University. Fellow graduate students had learned of his pending arrival and his past year on Southampton Island but knew little more.[1] His Ph.D. advisory committee was chaired by Arthur A. Allen and included Albert Hazen Wright, a herpetologist, and Walter King Stone from the fine arts department. He also worked with Professor Olaf Brauner in the fine arts department, and Stone and Brauner helped George in his efforts to paint birds in oils. As noted, George had contacted Allen and others in 1929 and they had agreed on his dissertation project, a study of the birds of Southampton Island, although he was also to collect specimens and information on the rest of the flora and fauna of the region. He had specific requests from scientists at both Cornell and Carnegie.

Unlike most students, George began his graduate student career at Cornell off campus, doing his research on Southampton Island. He then returned for class work and to write his dissertation. In Ithaca he shared a third-floor apartment in Louis Agassiz Fuertes's home with another graduate student in ornithology, Olin Sewall Pettingill, Jr. Each morning they had breakfast with Madge Sumner Fuertes, Louis's widow, and George learned much about the man from her. They remained close friends throughout their lives.[2]

The fall of 1930 was difficult for George. If he had harbored any hope of retrieving his relationship with Eloise, her marriage while he was away had ended that, and he was soon in financial difficulties. His salary at Cornell was inadequate.

Sale of paintings and writing were ways of paying his bills. Another was providing lectures for a fee. His father had done this; why shouldn't he? With Sewall's assistance, he prepared lantern slides (a larger format predecessor to modern 35 mm slides) of photos and paintings from his Southampton trip. He hand-colored the slides himself and did so well at it that he began drumming up business among other students and faculty.[3]

In addition to his friend Sewall Pettingill, George's fellow graduate students in the distinguished biology department based at McGraw Hall included many others who went on to become prominent scientists: Austin L. Rand, George B. Saunders, Wilfred A. Welter, James Crouch, Victor Coles, Adger Smythe, Victor Gould, Richard Weaver, Elizabeth Kingsbury, Lawrence Grinnell, Dorothy Compton, F. C. Edminster, and L. S. Vijjakich.[4] George was apparently the senior graduate student both in age and in professional experience. Yet he was in the thick of things, assisting fellow students with research projects, artwork, and lantern slides. He was also often the life of the party. What an environment McGraw Hall and his apartment in the Fuertes home were for him: surrounded by Fuertes's specimens and art, he was able to study them at his leisure, in essence continuing to receive lessons from the master. George described graduate student life and "Old McGraw" nostalgically in *Bird Student.*[5]

In June 1931 George returned to the Arctic, to an area forty miles north of Churchill, Manitoba. Again J. B. Semple sponsored the trip. Semple, Pettingill, and ornithologist Bert Lloyd from Saskatchewan rounded out the expedition. The purpose of the trip was to search for the nest and eggs of Harris's Sparrow, the only North American songbird for which eggs had not yet been described. Sutton had seen Harris's Sparrows in the area on his return from Southampton. A group of Canadian ornithologists was searching only a mile away for Harris's Sparrows. Having been scooped by Canadian Dewey Soper two years earlier in the discovery of nesting Blue Geese, George was determined to be on the winning side this time. On June 16, 1931, he was indeed the first scientist to discover a Harris's Sparrow nest with eggs and was so happy that he said he "hippity-hopped across the bogs."[6]

On July 5 George wrote back to his colleagues at the Pennsylvania Game Commission in Harrisburg to inform them of the expedition's success: "The eggs were beauties. I do not know how the man for whom this sparrow was named was related to the Harris family of Harrisburg, but I daresay they are cousins somehow or other! We have had a grand time. We have hardly been sick a bit, though the mosquitoes have led us an awful and dizzy chase, I tell you. . . . Our collection is fine and large."[7]

In late July the tale of the competition and American discovery was a major story in the science section of *Time* magazine.[8]

The next months were busy as George completed his dissertation and saw it through publication in the Carnegie Museum Memoir series. His graduate course work was minimal by today's standards: he went directly from a bachelor's degree to a doctorate, skipping the master's degree. He spent less time in residence as a student at Cornell than most students of his day because he was given "residential credit" for his time on Southampton. Cornell was generous and well ahead of its time in agreeing to accept the published version of George's Southampton Island research results as his dissertation. He was awarded a Ph.D. from Cornell on June 20, 1932. He had taken thirty semester hours of graduate work, including two zoology courses, a seminar, and German each semester during the 1930–31 academic year, two animal biology courses and a zoology seminar during the fall semester of 1931, and one animal biology course as he completed his dissertation during spring 1932. George's grades were all recorded as "S"—satisfactory—except for an A in Animal Biology 26; it is not clear what that course entailed.[9]

While at Cornell George provided color plates and line drawings for several books. His approaches to illustration showed dramatic change and improvement. Among these books one of the earliest and most frustrating was Thomas Roberts's *The Birds of Minnesota* (1932).[10] Roberts had intended that all of the plates be done by Louis Agassiz Fuertes, but when Fuertes was killed in 1927 he had to look elsewhere, opting for the work of several artists, including George. The request came shortly before George left for Southampton and thus he was very short on time. *The Birds of Minnesota* would be a major work, and Roberts had been a personal friend of Fuertes and was a close friend of George's new major professor, Arthur Allen. This was an assignment he could not turn down. He contributed four plates to the book: one including male and female Spruce and Ruffed grouse, two that included a total of nine species of flycatchers, and one with six species of vireos. Because of the multiple species per plate, the watercolor portraits are contrived, but they are pleasing, with a seminatural, appropriate habitat background in each. George was not particularly pleased with them, but he was simply out of time. According to Gustav Swanson, who was Roberts's assistant at the time, Roberts also felt that George's work was a rushed job and not as good as it might have been.[11]

When George had stopped by the University of Minnesota en route home from his year in the Arctic, he had learned that all of the original artwork for *The Birds of Minnesota* had been stolen from the lithographer's office after the plates for the book had been made. The artwork had been insured, and Roberts wanted all the artists to redo their originals from the plates—exactly as they had been. All agreed, but Sutton was chagrined because he did not want to copy illustrations that he now felt he could greatly improve. While the others charged less the second time around, Sutton charged more, about $150 for each of the paintings.[12]

With a fresh Ph.D. in hand and no paying job, in September 1932 George headed afield with JB to collect prairie chickens for the Carnegie Museum. He returned to Cornell and then headed north to attend the annual meeting of the American Ornithologists' Union in Quebec in late October. At the meeting George presented a paper on his "First Impressions of Some Saskatchewan Birds," and another on "Topsell's Fowles of Heaven" on behalf of his friend Bayard Christy.[13] He also contributed fifteen paintings to an exhibition of bird art at the meeting. Six of those paintings were oils (Great Horned Owl, Canvasback, a pair of Canvasbacks, Mallard, a flock of King Eiders, and a pair of Redheads); the other nine were watercolors. This was perhaps the greatest exhibition of George's work with oil. The paintings were on loan from the Carnegie Museum and included none of his recent Arctic work. Instead of Cornell, George listed his address in the catalog of the exhibit as "Pebble Hearths, Bethany, West Virginia." At the time there seems to have been some uncertainty as to where his next "home" would be, although even later he often used the Pebble Hearths address—it was his home and refuge.[14]

At the AOU meeting in Quebec, George was a rising star. His year in the Arctic had been well publicized, his affiliation with and recent Ph.D. from Cornell placed him at the forefront of American ornithology, and his link to Fuertes and contribution of fifteen paintings to the display of art at the meeting placed him among the leading North American bird illustrators. With the fiftieth anniversary of the founding of the American Ornithologists' Union to be celebrated in 1933, the AOU Council decided at the Quebec meeting to publish a volume on progress in American ornithology. George was asked to report on "Fifty Years of Progress in American Bird Art." I believe this was an exceptionally important endeavor in that it required an evaluation of the work of his predecessors and contemporaries, of the functions of bird art, and of the evolution of printing processes upon which reproduction of bird art depended. The effort must have resulted in considerable introspection and it was done with finesse, dwelling on the strengths he found in the work of each of his contemporaries.[15]

With ornithological jobs difficult to come by, George opted to remain at Cornell as a poorly paid curator of birds, building up the collection and cataloging Fuertes's specimens, supplementing his salary with income from artwork and lectures. In November 1932, now truly "Dr. Sutton," George mailed out cards advertising his availability as a speaker:

> You may be interested in knowing that during the season of 1932–1933
> George Miksch Sutton
> will be available as a lecturer on the following subjects:
> "A Year in the Arctic with Camera and Brush"
> "Bird Personalities of the Far North"
> These lectures are illustrated.
> Communicate with Dr. Sutton at McGraw Hall, Cornell University,
> Ithaca, New York.[16]

Funding for George's position as curator of birds at Cornell was split between federal and state sources, and he was employed for only nine months each year. Each summer he had to search elsewhere for support. There was neither job security nor opportunity for advancement. But his financial woes soon took on crisis proportions. On his return from Southampton Island he had put all his savings in a bank in Ithaca. In the spring of 1933, during the aftermath of the stock market crash of 1929, his bank became insolvent; his meager savings could not be retrieved, and George lost everything. With such lemons, George made lemonade.[17] His position at Cornell had the advantage of providing free time to do free-lance illustration and writing and gave him an academic affiliation that opened doors and generated sponsorship of expeditions.

One of these paying endeavors involved some unusual Sutton art I learned of on the Internet when I typed "George Miksch Sutton" into the search engine for E-bay's online auction. Up popped an auction in progress, through which a seller was offering some trade cards issued during the 1930s that George had illustrated. These were the product of a commission from the Coca-Cola Company to paint illustrations for trade cards in a set called "The World of Nature." The set included eight series of twelve cards each, featuring everything from planets to diverse plants and animals. Several artists contributed to the set, but it was Lynn Bogue Hunt, a prominent wildlife artist of the era, who painted all the birds. George painted ten of the twelve cards in Series 7, "Life in and around the Water." His subjects included eight fish (speckled trout, black bass, pickerel, pike, common sucker, salmon, cod, common eel), the bullfrog, and "the toad." The remaining two cards in the series included one of oyster, scallop, and mussel, painted by Lynn Bogue Hunt, and one of a lobster, painted by David Frances Thomson. The illustration on each card is signed and the cards include brief natural history information about their subject. None of the cards is dated, but the entire set was produced between 1929 and 1934.[18]

These seem strange subjects for a bird artist, and no reference to these cards appears in George's correspondence or in the archives at the University of Oklahoma or at Cornell. The assignment came close on the heels of his year in the Arctic, during which George did exquisite paintings of Arctic fish. He may have come to the attention of Coca-Cola as a result of his contacts at Cornell, and may well have earned this job as a result of his portraits of Arctic fish, some of which are reproduced in *Bird Student*.[19]

Another outlet for George's art at about this time was a set of seven postcards issued by the Cranbrook Institute of Science at Bloomfield Hills, Michigan, the institute that supported Sutton's research at the George Reserve in Michigan beginning in 1934. Each postcard features one of the baby bird portraits that George painted while studying the development of plumages in Michigan sparrows at the George Reserve; the cards are not dated. Five of the seven also appear in Paul Johnsgard's *Baby Bird Portraits by George Miksch Sutton*, and the original of the nestling Indigo Bunting was dated by Sutton on August 9, 1934.[20] Each card identifies the species and indicates the nestling's approximate age on the front, and on the back identifies the Cranbrook Institute and provides a few sentences about the species. These postcards I also found on E-bay, and I have found no other mention of them.

In spite of the seemingly tenuous nature of George's position, he seemed to thrive at Cornell, busying himself with numerous projects, working with students, and becoming part of the social fabric of the university community. His influence on both undergraduate and graduate students was often profound. H. Albert Hochbaum, one of the great waterfowl biologists and conservationists of the twentieth century, attended Cornell in the 1930s to earn a degree in agriculture, but he took a course from George, who convinced him to expand his horizons to include science and art with a special focus on birds. So profound was George's impact on Hochbaum that he named his son "George Sutton Hochbaum."[21]

George took an active interest in Cornell's chapter of Beta Theta Pi, the fraternity of which he had been a member at Bethany. Harry C. House, an undergraduate and Beta Theta Pi member at Cornell in the 1930s said "Doc" was a frequent visitor at the fraternity and that he had given the fraternity a gorgeous painting of an eagle. George had also invited the fraternity members to a party at his apartment when he was elected a member of the Explorer's Club of New York.[22]

On March 30, 1933, Josselyn Van Tyne invited George to join him on some trips around Michigan, suggesting that they might visit the Beaver Islands, Drummond Island, or the Kirtland Warbler nesting areas. He noted the hard financial times in which the country was mired but added that the drive was only a day and half from Ithaca and that the cost would be minimal. Van Tyne offered use of his car, and the depth of his invitation was shown by his final comment: "We can . . . look up any part of Michigan that appeals to you." He wanted to get to know George better and to spend time in the field with him.[23]

George, however, was preoccupied with a scheduled trip to the Chisos Mountains of southwest Texas. He was also working on his book *Eskimo Year* and writing his chapter for the memorial volume celebrating the first fifty years of the American Ornithologists' Union. He had to say no, but he expressed considerable disappointment at having to do so. Van Tyne then provided George with useful logistical information and contacts for his Texas trip.[24]

George and JB spent more than two months in the Chisos in late spring 1933, venturing south to the Rio Grande and elsewhere in the Big Bend country. On his return to Cornell George contacted Van Tyne, expounded on the approximately four hundred specimens they had collected, and suggested a collaboration combining most of his and Van Tyne's independent Texas efforts. Van Tyne readily concurred, and in 1937 they published *The Birds of Brewster County, Texas*.[25]

In the fall of 1933 George and JB traveled to Oklahoma, then in mid-April 1934 they left for a collecting visit to British Columbia—a "tea party" trip, according to George, since they would not be getting into some of the remote areas he had hoped to visit. The trip was a good one for the experience, and it was good to be within easy contact of family, because his mother was quite ill at the time. One of the highlights was the collection of the second known egg of the Marbled Murrelet.[26]

In 1934 and several subsequent summers Van Tyne facilitated a summer stipend for George to do fieldwork at the Edwin S. George Reserve, the University of Michigan's field station. George loved the work there, seeing it as "real science" rather than the "popular science" that seemed to be dominant at Cornell. At the George Reserve he was much involved with studying the development of plumages of finches that nested there, raising the young of many species in captivity. Later that summer he was photographed at a West Virginia bird meeting at the state 4-H camp, Camp Frame, near Hedgesville, holding his pet Rose-breasted Grosbeak Rosie (fig. 8.1). Rosie was one of many birds George reared in order to study plumage development. George, the consummate collector of birds, was mimicked in another photo at the meeting by Chuck Conrad, a friend and West Virginia ornithologist, who posed with a stick next to George with his gun (fig. 8.2).[27]

Although he was very active and able to spend considerable time afield, George felt he was stagnating at Cornell and both underpaid and underappreciated. He repeatedly told Van Tyne he wanted a full-time position at Michigan.

George's first summer in Michigan went exceptionally well—so well that Van Tyne and Frederick M. Gaige, director of the Museum of Zoology, acted on George's wishes to leave Cornell. At the end of the summer in 1934 they offered him a position at the Museum of Zoology funded in part by the Cranbrook Institute and in part by the University of Michigan. On September 10, 1934, Van Tyne wrote to George: "You must make the right decision. We *have* to have you."[28]

Instead of taking the position, however, George took the Michigan offer to President Livingston Farrand at Cornell and used it to improve his position there. He broke the news to Van Tyne on October 2:

> It is not going to be easy to write this letter. . . . I have decided to stay at Cornell. I am writing to you rather than to Director Gaige, for I know you better than I do him; and I shall ask you to tell him, please.
>
> Your offer tempted me greatly—really very greatly. I should have been with you long since had I not so often expressed my desire to help build up Cornell's bird department. My salary has been increased. . . . When I talked to my good friend President Farrand yesterday morning, I perceived that my deepest allegiance is here. Not that anyone has coerced me in the least. It is just that I love the place.[29]

8.1. *George and his pet Rose-breasted Grosbeak, Rosie, along with a friend identified only as Colin, at a bird meeting at Camp Frame, the state 4-H camp near Hedgesville, West Virginia, in 1934. Courtesy of Albert R. Buckelew, Jr., and Bethany College, Bethany, West Virginia.*

8.2. *George and West Virginia ornithologist Chuck Conrad at Camp Frame, West Virginia, in 1934. Conrad, with a stick, was mimicking George and his gun. Courtesy of Albert R. Buckelew, Jr., and Bethany College, Bethany, West Virginia.*

Nonetheless, George left the door open for a later move—perhaps a better offer: "If our department does not show definite signs of moving forward this year I shall have to consider a change." He also sought additional support from Van Tyne and noted the continued insecurity of his Cornell position: "Josselyn, is there any chance I might go to Yucatan for you, or with you, this winter? I'd like to see Yucatan. I believe a leave of absence could be arranged (with salary if certain specimens come to us; without salary if they don't), for as you know I continue to be what is sometimes called—perhaps unadvisedly—a 'free lance.' "

The Yucatan trip did not materialize, but George's schedule in the spring of 1935 included extensive fieldwork. Ivory-billed Woodpeckers had been discovered in swamps along the Tensas River in northeastern Louisiana, and Arthur Allen, George Sutton, Albert Brand, James Tanner, and Louisiana game warden J. J. Kuhn spent several days there searching for them. It was George and Kuhn who found the Ivory-bill nest at which they studied, photographed, and recorded the birds. George described his encounter with Ivory-bills vividly in *Birds in the Wilderness*, illustrating his account with some of his field sketches.[30]

George later did an oil painting of the pair of Ivory-billed Woodpeckers they observed. The New York Zoological Society commissioned the painting, a portrait of the birds at their nest cavity in early morning light. It is an outstanding example of Sutton's abilities with oils. The portrait was used as a frontispiece in H. C. Oberholser's *The Bird Life of Louisiana* and later as the frontispiece for J. T. Tanner's monograph *The Ivory-billed Woodpecker*.[31] The painting is stunning, a result of George's observations of these birds at their nest in Louisiana's Tensas River Swamp. The nest cavity, placed directly below a broken-off branch where water could seep in to create a perfect microhabitat for wood-rotting fungi, shows understanding of the ecological relationships of the birds. The glossy black of the birds' plumage reflects the green world around them. The chisel-tipped bills (rather than sharply pointed, as in the work of many artists), strongly curved claws, and the more acutely pointed crest of the female demonstrate Sutton's keen observations and first-hand knowledge of the birds and their functional anatomy. George also painted other Ivory-bills based on his field sketches and work in the Singer Tract (plate 13).[32]

On leaving Louisiana George joined J. B. Semple and returned to the Big Bend country of West Texas, while Allen and the rest of the party continued elsewhere to record sounds of other rare birds. A news release on April 26 reflected high optimism on the heels of the Louisiana Ivory-bill sightings, suggesting that George and JB had hopes of finding the Imperial Woodpecker, a close relative of the Ivory-bill. They did not, nor are there any records of that species from the area.[33]

During the summer of 1935 George again went to Michigan to work on sparrows at the George Reserve. On weekends he and Van Tyne regularly got together to work on joint manuscripts. One was a description of a new subspecies, Fuertes' Red-tailed Hawk, *Buteo jamaicensis fuertesi* (plate 14), honoring George's mentor. The relationship between Sutton and Van Tyne may be somewhat reflected in the co-authorship in that George and Semple collected the bird, and George had wanted to name the new subspecies by himself: "I hope too you will not think me piggish in wishing to present this description by myself rather than with you. I told Mrs. Fuertes that I thought Mr. Semple and I had taken a new subspecies of Red-tail, and that I wanted the bird to bear Louis' name. I think I shall never have a better chance than this to do peculiar honor to a man whose memory I revere. Do you understand?"[34]

In the end, Fuertes' Red-tailed Hawk was described by Sutton and Van Tyne—with Sutton's name first, although Van Tyne took lead authorship of the publication in which the description appeared.[35]

George was effusive with praise of Van Tyne, the museum, the university, and all things Michigan. He wrote to Van Tyne's wife, Helen, again setting the stage for a possible move to Michigan: "You and Josselyn have given me a summer I will never forget. When I hinted that Michigan 'was growing on me' I was not exaggerating. And a fondness for a place that comes about as this fondness has is a most satisfactory sort of feeling. I need not tell you again that I like your friends. I feel as if some of them (one or two at least) might be my friends for life. And they all contributed much to my happiness these past several weeks."[36]

At summer's end George returned to Bethany, West Virginia, to spend time with his mother, who as mentioned had been ill. He found her much improved and in late August took his parents on a vacation to Maine, returning in mid-September. He noted in a letter to Van Tyne: "The trip did us good. It's the first real outing mother's had for years and she responded amazingly."[37]

In addition to his curatorial duties at Cornell, George was obviously "resident illustrator" for Arthur Allen's projects. His watercolors for Allen's *American Bird Biographies* and its sequel, *The Golden Plover and Other Birds* are exquisite portraits of birds in action within their habitat.[38] George also found a new use for the black-and-white line drawings he had done for *An Introduction to the Birds of Pennsylvania*:

several of them are printed on the phonograph records that accompany Albert Brand's books on bird songs, and others are included in the books (fig. 8.3).[39]

Book illustrations continued to occupy a great deal of George's time. In 1936 he provided a color plate of a Ring-necked Pheasant and thirty-three black-and-white line drawings for Robert Vale's *Wings, Fur and Shot*. These are among the most unusual of George's book illustrations. Later reprinted under the title *How to Hunt American Game*, the book went through at least five printings. Although it included a color frontispiece of a male Ring-necked Pheasant, the unique Sutton illustrations

8.3. *A new use for George's line drawings from* An Introduction to the Birds of Pennsylvania—*illustrations on the phonograph records accompanying Albert Brand's* More Songs of Wild Birds, *1936.*

are the pen-and-ink sketches of hunters and dogs and a cottontail that leaps off the page toward the reader. When Vale's book was reprinted in 1946, George altered the cottontail drawing, adding another footprint and a shadow, making the rabbit much more earthbound. Vale's book includes a few Sutton drawings that are of lesser quality or that have been poorly reproduced. A flock of ducks (Northern Shovelers?) facing page 75 leaves much to be desired; their feet seem "rubber-stamped" and the hatchwork background seems unnatural. The job illustrating Vale's book likely came about as a result of George's earlier job with the Pennsylvania Game Commission, since the publisher's offices were in Harrisburg.[40]

In late April 1936 George headed for Oklahoma, spending a few days along the way with family in West Virginia. In Oklahoma he focused his efforts on the northwestern counties, an arid area where east meets west. That spring his third book appeared and was well received. *Birds in the Wilderness*, a collection of his adventures with birds, included a color plate of his watercolor portrait of a Harris's Sparrow.[41]

In an interesting moment of recycling, George made use of his hovering male Ruby-throated Hummingbird, included with a female and cardinal flowers in *American Bird Biographies*, to illustrate "Lines to a Hummingbird," a poem by E. G. Palmer that appeared in the July 1936 issue of *Woman's Home Companion*. The *Woman's Home Companion* illustration includes the hovering male and another male at larkspurs, but the hovering bird in the magazine is clearly a repetition of what George must have considered a successful effort with a difficult subject (plate 15).[42]

The 1936 meeting of the American Ornithologists' Union was held at the Carnegie Museum and, of course, George attended; it was a welcome trip "home." He presented a paper on his spring study of nesting Mississippi Kites in Oklahoma and was also honored with a special exhibit of his paintings of the birds of western Pennsylvania. At the meeting George, Van Tyne, and Herb Stoddard, a close friend of George's from Georgia, were elected as fellows of the AOU, fitting recognition of their many contributions to ornithology.[43] George was also royally roasted in the *Auklet* distributed at the annual banquet. The *Auklet* is an irregular and irreverent parody of the AOU's scientific journal, the *Auk*. The anonymous author of the three-page mock review of *Birds in the Wilderness* notes that George "excels in these true tales of reckless adventure and peril in far places of earth for the sake of scientific achievement. Who but this one would have captured a Whooping Crane barehanded and without help at the age of eight months? (The Crane had no help, either.) And in the barren wastes of the Loop in the *Chi-ca-go* country, at that!"[44]

Kenneth Washburn, then an assistant professor in fine arts at Cornell, painted an oil portrait of George in 1937 (plate 16). The portrait includes a portion of an oil painting of ptarmigan done by Fuertes in 1910, hanging on the wall behind George. It is unclear how this portrait came about and how it got to the Sutton Biology Lab at Bethany College in Bethany, West Virginia, where it has been hanging for a long time. The fact that it was signed and dated by the artist is the only lead. Washburn is known for his artwork for the Works Progress Administration (WPA) during the 1930s. He left Cornell in 1950 to establish a studio in California, where he trained many students. The Fuertes ptarmigan painting currently resides at the Cornell Laboratory of Ornithology.[45]

During the 1930s George also wrote many book reviews for the *New York Herald-Tribune*. He enjoyed doing reviews not only because this meant keeping up with the most recent books in ornithology and natural history but also because he became known as a literary critic—and he got to keep the books he reviewed. Most of those books were donated to the DeGolyer Collection of the History of Science at the University of Oklahoma in the late 1970s.[46]

George's first trip to Mexico was from late January into early March 1938 with JB and ornithologist Thomas D. Burleigh. The three of them traveled about the northeastern Mexican states of Nuevo León, Coahuila, and Tamaulipas, and it was this exploration that stimulated George's love for Mexico, and specifically for the area along the Río Sabinas near the hill-top village of Gómez Farías in southern Tamaulipas. He would return there time and again. This first trip resulted in many specimens for the Carnegie, forty watercolors, and ultimately in George's book *Mexican Birds: First Impressions*. On this first trip, too, near Monterrey, JB collected a Sharp-shinned Hawk, which proved to be so different from other Sharp-shins (paler, redder, less spotted, with dark brown eyes) that A. J. Van Rossem described it as a new race. George had painted the bird and had shown the painting to Van Rossem, who was immediately intrigued by it. In describing the new race, Van Rossem honored George by naming it *Accipiter striatus suttoni*. Van Rossem did not suggest a common name for the new sharp-shin; in *Mexican Birds: First Impressions* George refers to it as the "Mexican Sharp-shinned Hawk."[47]

When George returned from Mexico the first 1938 issue of the *Wilson Bulletin* had arrived, and he was surprised to find that his drawing of the Wilson's Warbler was no longer on the cover. Indeed there was no cover illustration. He said nothing, but there was a firestorm of protest from Wilson members, including the president, Margaret Morse Nice. In the next issue long-time editor T. C. Stephens addressed the change, and acknowledged the criticism, but said he was reluctant to change the cover in the middle of a volume. For the rest of the year the unadorned cover persisted. At the end of the year Stephens resigned, Josselyn Van Tyne became editor, and George's Wilson's Warbler drawing was restored to the cover.[48]

Shortly after his return from Mexico George boarded a ship bound for France, where he attended the International Ornithological Congress. While crossing the Atlantic aboard the *SS City of Baltimore*, he prepared the first draft of *Mexican Birds: First Impressions*. He presented a paper at the meeting on his recent work in Mexico and had a well-received showing of his Mexican bird portraits. His portrait of an Elegant Trogan was later published in the congress proceedings, as a frontispiece in the French journal *L'Oiseau*, in *Mexican Birds*, and in 2003 on the dust jacket of *Dictionary of Birds of the United States*, by Joel E. Holloway (plate 17).[49]

Another striking painting from George's first Mexican trip is that of an Acorn Woodpecker (plate 18). Although it did not appear in *Mexican Birds*, George described the conditions under which he painted it: "February 13 was Sunday, a quiet, cloud-smothered day. While my companions were skinning specimens, I took myself to the porch to paint an Acorn Woodpecker in watercolor. So damp was the atmosphere that I had a bad time with the paper, and the brush strokes would not dry. The all-pervasive cloud flowed in round the pillars, trailing past at arm's length between me and the door."[50]

Although Van Tyne asked George to return to Michigan that summer to work at the George Reserve and had even offered a small stipend, George was busy working on his Mexican book and paintings and specimens from the trip. Then his father became ill, and family came first. He spent the summer in West Virginia. Through the summer George corresponded with Van Tyne and other bird artists, making arrangements for a show of bird art for the fiftieth anniversary meeting of the Wilson Club, which was to be held in late November at the University of Michigan.

At the Wilson meeting George seemed to be the man of the hour. He gave a lecture on the bird art exhibit that had been held at the International Ornithological Congress in France; gave an introductory gallery talk on the history of bird art in conjunction with the art exhibit he had organized for the Wilson meeting; and was also the after dinner speaker for the annual banquet. For the latter he captivated his audience with tales of his recent Mexican adventures while passing around some of his paintings of Mexican birds. His involvement with the Wilson Club deepened: he was elected second vice president of the organization and would be serving with Pettingill, who was Wilson secretary, and Van Tyne, the new editor of the *Wilson Bulletin*.[51]

Following the meeting George wrote to thank Helen Van Tyne for their hospitality. He was fairly bubbling over: "You and Josselyn (with your friendliness and gaiety and a way of giving me a feeling of great importance) certainly gave me the time of my life there in Ann Arbor. I did have a sense of responsibility about the meeting and I never do have a normal appetite when speeches are in the offing: all the same I was on a real spree the whole time and I have you, my good friends, to thank for that. It did me so much good just to work in the fine atmosphere of the museum building and bird range."[52]

Just after Christmas 1938, George wrote to Van Tyne of an exciting new opportunity with which he had been presented: John Baker, president of the National Association of Audubon Societies, Bob Murphy, and Guy Emerson, also of Audubon, had asked him to become editor of *Bird-Lore*, Audubon's official magazine and the prominent bridge between amateur and professional ornithology. They wanted him immediately, but George had promised to accompany JB on a return visit to Mexico. He also told Van Tyne that he hoped Audubon would allow him to remain at Cornell as curator of birds while assuming the duties of editor. Baker did not like the idea. Sutton pondered the position, writing to Van Tyne:

> They offer a good salary, and editing the magazine would doubtless be all right for me, providing I did it well. The idea of living in New York somewhat floors me to be sure, but I've grown weary with trying to push things forward here and am fairly well convinced by this time that neither Allen nor Brand is really interested in the building up of the collection that I have had in mind. The whole story here is motion pictures and sound recording and color photography, with some courses worked in here and there. I'm no photographer, so there's not much hope for me, I fear.
>
> So perhaps we will be fellow editors. What will become of my taxonomy & bird painting & so on I don't know. I never dreamed (a year or so ago) I'd turn so strongly to writing, but this field has opened up for me surprisingly and I feel [*sic*] to make the best of it.[53]

Van Tyne responded quickly and emphatically:

George, I am not sure I approve of your taking the job of editing *Bird-Lore*. You are an artist, a writer, and a research zoologist—and you are top-notch in all three. But does that mean that you would be serving your greatest usefulness if you took a job in which you would spend a very large part of your time in a city office editing America's leading magazine of conservation propaganda? We all know that if you took the job you would make a big success of it and we know that you must be pleased, as we are, that you were honored by the offer of a big job like that. We, along with Sewall, are happy to see you being given recognition. But *I* wonder seriously how long you could be happy at it? There must be a very large amount of business drudgery to editing a bimonthly of that size and importance. Two years ago Bill Vogt told me confidentially that he must give up the job soon because it consumed his time and energy so completely that he could not even keep up with what was being done in ornithology, let alone do much research himself. If as keen a man as Bill Vogt with a newspaper background found that to be the case, will you not find it also? No, George, I feel very strongly that your work in zoological research, art, and writing is too valuable to be crowded into the background by a full-time job editing a journal of conservation propaganda.[54]

George took the advice and declined the position, continuing his activities at Cornell, becoming more deeply involved with the Wilson Ornithological Club. In the spring of 1939 George, JB, and Tom Burleigh returned to the same region of Mexico, this time also visiting Vera Cruz, where Fred Loetscher, a graduate student from Cornell, joined them.[55]

In 1939 George's good friend Karl Haller discovered and collected a new warbler in West Virginia and named it in George's honor. George was pleased with the honor and painted a color plate of the new bird to accompany its description (plate 19). Bayard Christy offered the *Cardinal* as a place for publication of the description, and that was where it appeared, although George would have preferred that it be described in the *Wilson Bulletin*. The discovery of Sutton's Warbler (*Dendroica suttoni*) made national news at a time when the world news was bleak.[56]

The discovery of Sutton's Warbler generated a great deal of interest and discussion as to whether it was indeed a new species or, instead, a hybrid between two known species. Others have reported Sutton's Warblers from West Virginia, Virginia, the District of Columbia, South Carolina, Florida, Indiana, and Texas—but rarely. George himself weighed in on the discussion, and many consider the bird to be a hybrid between a Yellow-throated Warbler (*Dendroica dominica*) and a Northern Parula (*Parula americana*). Although the AOU suggests such a hybrid origin for Sutton's Warbler, their treatment reflects some ambivalence.[57]

George was soon presented with another unusual outlet for his art; he was asked to do a painting for a stamp to be included in the National Wildlife Federation's third annual series of conservation stamps. Issued in 1940, the stamp features a Red-headed Woodpecker atop a dead stub (plate 20). The same illustration is included in Roger Tory Peterson's *Wildlife in Color,* which is illustrated by the conservation stamp art of several artists.[58]

In 1940 Todd's mammoth *Birds of Western Pennsylvania* appeared. It included 108 bird portraits by George. These were arranged on twenty-two plates, each bird deliberately placed in an appropriate habitat and often illustrating a characteristic pose or behavior. With these George demonstrated his mastery of use of background washes. His Cliff Swallows are gathering mud, one in the difficult pose of facing the observer. His pair of Carolina Chickadees includes one clinging to a branch upside down. The iridescence of his grackles truly shines, showing a keen depth of understanding of the interplay of light and color. Vegetation shown is identifiable, but subdued, placing the bird in a unique habitat while clearly focusing on the bird. His Spotted Sandpipers are especially three-dimensional and in motion. One immediately senses their characteristic tipping. A unique feature of the plates is that he did them all at the same scale—about one-third life size.[59]

Just as *Birds of Western Pennsylvania* appeared, George was asked to provide color plates for the "bird" entry in the 1942 twenty-fifth anniversary edition of *The World Book Encyclopedia.* He considered this assignment the "biggest illustrating job" he had yet tackled. *The World Book Encyclopedia* became a broad public showcase for his art, featuring portraits of seventy-two species of birds, including each state bird that had been designated. His friend from the Carnegie, Rudyerd Boulton, then at the Field Museum in Chicago, wrote the accompanying text.[60]

He finished the color plates during January 1941. Most are of single species, but a few plates include multiple species. While most plates are of North American birds, a few show exotic species—some of which George had never seen alive—such as the King Bird of Paradise, Keel-billed Toucan, and Cock-of-the-Rock. He also included extinct birds, such as the Carolina Parakeet, Passenger Pigeon, Great Auk, and Labrador Duck. Most of the plates show the birds in natural habitats and often in action—a Great Blue Heron with a fish, and several species feeding nestlings. An apparent error in this series is his portrait of a European Starling with yellow legs.

George had fun doing the *World Book* plates, in part because of his interactions with the "head man" For the project. He noted that correspondence with the fellow had been "a lark from start to finish. Never was business carried on so gaily. You'd have thought we were a couple of college fellows writing about frat doings and such rather than a couple of very hard-headed business men." [61]

From mid-February to June 1941, George and Sewall traveled to Tamaulipas and the Rancho Rinconada. Obtaining permits to collect birds in Mexico had been a serious and complicated problem. Permits were required in order to take guns and ammunition into the country, to collect the birds, and to take specimens from the country. But letters requesting permits went unanswered, and George was particularly frustrated by a stipulation on the permits that one-third of the specimens collected should be returned to Mexico. He was concerned that specimens returned to Mexico would not receive proper care. Alexander Wetmore of the Smithsonian provided guidance and firm instructions that all terms of the permits must be adhered to; he indicated that what happened to specimens that stayed in Mexico was simply of no concern.[62]

At the last minute permits came through and the expedition went well. Sutton collected and painted birds (fig. 8.4); Pettingill photographed them. One of the products of the trip was a film titled *Bird Magic in Mexico* that both Sutton and Pettingill presented to Audubon Screen Tour audiences.[63]

George was obviously restless as World War II heated up. He was unhappy at Cornell, saw younger men heading off to distant lands and the adventure of war, and longed to be among them. His restlessness was tempered, however, with frequent trips away from campus and with new honors. In March 1942 George was honored by having a river on Southampton Island named after him.[64] In a letter to George Breiding, a friend from West Virginia, he noted: "It is probably the second largest stream of the island and is important to the Eskimos because of the steady fish supply available all winter long."[65] Later in the spring he joined his friends George Lowery and Henry Bruns in Louisiana, following Audubon's trail and collecting birds.[66]

In early August, while finishing his summer's work at the George Reserve in Michigan, he received his renewed contract from Cornell. He had applied for promotion from assistant professor to associate professor, and although he had Allen's backing, he was turned down. He wrote to Allen: "People in general seem to approve of my work there in Ithaca,

8.4. *George at work painting in Tamaulipas, Mexico, spring 1941. Photo by Olin Sewall Pettingill, Jr. Courtesy of Olin Sewall Pettingill, Jr.*

but officially I feel as if someone were trying to 'put the skids under me.' . . . Feeling as I now do, and have been feeling for some time, I'm not sure that I'm really worth much to the institution. A relationship ought to be mutually helpful and stimulating."[67]

Allen responded with a sympathetic note, letting George know that he was appreciated and asserting that both Allen himself and the laboratory of ornithology did "benefit tremendously" by having George on the faculty.[68] George was not convinced. In answer to Allen he observed of the determination made by the university president:

The significance of Dr. Day's decision is simply this, as I understand it: I am one of those 'on the fence' faculty members likely to be dropped at any time. I am sorry he has taken this attitude for I don't think it's warranted. I have taken the attitude right along that Cornell was a sort of permanent working place for me. . . . We do not know what the year will bring forth, of course. If I were drafted, the whole picture might be considerably simplified. Since I have the appointment for the year I believe the thing to do is stay, do my best to get the collection of birds into good shape so that some one else may carry on, and then find a new connection. I shall leave feeling that Cornell hasn't begun to tap my resources.[69]

Allen pleaded George's case with the new department chairman, F. B. Hutt:

> I have written George assuring him that it was a great disappointment to me also that his title was not changed and that we all have the greatest appreciation and admiration for his work here and that I would do anything within my ability to make his tenure more satisfying. However, I feel quite sure that he would appreciate a word from you. . . .
>
> George certainly has done a fine job on our collection and he is a most prolific worker as you doubtless know. He is rapidly gaining recognition not only as one of the best bird artists in this country, but also as a leading taxonomist. . . . You don't suppose Dr. Day would change his mind on the subject, do you, under the circumstances?[70]

Hutt discussed the problem with the dean of the College of Agriculture, then responded directly to George on August 21. The answer was negative: no promotion, no raise. George's position, funded by a mix of federal and state funds, simply limited the options.[71]

The next day, apparently with mixed emotions about his patriotic duty and his unhappiness at Cornell, George filled out a selective service questionnaire and deliberately listed himself as 1A. He told Allen: "We'll call it my duty since that's a convenient, cover-all term."[72] In truth George had been corresponding with Van Tyne and others since March about going into the armed services. By spring he had contacted both the navy and the army regarding possible positions he might obtain. He apparently did not share his possible plans with Allen until he found that he was not receiving a promotion and raise at Cornell.

The fall of 1942 was full of anticipation. George sought to enlist in the army or navy, feeling that he had expertise to share. He visited recruiting offices in New York City for interviews, but heard nothing from military authorities. Working with William Dilger, then an undergraduate student, George busied himself in cataloging a sizable collection of birds that had been donated to Cornell. Dilger was also interested in painting birds, and George provided guidance, but all around them young men were leaving for the war and George wanted to join them.

CHAPTER 9

World War II

One blessing of war is that we're obliged to become familiar with new country and to have to see new birds and mammals and plants.

GEORGE MIKSCH SUTTON

G eorge had been party to what some had perceived as an "anti-war" protest during his senior year at Bethany College, but in truth it had been an opposition only to the establishment of an ROTC unit at the college. He had felt the unit inappropriate at a church-supported school. It was thus, perhaps, with a twinge of guilt as well as with a feeling of duty and an anticipation of adventure that George wanted to enlist in the military. Many of those around him and younger ornithologists had already gone, and by the spring of 1942 he was hearing of their travels. He wrote to congratulate his West Virginia friend George Breiding on attaining the rank of corporal. "Go ahead and be tough as you like," he admonished. Your men may cuss you under their breath, but they won't really hold anything against you."[1]

Although volunteering for military duty, George was specific in what he wanted to do. In his letter to Breiding, he noted: "I have written down a long list of my special qualifications for the use of the Adjutant General and his cohorts, but have no idea whether this will convince them that I can be of some real assistance in the Far East or in Alaska. If I do not go off on some military adventure, I hope to get down to the eastern panhandle of West Virginia . . . or into Mexico."

Getting into the military was not that easy for George, however. On March 17, 1942, he wrote to Van Tyne: "There is no assurance that I will be taking an active part in the present war, though I have, as you know, been in correspondence about it." On March 23 he again wrote to Van Tyne: "I wonder where I'll be! This correspondence about Army and Navy seems to be getting me nowhere." In April he told Van Tyne that he was planning to spend the summer in Michigan if at all possible, noting: "There is no assurance whatever that I shall be allowed to take part in the Army's camouflage work though some good letters of recommendation have gone in."[2]

On May 27 he wrote again to George Breiding, now a sergeant: "I thought by this time I'd be writing on Army or Navy stationery, but it doesn't seem to be working out that way."[3] With still no word from the army, on June 10, Sutton wrote to Van Tyne: "I'm planning to come to Michigan toward the end of this month unless I hear from the Army. If I have to pack up and leave from there, I have to, that's all." On September 7 he told Van Tyne: "I am going to New York tomorrow or Wednesday night for an interview with the Navy and I have no idea what may be in store for me." On September 21 he lamented: "Why the Navy doesn't do something, I don't know. Can it be that just because I'm 44 I'm considered old? Perhaps that's the trouble." On September 30: "No word yet from the Navy. I'll have to whip my topcoat out of storage if I wait much longer." On October 2: "My Navy papers are in Washington now—or at least were there day before yesterday when we spoke with them direct. A guess has been expressed that I shall be waiting hereabouts a few weeks more but apparently it is impossible to make any definite plans under the circumstances." On November 4: "I still am marking time, wondering what is going to happen next." On November 12: "I have just had another Army interview and now feel myself so definitely on the fence between Army and Navy that I have no idea which way I'll fall."[4]

In truth George probably had higher hopes for the army. Pettingill, then a professor at Carlton College in Northfield, Minnesota, had contacted Laurence McKinley Gould of the Arctic Section of the Arctic, Desert and Tropic Information Center of the Army Air Forces on George's behalf. As a civilian, Gould had been a professor of geology at Carlton College. As an academic with research experience in the Arctic, George had a great deal to offer with regard to arctic survival training.[5]

In anticipation of military service George shipped his paintings to Van Tyne for storage at the University of Michigan and made arrangements with S. Charles Kendeigh to take over in the event that he had to step down as president of the Wilson Club.[6] At last the call came in late December 1942. George entered the U.S. Army Air Corps as a captain and was sent to Eglin Field near Valparaiso, Florida. On March 20, 1943, he reported for duty at the Army Air Forces Officer Training School in Miami Beach, where he stayed at the Roney Plaza Hotel (fig. 9.1). The training was punctuated with close-order drills and critiques of how he wore his uniform. An officer in charge of a drill once barked: "You're a bunch of conceited, high-handed, prima donnas." And George had to agree with him. His fellow recruits were all from the ranks of businessmen and professionals; the reality of war had not really set in. On May 1, 1943, George was given a diploma and a commission: he was Captain George Miksch Sutton. He was also on his way to the Army Air Forces Arctic, Desert and Tropic Information Center at the University of Minnesota campus in Minneapolis.[7]

In Minnesota George began pulling together information on survival of downed pilots in the Arctic and quickly learned that most did not sur-

9.1. George Miksch Sutton, army recruit. The portrait photo in his new uniform was taken before he had completed officer training to become Captain George Miksch Sutton. Courtesy of Dorothy Miksch Sutton Fuller.

vive. His task was to develop gear and educational materials to improve the odds for survival. In his free time, George renewed his friendship with Walter Breckenridge at the Minnesota (later James Ford Bell) Museum of Natural History and was able to use the museum as a research base. He also spent time there afield with his college roommate, Sewall Pettingill, who was teaching at nearby Carlton College. He often visited with Pettingill's family, taking special delight in the Pettingills' two young daughters—George's god-daughters.[8]

While working in Minneapolis George provided funds to create the exhibit of Swallow-tailed Kites that remains, to this day, just inside the front door of the James Ford Bell Museum. The exhibit features one mounted kite and three painted ones flying in the background at a site seventeen miles below Winona, Minnesota, at Guinn's Bluff, overlooking Mississippi River bottomland. The diorama was constructed by Breckenridge, and the background painting was done by Francis Lee Jaques. George's sponsorship of the exhibit was to provide a memorial for his mother, Lola Mix Sutton.[9]

Although he longed to get to the Arctic, instead George was selected for another very unusual assignment: he was sent to Hollywood to represent his unit at "Fort Roach"—formerly the Hal Roach Studios in Culver City, California. That studio had shut down when Roach had been called to active duty, and the Army Air Force took it over for use as the home base for its First Motion Picture Unit (FMPU, pronounced *"fum-poo"*). George's task was to guide production of a training film on survival following a crash in the Arctic.[10]

When George got the assignment, he was certain he would be working "on location" in the Arctic and he began carefully outlining what the film should cover. His script included hordes of mosquitoes, ptarmigan, sundogs, snow and ice— but Hollywood would hear nothing of the real thing. They would create mosquitoes, ptarmigan, sundogs, and whatever weather affects George wanted. And they did. The completed film was titled *How to Survive in the Arctic*.

During his Hollywood tour of duty George saw Betty Grable "at ease off-stage," was "observed (or at least looked at)" by Tallulah Bankhead, and discussed the polar regions with George Montgomery. The actors and actresses had been given copies of George's script and a little background information about him, although they apparently did not believe it or think much about it. At one point during a discussion with Montgomery it became evident to George that Montgomery had read the script. A while later, as he and Montgomery found a common interest in pheasants,

George described geographic differences in them and drew a sketch to illustrate. At that point Montgomery suddenly exclaimed, "Holy smoke! You really do draw birds, don't you?"

On September 12 George wrote to his sister Dorothy that he had been ordered back from Hollywood before being sent to the Arctic.[11] But he was wrong again. In early October his section was relocated to the heart of the financial district in New York City.[12] There he stayed with his sister Evie, who lived in Greenwich Village. In New York George was a regular visitor to the bird range at the American Museum of Natural History, to the Metropolitan Museum of Art, and to the offices of the National Audubon Society. Throughout the war he was a contributing editor to *Audubon Magazine*, where in 1944–45 he published a serialized predecessor to his book *At a Bend in a Mexican River*. George took advantage of museum collections to make a few sketches (fig. 9.2), but to a great degree his artistic career was on hold.[13]

9.2. Captain George Miksch Sutton at work sketching American Woodcock during free time from his military duties. (The photo incorrectly shows him sketching with his left hand; apparently it was printed in reverse.) Courtesy of Olin Sewall Pettingill, Jr.

Although his section was now headquartered in New York, aspects of the arctic survival research program were being conducted elsewhere, and in early December 1943 George was reassigned to Wright-Patterson Army Air Base near Dayton, Ohio, from which he made frequent trips back to New York. At Wright-Patterson he came to know Nicholas Collias, an ornithologist who later became a professor at the University of California in Los Angeles.[14] There he also met the famed arctic explorer Vilhjalmur Stefansson, who was not only working for the war effort but was preparing an *Encyclopedia Arctica*—a *vade mecum* for Arctic research. Stefansson was of Icelandic heritage, Canadian by birth, but an American citizen. He had begun the project in 1935 and it was continuing during the war, supported by the U.S. Army. Stefansson and Sutton became good friends, and George was recruited to prepare ornithological materials for the *Encyclopedia*.[15]

Although much of George's wartime military activity was in developing and testing survival gear and preparing training materials, he occasionally participated in real rescue missions. On March 28, 1944, he wrote to Van Tyne that he had just returned from such a mission. He was excited, noting that he found the work extremely interesting and worthwhile, especially when he got out and grappled with the elements.[16] Two weeks later, however, he lamented to Alexander Wetmore that there was then little ornithological in his life and that he seemed to have a real job in the Army Air Force. He noted that since he was over draft age he had considered resigning his commission but that being "into the thick of the thing I feel that my knowledge is perhaps of some real use; so I intend to stay until the job's done whether I ever get back to birds again or not. I suppose this sounds a bit doleful. I don't intend it to."[17]

Although he was often totally immersed in his military efforts, and those efforts had earned him a promotion to major, when the opportunity arose George joined local birders wherever he was. These included naturalist and writer John Kieran. A visit to section headquarters in New York in August 1944 was immortalized by Kieran's devilish description of a local field trip to a swamp, with George in the group. Kieran was well known as a competent naturalist and birder but had never been afield with an individual as familiar with bird sounds as George was. With George calling out bird names at the slightest pip and "squeaking" birds into view by sucking on the back of his hand, Kieran began to feel professionally threatened. He decided to show Major Sutton a thing or two and led the group into the depths and briars of the swamp. George never hesitated. When it was time for him to leave for his meeting his only uniform was wet, bedraggled, and covered with yellow ragweed pollen. Kieran noted that he looked "more like an ill-used prisoner of war than a well-dressed officer . . . tokens of my displeasure marking him from head to foot."[18]

In early October 1944 the Arctic Section and George were again transferred, this time to the Army Air Force's Technical Center at McCoy Field in Orlando, Florida. There he lived off the base and purchased a bicycle for transportation to and from his office. George arrived just in time to experience a Florida hurricane and took careful notes on the responses of birds to it.[19] His birding companions at McCoy included Sergeant Roger Tory Peterson (known to all because of his field guides) and Lieutenant Frank McCamey, a meteorologist with the Army Air Corps at Orlando and a prominent amateur ornithologist and bird bander well known among banders today for his design of the "McCamey Chickadee Trap." George also quickly made friends with longtime Florida birders Lieutenant Joseph G. Howell, home on leave from the navy, and brothers Donald J. and Wray Nicholson.[20] It was easier to find time for birding and writing in Florida, and George's tenure there resulted in publication of several scientific notes in the *Auk*.[21]

In February and March 1945 George finally got the chance he was waiting for. He was sent on a short-term assignment to Ladd Field, near Fairbanks, Alaska, where he tested sleeping bags and snowshoes under field conditions. Although his official work was testing survival gear, George kept careful notes of birds and other wildlife seen and collected several specimens during daily trips afield. His "Notes on the Winter Bird-Life of Fairbanks, Alaska" appeared in the *Condor* before the end of the year.[22] From there he made two trips to Attu, at the western end of the Aleutian Islands. There he tested life rafts, assessed the length of time one might be able to survive in one, and happily recorded diving times of birds, salvaged and collected specimens, and birded with Rowland Wilson. Again his incidental bird observations became the subject of scientific publication.[23]

Back in Florida, on June 23 he wrote to his former student Robert M. Mengel, now a sergeant, with exuberance: "My Aleutians experience was great. I had a month on Attu—a gift straight from Heaven." He also noted that he had become "Chief" of the Arctic Section.[24]

In mid-August McCamey and his wife invited his two birding friends, Sutton and Peterson, to their home off base for dinner. Their dinner date was for August 14, which turned out to be the date of victory in Japan. As luck would have it the base commander, fearing that V-J Day celebrations might become too exuberant, confined all enlisted men to the base. Major Sutton could go for dinner; Sergeant Peterson could not. But George found a solution: he got a Jeep, picked Peterson up at his barracks, drove to the gate, and told the guard that he needed "this enlisted man for important duty off base." The ruse worked.[25]

A few days later Sutton and Peterson both received an assignment at Crowsbluff Landing, a remote site along the St. John's River. For them it was like Brer Rabbit being tossed into the briar patch. They were excited about the opportunity to work in a habitat where they might find Bachman's Warbler, a potential life bird for both of them. The birding was good, but they found no Bachman's Warbler. One day during this assignment they stopped at a small country store, and George drank some fresh local milk. Soon after returning to Orlando he sensed that he was not well. The war was over, however, and he was sent to Fort Bragg, North Carolina, to be discharged. He was feverish at the time, having contracted undulant fever, the human form of the cattle disease brucellosis, from drinking the unpasteurized milk of an infected cow in Florida. George was seriously ill and weak for months, and the disease would lay him low repeatedly in the years to come. Symptoms including a high fever, weakness, and depression can be recurring and can last for days or months.[26]

George was president of the Wilson Ornithological Club at the beginning of 1943 and became a life member of the organization, but when he entered military service he turned the reins of the society over to Vice President S. Charles Kendeigh. Having done so, he still remained vigorously active in the organization. The war delayed club meetings until November 1946, but while most business was carried out by mail, the executive council met in Ohio in August 1944. In 1944 and 1945 the same officers, with Kendeigh as president, were reelected by mail ballot. In 1946 a mail ballot was used again for the election of officers, and a new slate of officers was put forward. George was again elected president, with his friend Sewall Pettingill elected first vice president. Throughout the war Josselyn Van Tyne served as editor of the *Wilson Bulletin*, and George had remained intimately involved in Wilson affairs, especially in promoting membership, the bulletin, and the publication of color plates. At the 1946 meeting George was able to announce that the Wilson membership stood at 1,301, the highest to that date.[27]

Although George was most active with the Wilson Club, he was also active with the American Ornithologists' Union. He had been elected to a three-year term as a member of the AOU Council at their annual meeting in Denver in 1941, but due to the exigencies of war he was unable to attend the 1942 meeting or the limited council meetings that were held in 1943 and 1944.

In the fall of 1945, after being discharged from the army, George convalesced in Ann Arbor, Michigan, with Josselyn Van Tyne and his wife. In early February 1946 he returned to Cornell to finish cataloguing the Fuertes bird collection. But Cornell was not on his mind—he was only tying up loose ends. Van Tyne had found him a position at the University of Michigan, and he joyfully accepted it.

1. *George Sutton's watercolor of a male Mallard provided as a prize to Ed Miller for his essay "Why the Mallard Duck is My Favorite Bird." Courtesy of John Wiens.*

2. George Sutton's watercolor of an Eastern Wood-Pewee, painted in the spring of 1916 from a specimen that had been collected in Ypsilanti, Michigan. Fuertes praised the painting in a letter to George on May 26, 1916. Courtesy of William R. Johnson.

3. *Portrait of a Purple Finch given by George to H. Newton Miller and his family in appreciation of their hospitality during the spring of 1923. George had stayed at their home on weekends while taking an English course at Bethany College so that he might graduate. Courtesy of John Wiens.*

4. A tightly crowded plate illustrating a diversity of world birds; published in a 1925 dictionary under "bird" and also as a frontispiece for W. A. DuPuy's Our Bird Friends and Foes.

5. *A sample of the covers George painted for* Outdoor Life.

6. *George's original painting of a pair of Hooded Mergansers; published
on the cover of* Outdoor Life. *Courtesy of Albert R. Buckelew, Jr.;
Bethany College, Bethany, West Virginia; and Action
Images of Wellsburg, West Virginia.*

7. *Portrait of a Herring Gull and Common Terns done for Thornton W.
Burgess's* The Burgess Seashore Book for Children *(1929).*

8. Portrait of a Northern Cardinal and forsythia on the dust jacket of An Introduction to the Birds of Pennsylvania *(1928).*

9. *These Yellow-billed and Black-billed cuckoos exemplify the series of plates George did for* Bird-Lore *focusing on the characteristics of North American birds. Courtesy of Martin Sidor.*

10. *Downy chicks of thirteen species of shore and water birds painted by Sutton during his year on Southampton Island. These include: (1) Canada Goose,* Branta canadensis hutchinsi, *(2) Semipalmated Plover, (3) White-rumped Sandpiper, (4) Red Phalarope, (5) Pacific Loon,* Gavia arctica pacifica, *(6) Dunlin,* Pelidna alpina sakhalina, *(7) Long-tailed Jaeger, (8) Long-tailed Jaeger, (9) Arctic Tern, (10) Arctic Tern, (11) Semipalmated Sandpiper, (12) Ruddy Turnstone,* Arenaria interpres morinella, *(13) American Golden-Plover,* Pluvialis dominica dominica, *(14) Sabine's Gull, (15) Ruddy Turnstone,* A. i. morinella, *(16) King Eider. He also provided approximate age for each. From George's dissertation, plate 22,* The Birds of Southampton Island.

11. *Blue Geese on tidal flats at Cape Low, Southampton Island. From George's dissertation, plate 24, figure 2,* The Birds of Southampton Island. *Courtesy of William R. Johnson and the Carnegie Museum of Natural History*

12. *Mushrooms George found and painted on Southampton Island. This plate was included in O. E. Jennings's assessment of George's collections of algae and fungi during his year on Southampton Island. Courtesy of the Carnegie Museum of Natural History.*

George Miksch Sutton

13. *A Sutton watercolor of an Ivory-billed Woodpecker male based on work in the Singer Tract near Tallulah, Louisiana. This painting was done in the 1930s and touched up, especially to restore the red, so that it could be used on the cover of the Cornell Laboratory of Ornithology's record* Florida Bird Songs. *Courtesy of the Cornell Laboratory of Ornithology.*

14. *Fuertes' Red-tailed Hawk,* Buteo jamaicensis fuertesi, *discovered in West Texas and named by George Miksch Sutton and Josselyn Van Tyne to honor Sutton's mentor. Courtesy of the University of Michigan Museum of Zoology.*

15. *The hovering male in Sutton's 1934 painting of a pair of Ruby-throated Hummingbirds with cardinal flowers from Arthur Allen's* American Bird Biographies *(left) was a successful pose. He used it again in a portrait of two male Ruby-throated Hummingbirds with blue larkspur that appeared in a 1936 issue of* Woman's Home Companion *(right).*

16. *A 1937 oil portrait of George Miksch Sutton by Kenneth Washburn, then a faculty member in fine art at Cornell University. The ptarmigan painting in the background is by Louis Agassiz Fuertes and is at the Cornell Laboratory of Ornithology. Courtesy of Albert R. Buckelew, Jr.; Bethany College, Bethany, West Virginia; and Action Images of Wellsburg, West Virginia.*

17. *Elegant Trogon painted by George Miksch Sutton in Mexico.*
Courtesy of William R. Johnson.

18. *Acorn Woodpecker painted by George Miksch Sutton in Mexico in 1938. Courtesy of Lew and Kay Oring.*

19. *Sutton's Warblers, painted by George Miksch Sutton to illustrate Karl Haller's original description of the bird. George himself questioned that this was a true species, and it is generally considered to be a hybrid between a Yellow-throated Warbler and a Northern Parula. From the Collection of the Leigh Yawkey Woodson Art Museum, Wausau, Wisconsin.*

RED-HEADED WOODPECKER

RESTORE YOUR OUTDOORS
CONSERVATION STAMP
COPYRIGHT 1940.   NATIONAL WILDLIFE FEDERATION, WASHINGTON, D. C.

20. *George Miksch Sutton's illustration of a Red-headed Woodpecker on one of the conservation stamps issued by the National Wildlife Federation in 1940. Image copyright © the National Wildlife Federation.*

21. *A Common Nighthawk broods newly hatched young on the roof of the Museum of Zoology, University of Michigan. Sutton sat in the broiling sun, almost within reach of the bird, as he painted it from life. Courtesy of the Cornell Laboratory of Ornithology.*

22. *Sutton's medal received when he was honored by being named to the Knight Cross Order of the Falcon by the Icelandic government. Courtesy of the Museum of Natural History, Reykjavik.*

23. *A pair of Ivory-billed Woodpeckers along with Carolina Parakeets and Hairy Woodpeckers painted by George for Bailey's* The Birds of Florida *(1925). For this early assignment George worked primarily from specimens. It was not until he was nearly finished with the plates that he first visited Florida, and he had not yet seen Ivory-billed Woodpeckers in the wild. Note the rounded head, smoothly sculpted body, extensive white on the neck, and sharply pointed bill, contrasting with his rendering of these characters in the Ivory-bill portrait he painted after having observed the birds in 1935 (plate 15).*

24. *An adult Northern Goshawk captured in oil by Sutton. At the time he was learning the techniques of oil while documenting an invasion of Goshawks into Pennsylvania and educating hunters on the values of raptors. His views of Goshawks during his tenure at the Pennsylvania Game Commission were somewhat negative because of this bird's taste for game birds. Courtesy of William R. Johnson.*

25. *Sutton captured the expansiveness of the landscape in the work he did for* High Arctic. *This portrait of the dark morph of the Snow Goose—the "Blue Goose" for which he sought the nesting area in the 1920s—shows the bird heading toward open water in spring, the vastness, the subtle colors, and the bleakness of the landscape. This painting was not included in* High Arctic *(1971). Courtesy of William R. Johnson.*

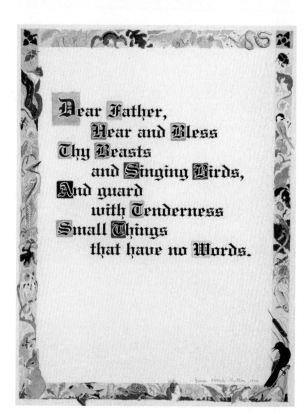

Dear Father,
Hear and Bless
Thy Beasts
and Singing Birds,
And guard
with Tenderness
Small Things
that have no Words.

26. *Dr. Harry Gifford Bull's* Prayer of St. Francis of Assisi, *the calligraphy illustrated with a border by George Miksch Sutton. Courtesy of Gifford and Grace Bull.*

27. *A fox squirrel painted by Sutton and used as the frontispiece for* Mammals of Oklahoma. *Courtesy of William R. Johnson.*

CHAPTER 10

The Michigan Years

One hill cannot shelter two tigers.

ROBERT B. PAYNE

Josselyn Van Tyne and George Miksch Sutton rank among the most distinguished ornithologists of the first half of the twentieth century, and they were longtime friends.[1] Their first meeting seems to have been about 1931, probably at a Wilson or AOU conference. Sutton was completing his doctoral work at Cornell and Van Tyne was well established as curator of birds at the Museum of Zoology at the University of Michigan in Ann Arbor. Early correspondence from Sutton to Van Tyne was most formal: "My dear Doctor Van Tyne," began Sutton's letter of November 7, 1931, requesting specimens of Horned Larks to compare with his Southampton Island materials. The return salutation was "Dear Mr. Sutton," and the response was terse, polite, and negative. There were no specimens at Michigan from the Hudson Bay region, but if there had been, they would have been lent.[2]

Sutton and Van Tyne kept up a lively correspondence for more than thirty years. They sometimes collaborated on research, they worked strongly together for the Wilson Ornithological Club, and Van Tyne provided research funds and opportunities for George, ultimately leading to his full-time employment at the University of Michigan. Beginning in 1934, George worked many summers at the Colonel Edwin S. George Reserve of the University of Michigan, twenty-two miles from the main campus in Ann Arbor. The George Reserve in Livingston County is an area of high hills, deep valleys, and a variety of bogs and other wetlands.

George's first position in Michigan came about as a result of a donation made to the Cranbrook Institute of Science. Van Tyne had been approached by Cranbrook about possible research funding for someone who could complete a study in a short time and present them with a manuscript for publication. He jumped at the opportunity. If this money produced good work, regular funding might be made available by Cranbrook for his students. He decided that George Sutton would be the man most likely to get the job done for Cranbrook. George's support that summer amounted to an honorarium of three hundred dollars from Cranbrook and living quarters at the George Reserve.[3]

After several letters were exchanged, George accepted the proposition. He noted his dissatisfaction at Cornell and that he was really interested in a more permanent position associated with the university—although *not* a teaching position. He was emphatic that the position must allow him time for painting and occasional expeditions as well as the opportunity for "good, solid, scientific work." Could Van Tyne get him a part-time position at the museum as well as the summer work at the George Reserve? George was given an "honorary" appointment at the museum and freedom to use museum facilities.[4]

During the summer of 1934 George studied plumage development in several species of sparrows at the George Reserve. He hand-raised nestlings for detailed study, using his screened-in porch as an aviary. There were so many birds to care for that he came to be known as a "sparrow rancher." Some of this work was published in the *Bulletin of the Cranbrook Institute of Science*, providing the institute with the quick publication they had desired and establishing George as a researcher that Cranbrook and Van Tyne could count on.[5] Popular accounts appeared in the *Detroit Free Press*, *Audubon Magazine*, and in the children's book *Real Boys and Girls Go Birding*.[6]

Finches were always favorites, and some of George's more important contributions to our knowledge of birds relate to them. His watercolor studies of nestling finches are unsurpassed, but there is much more to the many nestlings he painted than endearing portraits. Each painting documents the plumage development of its species. Through the 1930s and 1940s George continued his studies of Michigan finches. In a seven-part series published in the *Jack-Pine Warbler* he summarized fourteen years of work on fourteen species of finches at the George Reserve.[7] Any student of finch behavioral ecology would do well to read these accounts. Many of the paintings, now at the Field Museum in Chicago, have been exquisitely reproduced in Paul Johnsgard's *Baby Bird Portraits by George Miksch Sutton*.[8]

Throughout the war George and Josselyn kept in close contact, and Josselyn pieced together a position for his friend at war's end. During a brief visit to the University of Michigan in January 1946, George wrote to Robert M. Mengel: "Because of the fever, etc., I'm not really functioning here yet, save perhaps as the Wilson Club president."[9] He was, however, getting to know Ann Arbor, the university, and the birding community. Michigan was going to be his home. Then it was back to Cornell to complete cataloging of the collection there and to wrap things up in Ithaca.

On May 7, 1946, still suffering from the effects of undulant fever, George left Cornell by train for Minnesota to join Sewall Pettingill for a trip to the Nebraska Ornithologists' Union (NOU) meeting in Lincoln. There he formalized an affiliation between the NOU and the Wilson Ornithological Club. After traveling to see and paint a captive Whooping Crane and make a brief visit to the Black Hills, George headed to Ann Arbor and his new home.[10]

George's dependence on Van Tyne during the war and the transition from Cornell to Michigan was considerable. While at the NOU meeting in Nebraska he wrote to ask if the Van Tynes could put him up for a while. He said he did not want to get a place just yet as he might be going to Mexico. Van Tyne and his wife took George into their home and looked after him, assisting him with both personal and professional needs.[11]

George's move to Michigan was paralleled by moves of several students from Cornell to Michigan. He was not their only reason for moving, but he certainly influenced their decision. Within the year, for example, Robert M. Mengel and Harrison B. Tordoff had made the move. Mengel had worked with Sutton as an undergraduate at Cornell; at Michigan, Mengel did his dissertation on the birds of Kentucky and honed his artistic skills with guidance from George.[12] Tordoff had helped George complete his work on the Cornell collection, and George wrote of him to Van Tyne: "He thinks of coming to Michigan for graduate work and I do not hesitate to describe him as a very able and promising young man. . . . He puts up good skins and is helping me daily with the fierce cataloging job."[13]

In 1946 George was high on Michigan, heaped praise on Van Tyne, and was critical of Cornell, a human foible associated with transfer of allegiance and high expectations for a new beginning; the grass was clearly looking greener in Michigan. In October, after an exasperating exchange with Cornell regarding a student, he wrote to Van Tyne:

Do you know, Josselyn, I believe I have lost faith *completely* in that Cornell outfit? The atmosphere of cynicism and anything-will-get-by and pleasant inaccuracy there I call downright harmful to what I choose to call our cause and I feel that I'm doing a downright injustice to prospective bird students in advertising the place at all. Not that my advertising it or not advertising it will make very much difference: I fully realize that. But I can't bear to see those false standards in control. I believe your standards are real; that's one of the very special reasons why I am back of you now.[14]

The position George held at Michigan was a makeshift one with a relatively low salary and duties split among the museum, the George Reserve, and Van Tyne's ornithology textbook project. George anticipated a full faculty position in due time. He lists his position at Michigan on a curriculum vitae that dates from about 1968 as having been "Curator of Birds and Associate Professor of Zoology" at the University of Michigan from 1945 to 1952, although in his history of ornithology at the University of Michigan, Bob Payne indicates that George's position was as "half-time Curator of Birds and Consultant in Research, working in the museum, skinning birds, painting, writing and advising graduate students." George served on at least one graduate committee while he was at Michigan and was listed on the signature page as "Associate Professor." He also taught at least two courses, "Arctic Birdlife" in 1949, and "Life Drawing" in 1950.[15]

By early 1947 George seemed recovered from his undulant fever and was hard at work at the George Reserve and assisting with curating the bird collection at the museum. He frequently interacted with graduate students, although he was not on the graduate faculty and thus could not chair graduate advisory committees. In January he signed a contract with Oxford University Press for his book on Mexican birds. Things seemed to be going well.[16]

Within a matter of months, however, George and Van Tyne were at odds. Van Tyne did not like the fraternity that developed between many of the students and Sutton. George was eager to help students with their projects and enjoyed long discussions about all things relating to birds. In the museum George had an office close to Van Tyne's, and that contributed to growing problems between these two highly respected scientists. From afar they had been the best of professional colleagues. But George and Van Tyne were of considerably different temperaments, and their close association at Michigan, perhaps exacerbated by George's illness, led to trouble. George was "free-wheeling and in many ways sloppy," whereas Van Tyne was "meticulous and rigid."[17]

Sutton also did things that Van Tyne viewed as inappropriate or as not in the best interest of the museum. In his position at the George Reserve, George needed a vehicle and purchased a Jeep, which he loaned to students, including Tordoff, a young war veteran. Van Tyne was furious; students, he said, were *not* allowed to use the vehicle.[18] A continuing and festering problem was the disposition of specimens collected by students, such as Paul Slud, when they traveled to exotic places. Van Tyne felt that their specimens should belong to the museum, yet Sutton regularly purchased them for his personal collection. The students, of course, were delighted to be paid for their specimens, and George felt that he was helping to support their research.[19]

The final straw may have come one hot summer day when George was painting in his un-air-conditioned office without his shirt on. Van Tyne walked by the door and apparently gave Sutton such a verbal thrashing for his "unprofessional" appearance that from this point on, for George, there was no return.[20]

The next five years at the University of Michigan seemed to be a living hell for George, as can be seen in his own words in multiple letters to his family. Respite came only as result of periods of self-imposed exile to the George Reserve and frequent trips afield. The problem was not that George was right and Van Tyne was wrong; each owned his own share of the blame for difficulties. From afar the two had been admiring of each other's capabilities. During their years together in Michigan each found that the other did not meet expectations. George had been terribly dependent on Van Tyne, yet he was also fiercely independent. The conflict that ensued was more than just territoriality between two alpha males. For George it was the intersection of conflicting needs for dependence and independence, for financial and job security and freedom to do as he pleased.

Escape from his burdens in 1947 came in late spring with a trip to Tamaulipas, Mexico, followed in mid-June by a two-week collecting trip to the Black Hills with Pettingill and others. When the group visited Mount Rushmore, George "the tourist" Sutton could not resist a humorous photo. He and three of his comrades posed in front of the famous monument, mimicking as the historical figures represented. George, the elder statesman of the group, had to be George Washington, and the lanky Ernest P. Edwards had to be Abe Lincoln (fig. 10.1).[21]

10.1. *A lighter moment while studying birds of the Black Hills in June 1947: (from left) George Miksch Sutton, Robert B. Lea, John Boehm, and Ernest P. Edwards pose before Mount Rushmore. They titled the photo "The Big Eight." Courtesy of Olin Sewall Pettingill, Jr.*

Following the war the Museum of Zoology at the University of Michigan was clearly the hub of the Wilson Ornithological Club. George was president and Van Tyne was editor of the *Wilson Bulletin*. At the annual meeting of the club in Columbus, Ohio, in November 1947, George organized an auction of American and European bird paintings to raise funds for the relief of needy European ornithologists and contributed his own art to the effort. The event brought in $1,058.[22]

George was always the opportunist when it came to painting birds from life, and when a pair of Common Nighthawks was discovered nesting on a flat roof at the museum, he stripped to the waist to sit in the sun and paint an adult as it brooded newly hatched young nearly within his reach (plate 21).[23] As with some paintings in Mexico, he had to be ever alert to keep from dripping sweat onto his work in progress. He was enamored with how the birds survived the heat on the roof, and the subtlety of their plumage colors reminded him of Fuertes's mentor Thayer and his focus on concealing coloration.

In August 1948 George wrote to Alexander Wetmore at the Smithsonian that he had resigned his curatorship "in order to go ahead with certain work with a freer hand." He was devoting all his time to his portion of the *Encyclopedia Arctica* with the hope of completing it by mid-December. He added that he would not be attending the AOU meeting, that he was giving Audubon Screen Tour lectures, and that he would return to Mexico in December.[24] Although George was still a member of the AOU Council and in his letter to Wetmore asked if there was anything he could do for AOU "in absentia," he also indicated that he felt he should resign. In September George again wrote to Wetmore, this time concerning graduate student Charles O. Handley, praising his abilities and seeking support for his research in the Arctic. He added, however, that he was not on Handley's graduate committee and that "it looks as if I'd be steering away from directing graduate work from now on."[25] The truth seems to be that George was trying to distance himself from Van Tyne in every way possible.

In November there were other problems on the horizon. Although George had received a contract from Oxford University Press for his book *Mexican Birds: First Impressions*, the press had held the manuscript for more than a year and still had done nothing with it. It seems they wanted more of a field guide, which George was not prepared to write.[26]

Problems with Van Tyne and the frustration over his *Mexican Birds* manuscript were cast aside once more when, in mid-December 1948, George left with Roger Hurd for a long expedition to Mexico, returning to the Río Sabinas.[27] Back in Michigan by early May, he once again vented his frustration with Van Tyne in a letter to his family:

> I swear I would rather be *fired* from the University of Michigan than live a false sort of life such as might be expected of me with the Van Tyne military

channels system. I've always hated the idea of being fired, but right now I see how there are times when it is the only thing. At this moment it appears that I am too human for this place—too full of feelings for the students and the like. Nobody is going to tell *me* to stop loving and help- ing these students in ways that seem right to me. It's my way of living life. If I turn my Jeep over to Bud Tordoff to help him with his field work and so on that's my business. And the same goes for my library, paints, bird- skins and so on. I'll lend my name when I want to, also. And whatever prestige I have. Well, you see how stirred up I become! I wish another institution would offer me a job right now. I'd go and start again. Life is a series of startings again anyhow.[28]

With the summer of 1949 came nestlings, fledglings, and a crop of students from Cornell wanting to study George's Mexican bird collection. He was also incredibly busy doing pen-and-ink sketches for what he referred to as Van Tyne's "birds of the world book." Sometimes complet- ing two to three sketches per day, often of birds he had never seen alive, George was busy and sounded decidedly happier in letters to his family. He did the sketches at the George Reserve, sending the Jeep the twenty- two miles into town each afternoon with his day's drawings and speci- mens he was finished using, and it came back late at night with mail and specimens for the next day's drawings. The students bunked and ate at the George Reserve with him, and he was in his element. He wrote to his family in September: "I find I do so much better work out here at the Reserve, that I've just about resolved to stay (as long as I can—even pos- sibly through the winter). It's so wonderful to be able to shut the door and step right into the woods (or the swamp water if I want to)."[29]

Bad news arrived in September. Oxford University Press returned his manuscript for *Mexican Birds*. They suggested that the cost of the color plates made the project impossible. George was furious. He had a con- tract. They had held the manuscript for two years. George put it aside; his plate was full with other projects. Sewall Pettingill and his family joined him for the fall semester. Sewall had a one-semester sabbatical to write his *Guide to Bird Finding East of the Mississippi*. As soon as George finished the drawings for Van Tyne's book, he would do the drawings for Sewall's.[30]

In mid-September George was offered a position as curator of birds at the University of Kansas, but he had to turn it down because the museum director, E. Raymond Hall, wanted him to come immediately. George had too many projects in the works. His schedule continued to get busier, but he wrote to tell his family in October that he was "determined to get to Kansas U. for the spring semester" if he could.[31] Two weeks later he wrote to his family again: "I have had to tell Prof. Hall that I cannot take on the spring semester work in Lawrence. I've made too many promises and it seems to me I make new ones with every mail. A lady wants me to do 14 pictures to be used in calendars, writing paper, etc. The pay will be good (pot boiling) so I suspect I'll do them. But this will commit me until March 15! The semester in Lawrence begins January 30."[32]

At this point George was having trouble with finances, such that he said he could not even afford an apartment. His art was sustaining him but also restraining him. As an additional source of income he was on the Audubon Screen Tour circuit for that fall, scheduled to do about twenty lectures around the Midwest. He also spoke on his Mexican adventures at an Audubon convention in Detroit.

In late November he wrote to his Uncle Milton Fuller:

> The nominal connection with the University is not working. . . . I am going to form another connection as soon as I can, one paying a good salary so that I can ask Father and Anne to come live with me. I'd have gone to Kansas by this time but for the losing of momentum in getting these promised drawings done. My eye is on the southwest. . . .
>
> My relationships with Josselyn have settled down to a daily greeting or so and nothing more. He stooped very low in writing a complaint not long ago because an ornithologist visited this museum and came first to see me, not him. That's the 'lovely spirit' which exists around here. That's the 'incredible friendship' Helen Van Tyne wrote you about. The situation, with all its hatreds and jealousies, has made me bitter indeed, and the only light I see seems to be off in the southwest somewhere.

Then, in a strange conclusion to a long and negative letter, George added: "In some ways I believe I am happier than I have ever been. I seem to know as I never knew before what makes me truly happy, what makes a good friendship, what is worth spending money on."[33]

George mentioned in a letter to his family in December 1949 the possibility of a job with the navy at Point Barrow, Alaska, for a year. The letter was full of reminiscences, but it was obviously not the job he wanted.[34] In February 1950 he had another promising job possibility. Oklahoma State University had asked what might induce him to go there. A fireproof building for specimens and drawings were the essentials. He wrote to his family: "Let us keep our fingers crossed. I think it would be wonderful out in that country of wind and bright sun and dust, etc., etc. And only a stone's throw or so to the beautiful Black Mesa country."[35]

A crisis in the Wilson Ornithological Club brought another job for George. Van Tyne had stepped down as editor of the *Wilson Bulletin* following the 1948 volume, and David E. Davis had taken the reins as editor. Without consulting anyone, Davis changed the journal's size to a smaller format, published fewer manuscripts, and focused more on papers with tables of statistics. It was not what the members wanted, and Davis resigned after editing only one and a half volumes. George was elected editor to take over for the second half of the 1950 volume. He found it very time-consuming but continued through 1951.[36]

On March 3, the job *du jour* was again at the University of Kansas. E. Raymond Hall had been to see him again. He told his family: "I think he expected me to fall all over myself to take that job there; but I'm not at all sure I could get along with him. There is still talk of my locating in Oklahoma. Wouldn't that be wonderful." George apparently sensed the possibility of a personality clash with Hall and was showing some caution; he was not going to make the same mistake again.[37] His next letter continued the questing:: "More talk of going to Oklahoma, but to another school than the State University. Well, we'll see. I thought by this time they'd be asking me to the Univ. of Texas. But these things take time and lots of times the right persons aren't sufficiently interested."[38]

A week later George really released his frustration on his family, putting the focus of his ire clearly on Van Tyne:

> May I say, in all sincerity, that the administration will probably dislike seeing me leave here. . . . I believe Director Rogers will actually be hurt, for he'll feel that he's failed to help me adjust. But no one who understands this situation at all would want me to go on half-living the way I seem obliged to. There is a round of suspicion from morning to night. I hardly feel at ease with anyone because of the bitterness of the politics. I think the students sense the trouble and it's hard on them. It's got to the place where I hate to have them come to me for advice for fear Van Tyne will take out his jealousy *on them*.[39]

Uncertainties persisted through the spring of 1950. On April 2 George wrote: "I badly need an apartment, there's no doubt of that, but I can't afford one. The only answer is to change, draw a decent salary, and have a lot of these things. If I weren't so all-fired stubborn, I'd capitulate, knuckle under and abide by all the thousand and one rules of the Bird

Division, and stay here drawing a fair salary, but I swear I believe I'd rather die first: that's how strongly I feel about it."[40] And on April 16: "The Oklahoma business is still up in the air. I think some folks down there thought it would be a simple matter getting the President to OK my coming; but they had a hail storm with a lot of damage, and the money that would have given Sutton some salary now goes towards putty and window glass I guess. Sounds like justice to me."[41]

In late May 1950, George wrote to his family: "I'm very busy here and not nearly as miserable as I was over personality clash. Perhaps that's because Van Tyne is in Europe."[34] The pot simmered. Letters for the next few weeks were positive, but there was no further word of possible jobs in Oklahoma or Kansas.[42]

For Thanksgiving he was invited back to Cornell. Mrs. Madge Fuertes was frail and ill, and he longed to see her again. It was a good trip, and he had a chance to discuss with Mary Fuertes the biography of her father that she was preparing. Family letters after Thanksgiving repeat the refrain of George's near poverty. He was again frustrated by developments at Michigan. Then on December 10, he wrote to his family that he had been offered a job at the Highlands Biological Station in North Carolina but had turned it down: "Can't keep my mind off Oklahoma! Sure enough, they asked me to consider the Highlands job, but when the Oklahoma offer came, with the possibility of my going there to stay, I seemed to grow deaf to other calls."[43]

In the midst of his turmoil, George was also seeking another outlet for his Mexican book. On May 28 he wrote to the family that the Cranbrook Institute had the manuscript and was making a trial reproduction of one of the plates. That possibility also fell through.[44]

Along with all his other projects and a constant eye to a different position, George continued his efforts in preparing ornithological materials for the *Encyclopedia Arctica*, then funded by the U.S. Office of Naval Research.[45] In 1950 George was in Michigan hard at work on articles for the *Encyclopedia* under contract to the navy. He wrote to Paul Slud: "The final revising of the *Encyclopedia Arctica* writeups is going on. As I may have told you, this ornithological material has become far more extensive than was first planned, and it may now appear as a volume of its own in the series. . . . Never has an ornithological assignment been as stimulating as this. I am beginning to feel that I really know northern birds. I shall never truly know them, though, until I see Siberia."[46]

Although it was not of George's doing, one of his greatest failures in terms of energy and time spent on a project relative to its ultimate fate was his work on the *Encyclopedia Arctica*. As the grip of the Cold War tightened, 1951 was not a time when things arctic seemed important to the navy, and financial support for the *Encyclopedia Arctica* was ended.[47]

George had other things on his mind than the Arctic in 1951. He funded publication of a series of eight color plates in the *Wilson Bulletin* to honor the memory of David Clark Hilton, his childhood family physician who had sat on the doorstep with him and talked of the economic value of birds.[48]

George now applied for jobs at two schools in Oklahoma and one in Texas. He was determined to leave Michigan, to get back to Oklahoma or at least to the southern Great Plains. When he did not hear back about his applications he began to fear that his age was a factor in jobs failing to materialize.[49]

In the spring of 1951 George tangled indirectly with another science luminary, Rachel Carson. While an employee of the U.S. Fish and Wildlife Service in Washington, D.C., Carson discovered the many illustrations of birds that Louis Agassiz Fuertes had painted decades earlier for the Biological Survey. Recognizing their quality, she proposed to republish them. The project she initiated, however, was dependent on her obtaining permission and paying a fee to Fuertes's heirs. The plan got as far as an agreement by Harper Publishing Company to publish them. At that point Fuertes's daughter, now Mary Boynton, intervened. She had her own publication plans for her father's work and abruptly removed Carson from the project. Boynton gave no reason for the change except to quote George Sutton in a letter to Carson's boss, the director of the Fish and Wildlife Service, Albert Day. Sutton, she declared, had asked: "What does Carson know either about Fuertes or about birds?"[50]

Here George was clearly coming to the defense of his mentor's daughter; he probably had little if any knowledge of Rachel Carson's familiarity with birds and perhaps no knowledge that his statement would be used in such a manner.

During the summer of 1951 he got a respite from his troubles at Michigan and a tentative foot in the door in Oklahoma. He taught ornithology at the Oklahoma Biological Station at Lake Texoma. While there he collected several specimens for the Museum in Ann Arbor. He may have been personally frustrated with Van Tyne, but he was a professional and was always on the lookout for specimens to fill gaps in the collections where he worked. Robert W. Storer acknowledged receipt of the birds, noting that the skeleton of a Chuck-will's-widow was new to the collection.[51]

Back in Ann Arbor and with minimal salary, George had been reduced to accepting as many illustration jobs as he could and often coped with multiple deadlines. He wrote to his family suggesting that the epitaph on his tombstone should read: "He met a deadline at last."[52] At times he felt that his art had suffered. As he told his family in December 1951: "*Arizona and Its Birdlife* has appeared, and my two colorplates there are the worst of my career. I should never have permitted their reproduction. I did them under pressure and felt no inspiration over them at all. Gore, let it be a lesson to me!"[53]

On December 1 George and Andy Berger observed a flock of Pine Grosbeaks in the University of Michigan arboretum. They marveled at how tame the birds were, and George immediately decided that they could and should be painted directly from life. That afternoon he returned with his paintbox, paper, and supplies and, without an easel or table, was able to paint three of the birds as they fed on crabapples. Perhaps they were an omen of the brighter days ahead.[54]

George received word that his book *Mexican Birds* was at last going to be published—by the University of Oklahoma Press. That alone brightened his world. In early 1952 he would join his friend Herb Stoddard for a few weeks to paint illustrations for Stoddard's book *Georgia Birds*. Then there was the Wilson meeting, and following that he was to be awarded an honorary doctorate from his alma mater, Bethany College.

Finally, in April 1952, George was offered and accepted a professorship at the University of Oklahoma. His joy and relief were tainted by pent-up frustrations. He wrote to his family: "How good it will be to be a simple receiver of salary and know what to count on again for a change! A very heartening thought, no matter what happens, is that I am to get away at last from Ann Arbor. I had no idea that a place could become so repulsive—this despite my having really good friends there."[55]

On August 15, as George was en route to his new position, Van Tyne wrote, continuing to haunt him: "Won't you send your keys in to me? . . . Since I drew out your master key and paid the $2.00 deposit, perhaps it will be simpler if I turn it in to the key office. . . . We are sorry to lose you George, but we all hope you will be much happier in Oklahoma than we were able to make you in Michigan. Yours, J. Van Tyne."[56]

George's reply of August 20 read: "If Andy Berger hasn't given you my key by this time then perhaps he has returned it direct to Mrs. Bruch. . . . If your records show that I have more keys than the above-mentioned, then I fear there has been a mistake. . . . You should have let me pay the

$2 deposit. If you do not get your money back, let me know. Sincerely, GMS."[57]

Even after his arrival in Oklahoma, George's letters to his family expressed the bitterness he had experienced, often showing more joy at being away from Ann Arbor than at being in Oklahoma: "Oh, the joy of being away from Ann Arbor!" and "Everything seems to be working out well here, and in some ways I feel as if I'm really living again after a half-dead period of seven years."[58]

A personal hell though it may have seemed as a result of the personality conflict between George and Josselyn Van Tyne, there remained a great deal of respect between them. Van Tyne was known at Michigan for the kinds of control he exerted over people. Indeed in 1946, just before George's sojourn at Michigan, ornithologist Pierce Brodkorb had left because of a similar clash.[59] But George had made many new friends in Michigan and had been a strong positive influence on the careers of many students. He did not regret having gone to Michigan; he regretted the circumstances of his employment.[60] Through it all, he continued to be incredibly productive as a bird illustrator and as an ornithologist. He had illustrated Van Tyne's ornithology text, Pettingill's bird-finding guide, Brandt's *Arizona and Its Birdlife*, and his own *Mexican Birds* book. He had provided dozens of illustrations for other efforts and to raise funds for charity. These included a color frontispiece for Theodora Stanwell-Fletcher's fictional account of a graduate student's studies on the tundra near Hudson Bay in the 1930s, *The Tundra World*. While George's graduate studies on Southampton Island immediately come to mind as a model for her work, the story was based in part on her own work there as a doctoral student of Arthur Allen's in the mid-1930s, and of course she knew George and his work well from her days at Cornell.[61]

Shortly before Van Tyne's death in 1957, he visited George at OU. Graduate students Richard and Jean Graber, who had known Van Tyne from Michigan, noted that it was "one of the nicest visits we ever had with him."[62]

CHAPTER 11

Visiting Oklahoma

*Here we have learned to expect the unusual, for
montane forms drift into it in winter, many western
species migrate regularly through it, and a paradox-
ically eastern element has a way of appearing among
the transients in spring.*

GEORGE MIKSCH SUTTON, *Oklahoma Birds*

In September 1932 George Sutton had accompanied J. B.
Semple on a trip to the Oklahoma Panhandle in order to
collect specimens of the Lesser Prairie-Chicken for the
Carnegie Museum. When they arrived in Lesser Prairie-Chicken habitat in
Ellis County, they found that the birds were still molting and not suitable
for the purposes of the museum. What should they do? Rather than return
empty-handed, they decided to explore the region. George was familiar
with Margaret Morse Nice's book *The Birds of Oklahoma* and drew upon
his knowledge of that book.[1] He had been led to suspect that the Black
Mesa country in Cimarron County in extreme northwestern Oklahoma
might be ornithologically interesting.[2] How prophetic a suspicion.

This was his first trip to the Black Mesa country, a place that
enchanted him, drawing him back time after time for the rest of his life.
His first description reveals its uniqueness:

Here we found ourselves suddenly among mountains. On the sides and
tops of the mesas about us grew trees we had seen nowhere in more east-
erly parts of the Panhandle: scrubby oaks, pines, pinyons, and cedars.

Here, to our surprise, we encountered no Scissor-tailed Flycatchers, no crows, no Horned Larks—species we had seen almost everywhere in the central part of the State. Here Canyon Towhees, House Finches, Texas Woodpeckers, and Say's Phoebes were familiar dooryard birds.

We were in the field every day for the following two weeks. So interesting was our every excursion through the cottonwoods that lined the Cimarron, the Carrizzoso and the Tequesquite, or through the aromatic conifers of the mesa tops, that it was with great reluctance that we departed on October 5, making our way back to the prairie chicken country of Ellis County.[3]

Identifying the material they had collected in 1932 was so "fascinating" that they decided to return in September of 1933, this time finding the Black Mesa country "gasping in the clutches of a terrific drouth." George reported: "Hot winds from the southwest blew almost incessantly during our ten-day sojourn. Clouds of sand dimmed the horizon, made the sky sullen, robbed the landscape of its color. The Cimarron was reduced to a chain of vicious quicksand holes. No weeds stood along the stream-banks where a year before we had made our way through dense tangles. The cattle that scaled the inhospitable mesa-sides were pitiably bony. Bird life was scarce everywhere."[4]

George returned to Oklahoma in 1936, this time accompanied by his sister Dorothy.[5] The major focus of his efforts was a nearly six-week study of nesting Mississippi Kites near Arnett in Ellis County. The resulting scientific paper published in the *Condor* is unusual in several respects. It is quite unlike most of Sutton's other research in that it is a detailed study of the behavioral ecology of a single species, is more quantitative than most such studies of the day, and has a strong conservation message. George took aim at egg collectors and did not mince words: "No Game Refuge is safe from an egg-hog. Silently he goes about his business of extermination, bland words on his tongue, an expression of innocence on his face."[6]

Another full paragraph attacks egg collectors in no uncertain terms, then he ends his barbs with an understanding that his words might come back to haunt him: "Let this plea be a boomerang if it must, for I have collected many a set of eggs, among them those of the Mississippi Kite. But all sincere ornithologists want living birds to see and study, not stuffed skins and egg shells. How dismal to visit the shinnery country of Oklahoma in spring, feeling the morning sun on one's hands and face, but hearing no Prairie Chicken gobbling from a distant rise, and seeing no Kite at play among the clouds!"

And his plea did boomerang. R. M. Barnes, editor of the *Oologist,* a now extinct bird journal that focused primarily on the interests of egg collectors, took the most strident of George's paragraphs and reprinted it in his journal. George's words reprinted from the *Condor* emphasized that the Mississippi Kite was common in western Oklahoma, although its numbers had declined to the east. He apparently believed egg collectors had had a lot to do with its declines and noted that publication of this information

> will expose the very birds I watched from day to day at Arnett to the unscrupulous egg collector. With an automobile, a light-weight step ladder and a boxful of cotton, any egg collector can go to Arnett today and gather in dozens of Mississippi Kite eggs without even scratching his hands on locust thorns! He can gather them in, hoard them, exchange them, have a great time gloating over them. With a dime here and a dime there he can put the farm lads to scouring the countryside for nests. For him, the rarer the Kite becomes, the better. For him, the sooner the Kite becomes extinct the sooner will he be able to command "fancy prices," the sooner a set of Kite eggs will bring a Crowned Eagle set in exchange, the sooner his fame as an "oologist" will circle the globe.[7]

The editorial comments that followed George's reprinted paragraph struck hard: "Wonder if the collectors of Bird Skins endeavoring to build up a series might not be fully as dangerous to these Kites, as the few oologists that are left? Why, George, lay all the blame on the egg hunters? Is it an outcrop of the 'holier than Thou' egotism that seems all to [*sic*] common with those who would, and do kill the bird and prevent it from ever again laying an egg, in place of taking the egg and letting the bird go elsewhere and lay another? 'Oh! consistency thou art a jewel.' "[8]

During the Spring of 1937 George led a major bird-collecting expedition to Oklahoma that included Leo Luttringer, once his assistant at the Pennsylvania Game Commission, J. B. Semple, and Karl W. Haller, a fellow graduate of Bethany College.[9] This trip, however, nearly got George off to a bad start in the eyes of Oklahomans. The trip had been planned well in advance, and appropriate Oklahoma authorities had been contacted. But authorities there had also informed Audubon Society members of Sutton's plans and schedule. At the last minute the plans were changed, and the expedition arrived in the state a week earlier than expected.

The earlier arrival in Oklahoma generated great concern among Oklahoma Audubon members; they feared the worst. They had apparently intended to keep an eye on Sutton to see to it that he did not collect any Oklahoma rarities, as had been reported in a *New York Times* article following George's 1933 trip to the Black Mesa. An article titled "Did Sutton Get State's Rare Birds?" appeared in the newspaper *Tulsa World* on May 16. The state's Audubon members were furious. Citing prominent Oklahoma ornithologist Margaret Morse Nice, the article noted: "Although both Tulsa and southeast Oklahoma bird lovers offered assistance to the Sutton expedition if they would not kill rare birds, the Cornell group moved in 'very quietly' three weeks ago, Mrs. Nice reports. They did not notify anyone of their arrival, and Tulsans interested in their expedition were amazed that they had come and gone."[10]

Hugh Davis, director of the Mohawk Park Zoo in Tulsa, suggested: "Of course, nobody will ever know just what the Sutton expedition is taking out of the state, but after the way they've done I believe they would have taken an Ivory-billed Woodpecker if they had a chance."[11]

Word got back to Cornell and to the president of the university—indeed, it had even reached Van Tyne in Michigan. Something had to be done. George wrote to Van Tyne:

> I was not aware of the proportions the Tulsa anti-expedition uprising had taken. But reverberations finally came my way (after Mr. Semple had left us) and I went to Tulsa, had a conference with everybody, doubled the cash reward offered for the finding of a nesting pair of Ivory-bills, and was photographed for the papers shaking hands with the Director of the Zoological Gardens (who was, it seems, the chief bearer of the 'To the Styx with Collectors' banner). And the upshot of the visit was that I now have two youthful collectors in Tulsa lined up to get me a nice series of Southern Robins; the President of the Audubon Society there is organizing a new drive in the study of *subspecies*, and well, you know how these things go. What I can't understand is how the story of our going after Ivory-bill specimens ever really started. Someone with the imagination of a calf which has seen lush grass on the other side of the fence, I suppose.[12]

George's interest in Oklahoma was already strong. While serving in the Army Air Corps, he wrote to Josselyn Van Tyne: "Mrs. Nice writes me further about the Oklahoma book. I was quite serious when I told her I would take over and do the third edition 'as soon as possible after the war.' Whenever that time comes round I hope I can get into Oklahoma again, do some more collecting in certain parts, and set to work with all the fine collection now at Cornell and Carnegie Museum.

I may be working more or less with you by that time, but I believe Oklahoma will finance me."[13]

Throughout his years at the University of Michigan, George's hopes were with the setting sun—south and west to the red, dusty prairie and the Black Mesa country of Oklahoma. Once he had made up his mind about his destination, this was where his allegiance would be, and here at last he would achieve the kind of academic stature and recognition that would match his already substantial scientific and artistic accomplishments.

CHAPTER 12

An Oklahoma Institution

We shall have a glorious time together studying birds.

GEORGE MIKSCH SUTTON

The spring of 1952 could hardly have been more glorious for George unless he had ridden into Norman in shining armor and on a white horse.[1] His latest book, *Mexican Birds: First Impressions*, had just been published by the University of Oklahoma Press—his new publisher. The book came out with a great deal of fanfare proclaiming his achievements as a scientist, artist, explorer, teacher, and raconteur. All of a sudden he was a big frog in the smaller pond of the University of Oklahoma. His duties in Oklahoma officially began on September 1, 1952.[2]

George was anxious to get ornithology "moving" in Oklahoma and he felt he had strong assets: Margaret Morse Nice's book, *The Birds of Oklahoma*; four good graduate students; beautiful birds and great places for birding near Norman; *and* the Cleveland County Bird Club.[3]

At the University of Oklahoma George found a small bird collection that was in sad shape and quickly moved to build it and to build enthusiasm for birds in the state. The Cleveland County Bird Club provided both a focus and a means for his efforts. Even before his official duties started, he set about building a bird range for housing and studying bird specimens, using as a foundation his personal library and collection of birds and the few birds already at the university. Club members were George's eyes and ears, reporting arrival of migrants and sightings of rare

116

birds and keeping him informed of conservation efforts and politics. He helped them establish a speakers' bureau and a "teaching collection" of specimens that could be used to enhance their programs. George himself gave dozens of civic club talks each year.

By the spring of 1952 the next book George would illustrate was well under way and was already being touted in ornithological circles. *Georgia Birds*, written by Tom Burleigh, would likewise be published by the University of Oklahoma Press.[4] George spent the weeks before arriving in Norman at Sherwood Plantation near Thomasville, Georgia, basking in the southern hospitality of his friend Herb Stoddard, drinking in the spring landscape and Georgia birds, and transferring his joy to paper. He completed thirty-five plates for *Georgia Birds*, showing the birds in their Georgia habitats, often with spring flowers at their best. To see these plates is to be with George on March 23, 1952, and to view south Georgia in spring as he described it to his family: "It was gray and drizzly, but when it cleared a bit in the later afternoon Stoddard and I drove over the place just to drink in the beauty of the opening flowers—wild azaleas in fresh, crisp clumps; trumpet vines flaming over the partly leafed out trees; tall, sturdy spikes of the indigo, its blossoms very white against the red of the soil; and an utter riot of dogwood."[5]

At the end of April George, Stoddard, and Leon Neel drove to the Wilson Club meeting in Gatlinburg, Tennessee. George took along his finished *Georgia Birds* paintings and shared them with attendees in an impromptu showing. In spite of the high acclaim received for his artwork, George was not completely satisfied with the end product. In a later letter to his friend Phil Street he wrote:

> The Georgia plates didn't come out as well as they should have largely because nickel-covered engravings were used. The engravings on which I corrected proofs were copper, of course; but to make them more durable, nickel covering was ordered and no proofs involving these nickel-covered plates were ever corrected. I'm afraid it was all my fault, in the last analysis. I simply did not know that adding the nickel could change the engravings so much. Worst of the lot, to my way of thinking, is the Wood Thrush. I really feel sick at times about that particular plate.[6]

Checking a copy of *Georgia Birds* to see the problem indeed shows the plate appearing as if slightly out of focus, with details simply not as sharp as in other plates.

Spring 1952 was capped off by George's return to Bethany College to receive an honorary doctorate (see chapter 3). The occasion brought together old friends and fond memories. It was with high morale that he swept into his new home in Norman and the University of Oklahoma.

Shortly after his arrival George heard from Stefansson, who urged him to go ahead and publish his material for the *Encyclopedia Arctica* separately.[7] He was perplexed, considered it, and went through the manuscript again. It was badly out of date and lacking firsthand information from the Old World. He put it aside, believing that the *Encyclopedia Arctica* was a project abandoned.[8]

David Parmelee had come to Oklahoma to work with George and had come under the spell of his arctic tales. A dissertation project was needed, and George obtained funding from the navy and the Arctic Institute of North America for bird work on Baffin Island. In the summer of 1953 George and David made the U.S. Air Force Base at the head of Frobisher Bay their base of operations. Parmelee's dissertation was to be on bird breeding cycles in the High Arctic, but over the next few years George and David co-authored thirteen scientific papers on their arctic observations (see Works by George Miksch Sutton at the end of this volume). They worked on foot, walking great distances each day to observe nesting Snowy Owls, Snow Buntings, Northern Wheatears, Horned Larks, and other tundra-nesting birds. As time and assistance permitted they explored other areas by canoe or small plane. Toward the end of the summer George developed a hernia that required surgery that fall.[9]

The Arctic cast its spell again, and the *Encyclopedia Arctica* weighed heavy on George's list of things to do. He studied maps of Siberia, pored over the Russian literature, and wrote to Russian ornithologists, but the Cold War, language barriers, and other projects kept him from moving forward.

The fall of 1953 brought renewal of George's fire for Mexico. The cloud forest habitat above Gómez Farías in Tamaulipas was threatened by logging. Paul Martin and others—including George, A. J. Sharp, Byron E. Harrell, C. F. Walker, C. R. (Dick) Robins, Irby Davis, and E. P. (Buck) Edwards—formed an ad hoc committee to raise funds for the purchase of habitat on the mountain at what is known as the Rancho del Cielo. Frank Harrison, the Canadian ex-patriot who lived there, was to serve as warden for any acquired land, and the land was to be used for research and education.

In 1955 George wrote to Paul Slud: "One thing is clear: the job I must finish this summer, if I possibly can, is this arctic book. My hewing to the line on the MS forces me to give less attention than I'd like to certain other matters."[10]

George's bird range quickly grew into a major research facility at the university. Located adjacent to the Stovall Museum in a building that had once been a "gun shed" for the military unit on campus, it was described in 1956 as a "spacious thirty by eighty foot . . . attractive area" containing "literally thousands of stuffed bird skins" and "a growing bird skeleton collection." Its usefulness was enhanced by George's extensive personal library housed in the range. Specimens included George's very large personal collection of birds from around the world as well as a growing Oklahoma collection that would serve as the foundation for his 1967 book *Oklahoma Birds*. The specimens served as reference materials for his art, and the well-lighted room with ample table and cabinet surfaces provided the needed conditions for efficient and careful examination. They also served ornithology classes, graduate students, visiting researchers and artists, and the Cleveland County Bird Club. All who used the collection and many in the community who simply admired George and shared his friendship were drawn by his enthusiasm to salvage birds found dead or to collect specimens needed. The collection grew rapidly, and the space became inadequate. More important, George became increasingly aware of the age and structure of the building and its vulnerability to fire and the region's tornados. He longed for a larger, more secure facility; he shared his dream with all who would listen, hoping that the state or a donor would make it possible.[11]

In the fall of 1957, Sewall Pettingill invited George to accompany him and his wife Eleanor to Iceland for a summer of studying Icelandic birds. Would he go? *Could anything stop him?* Although he had long studied birds of the American Arctic, a complete understanding of the avifauna of the far north required further study in Eurasia. Iceland was a stepping-stone in the right direction.

George arrived in Iceland on June 10, a few days before the Pettingills, but settled in and immediately got into the field. After the Pettingills had arrived but while he was working alone on June 14, a creek bank that was saturated with rainwater caved in underneath him, pinning George beneath mud and turf in the cold water for an hour. Although shaken and cold, he was unhurt. Day after day George and Sewall tromped the volcanic slopes, rocky coasts, and meadows of Iceland. They sought nests and young birds. Sewall took still photos and motion pictures, George sketched and painted, regularly using live chicks as models. On July 28 the Pettingills returned to the United States; George remained another two weeks. The summer had been glorious. In *Iceland Summer* George spins a most readable tale of his exploits and the history, natural history, and culture of Iceland. His paintings from the summer include the downy chicks of many Iceland birds and are among his finest.[12]

George arrived back in New York on August 15 in the midst of a family reunion. Gathered to greet him were his father Harry, now 90 but still spry, and Harry's wife Anne, sisters Dorothy and Evie, and Evie's husband Harry Swartz and their twelve-year-old son Mark: a perfect homecoming. Long into the night George spun his magic, recounting his adventures, showing them his paintings, and sharing the verbal mystique of the Icelandic names of birds, people, and places he had come to know. As he spoke he began to realize that he really did have a story to tell—a long and wonderful story. He had not intended to write a book about his summer, but all of a sudden the book began to take shape, and he organized and reorganized the threads of its fabric in his mind over the next few days as he traveled back to Oklahoma and readied himself for the fall semester.

As he wrote George sent chapters to his new friend Finnur Gudmundsson, director of the Museum of Natural History in Reykjavik. He wanted to be certain of Iceland's history and geography as well as its natural history. In 1961 *Iceland Summer* was published, including an Icelandic Gyrfalcon painting as a colored frontispiece and sixteen black-and-white illustrations, thirteen of chicks. Most of the birds had been painted directly from life. Not only did George's extended visit lead to publication of *Iceland Summer*, but the collaboration with Sewall also resulted in a 16 mm film that both Sewall and George used on Audubon Screen tours. The film was made by Sewall, but George modified his copy to fit the story from his perspective. In 1962 George was awarded the John Burroughs medal for *Iceland Summer*.[13]

Iceland Summer was heralded in Iceland as well as in North America, and George wanted some of his paintings to remain in Iceland, especially his painting of a Gyrfalcon, Iceland's national bird. How the painting would be presented to Iceland seemed to be in question. In a letter to Bob Furman on November 9, 1967, George commented on its fate: "There's been a second request for the Icelandic Gyrfalcon original. A branch of our government wants to present it to Iceland in one way or another. Last month the talk centered in President Johnson giving it to Iceland's President, but more recently Dillon Ripley [secretary of the Smithsonian] wanted to present it to some other dignitary. . . . I feel that the painting should be in Iceland."[14]

The painting is in Iceland today, at the Icelandic National Museum, but it is now more than just a gift. George's painting of the Gyrfalcon on a ledge was used as the model for a 25-krónur Icelandic postage stamp. For his book and artwork focusing on Iceland, George became Sir George Miksch Sutton in 1972, when he was awarded the Knight Cross Order of the Falcon by the Icelandic government (plate 22).[15]

The Iceland trip with the Pettingills in 1958 inevitably rekindled George's dream of seeing the bird section of the *Encyclopedia Arctica* in print. But he was never to see Siberia, he would never have the comparative material he wanted, and the section was never published. In 1974 most of the sixteen-volume effort was microfilmed to be made available for researchers.[16] He wrote to Lew Oring in 1981 that it "reposes 'in state' at Dartmouth, along with the rest of the Stef. library." The Dartmouth library wanted to microfilm his manuscript, but George refused permission since he felt it needed updating.[17] As we have seen, it was in part a victim of the Cold War and changing times. It was also compromised by surging postwar growth of knowledge about the Arctic, with which the authors could not keep up. And in some measure it also simply collapsed under its own weight. To say that George's efforts were in vain, however, is not correct. There were benefits derived: the project had been a reason for being, a challenge, a goal to strive for. George found in it many moments of satisfaction.

In the fall of 1958 George became faculty advisor to the OU chapter of Beta Theta Pi and state chairman for National Wildlife Week for 1959. That year, as a result of his books, scientific publications, and international stature, George was named Research Professor of Zoology at the University of Oklahoma, a step up that brought with it a half-time secretary and a half-time field assistant. The latter position would support one of his graduate students.[18]

George set about tying up loose ends, revisiting data he had collected on sparrows and their relatives at the George Reserve in Michigan. Published in the *Jack-Pine Warbler* in seven parts during 1959–60, his work provided solid data and a firm understanding of the breeding biology of several species.[19]

In early October 1963 George was busy preparing line drawings to illustrate R. Meyer De Schauensee's *The Birds of Colombia* and nearly had them completed when disaster struck. Shortly before 8:00 A.M. on October 9, George walked into the storeroom in the bird range and accidentally knocked a bottle of carbon disulfide off a shelf. The bottle shattered and a nearby water heater explosively ignited the highly volatile fumes. He fought the blaze until the fire department arrived, saving the collection, but he had breathed in toxic fumes and burned his hands. He was unable to complete the last two drawings, the albatrosses and shrike-vireos, which were done by Earle L. Poole. George's hopes for visiting the Siberian Arctic were dashed. The fire in the bird range so affected him that he wondered if he would ever be able to walk and talk normally again; he suffered lung problems the rest of his life as a result of the accident.[20]

The fire did little damage to the bird range, but it further convinced George that the building was not fireproof and that a safer structure was needed for scientific specimens that included some extinct species. Throughout George's tenure at OU, his dream was for a "real" museum—a solid museum of bricks and mortar that would provide a safe place for growing natural history collections and a work environment conducive to working with them. Many times he felt the museum was a possibility, that the legislature or donors would provide funding for it and the university would build it. It did not happen during George's lifetime, and it was a source of continual and increasing frustration. In 1967, for example, he wrote to Dean Amadon at the American Museum: "We have a real 'museum problem' here. My valuable collection is housed in a building that is far from fire-proof. I am after money for a good building, one that may cost three million or so."[21]

With *Iceland Summer* and other books, accolades for George were accumulating. In 1964 he was awarded the University of Oklahoma's highest honor, its Distinguished Service Citation.[22]

After an absence of sixteen years from the pages of *Audubon* magazine, George returned to the magazine's editorial board and as a contributor. His article "Footprint Thieves" recalled the experience of being temporarily lost in the Arctic as night approached and he could not find his footprints to retrace his steps. After considerable worry and darkening skies at temperatures well below zero degrees Fahrenheit, George discovered the trail. It had been hidden. In each of his footprints a snow-white ptarmigan had taken refuge, blending in perfectly except for the tiny black eyes that had caught his attention and reminded him of tiny black beetles on the snow.[23]

Almost as soon as he arrived in Oklahoma, George began planning to update Nice's book on Oklahoma birds. He wanted sound records and good coverage from throughout the state. For fifteen years he worked with his students and members of the Oklahoma Ornithological Society to create the scientific record base needed for such an endeavor. He made many friends along the way and repeatedly joined them in the field. Black Mesa was a destination to which he returned again and again. Most of his students and his closest friends visited the area with him—Warren

Harden, Jack Tyler, John Shackford, Bill Carter, Bill Johnson, and many others regularly accompanied him in the field. Others, like John and Eleanor Kirkpatrick and Robert and Mary Frances Furman, occasionally accompanied him but provided support for his work in many other ways. Finally, in 1967, his *Oklahoma Birds* appeared, putting Oklahoma ornithology on a sound footing. Curiously, for a Sutton book, it is illustrated by only a single color plate and a few pen-and-ink drawings. As a capstone for the year, for his many efforts that brought recognition to the university and the state, George was inducted into the Oklahoma Hall of Fame.[24]

The massive effort that went into preparing *Oklahoma Birds* convinced George of the need for a really fine state bird journal. Using the Cleveland County Bird Club as a foundation, he reached out to birders and other ornithologists across the state. What was needed was to get the Oklahoma Ornithological Society (OOS; founded in 1950) to support a state journal. He talked it up, encouraging Oklahoma birders, giving each a sense of ownership in the idea. In 1968 George's vision became a reality. The *Bulletin of the Oklahoma Ornithological Society* was a group effort, and the group included not only members of the society but any who might be able to help with any aspect of the publication process. At every turn there was George Sutton, pushing, prodding, and pulling, always encouraging, praising efforts even as he rewrote manuscripts so that they might truly make a contribution to Oklahoma ornithology. He noted that if it had been titled *Bulletin of the Oklahoma Audubon Society*, he would not have fought for it. The *Bulletin of the Oklahoma Ornithological Society* was not going to be a chatty newsletter but a strong state ornithological journal that could be recognized for its scientific value.[25] George provided the leadership, manuscripts, and much of the funding, but he insisted that another OOS member serve as the official editor, thus spreading important roles and skills throughout the membership. He created a sense of urgency that inspired members to take good field notes and to publish them, and he gave OOS members a sense of accomplishment for what they had done. Above all George Sutton taught OOS members how truly to observe birds and to question what they observed and what they did not observe, rather than merely to check off names on a checklist.

Among George's legacies to the OOS and Oklahoma ornithology are species files that he began shortly after arriving in the state. He kept these current, adding new records and details and constantly building a history from which he could quickly determine changes in a species' status or distribution. The files were invaluable in the preparation of his book *Oklahoma Birds*, and they were invaluable to Fred and Marguerite Baumgartner as they prepared their Oklahoma bird book.[26] Letter after letter in OOS files reveals George's use and nurturing of these files. For example, he wrote to OOS member Ella Delap about them:

> Truly do I appreciate your help. I am very proud of these summaries. I seriously question whether any state is even trying to do what I've been trying to do for Oklahoma. . . . Material on certain species has so accumulated that I've been obliged to abandon folders and use boxes. One whole shelf is devoted to these boxes here at the Bird Range. Species so covered include the two eagles, the Bobwhite, the Cattle Egret, the Mourning Dove, the Roadrunner, etc. The Bald Eagle summary runs over 20 double-spaced typewritten pages. The Golden Eagle summary is shorter. The Cattle Egret summary is sadly in need of filling-in. That bird's spread has been downright spectacular. The Great-tailed Grackle summary is not up to date, either—another species with phenomenal spread.
>
> Help me all you can. . . . Encourage observers to let you know whether the Rufous-sided Towhees are of the plain-backed *eastern* sort of the spotted-backed *western* sort. I am keeping separate summaries for those two forms. Same for the Myrtle and Audubon's warblers, the White-winged Junco, etc. There's no telling when there'll be a switchback to earlier concepts.[27]

In the spring of 1968 George was named to the Administrative Board of the Cornell Laboratory of Ornithology. He particularly cherished the position because it frequently took him back to his alma mater, to the Fuertes paintings that were there, and gave him the opportunity to once again work with his graduate roommate and lifelong friend Sewall Pettingill, who was director of the lab.[28]

In July 1968 at age seventy, George was forced by state rules to retire from the University of Oklahoma. Retirement by no means ended his career at the university. He merely shifted gears and proceeded full speed ahead as research professor emeritus—teaching some informal classes, working with students, painting, writing, and continuing his research and public lecturing.

A month later he received a letter from his old friend Tom Burleigh. Would he be willing to illustrate Burleigh's next book, *Birds of Idaho*? It seemed like old times; George remembered being with Burleigh in Mexico and the pleasant days in Georgia when he painted the plates for *Georgia Birds*. Of course he would do the plates, but now that he was retired and on a limited income, he would have to charge. The plates would probably require travel to Idaho. In the end the funds were simply not available for the artwork, and the book was illustrated with a few photographs.[29]

Late in 1968 George had an opportunity that he had long awaited. The New Jersey State Museum proposed a one-man show of his work, emphasizing not the birds but the art. He was thrilled, but under pressure of other obligations, including seeing to the publication of Hugh Land's guide to Guatemalan birds, he decided against it.[30]

Hugh C. Land had been one of George's Ph.D. students and had focused his dissertation research on the birds of Guatemala. He received his doctorate in 1960 and continued his work in Guatemala while holding academic positions in West Virginia and Louisiana. In December 1968 he died of Hodgkin's disease. Land had completed the manuscript for *Birds of Guatemala* and before his death had given it to the Pan American Section of the International Committee for Bird Preservation. George thought highly of Land and his work and assisted the publisher and Hugh's wife to see the book through to publication (see also chapter 13.)[31]

During the summer of 1969 George traveled again to the Arctic, this time to Cornwallis, Bathurst, and Ellesmere islands with Stewart D. MacDonald and David Parmelee. This was the expedition that was the focus of George's book *High Arctic*. The trip also marked an incredible transformation in George's art. Instead of emphasizing individual birds, the art resulting from this expedition focuses primarily on birds and mammals in the greater context of their habitats (see also chapter 14).[32]

The fall of 1969 was a very busy one for George and was especially filled with honors. On September 3 he was honored at the University of Arkansas at the annual meeting of the American Ornithologists' Union. There he gave a gallery lecture opening a display of his paintings and drawings. Ten days later he was at his alma mater, Cornell, to receive the Arthur A. Allen Award for his effectiveness in increasing public awareness, understanding, and appreciation of birds. On hand to honor George at the occasion was perhaps the largest, most distinguished contingent of bird artists ever assembled: Robert Gillmor, Albert E. Gilbert, Arthur B. Singer, Roger Tory Peterson, Don R. Eckelberry, Stewart MacDonald, and Guy Coheleach.[33]

On learning of George's selection as the recipient of the Arthur A. Allen Award, his friend Dewey F. Bartlett, governor of Oklahoma, declared Friday, September 13, 1969, as George M. Sutton Day in Oklahoma. Governor Bartlett proclaimed that George was of international stature, represented Oklahoma with dignity in all his travels, and had brought great esteem to Oklahoma, the University of Oklahoma, and himself.[34]

Late summer 1970 provided George with an unwelcome visitor from the past when he developed a bad case of shingles.[35] In late December he was back at the Black Mesa, then in January 1971 he headed for Colima with a group of friends. In February he accompanied John and Eleanor Kirkpatrick and a group from the Oklahoma Zoological Society to the Galapagos—the trip of a lifetime for any biologist. The trip was a gift from the Zoological Society, but upon his return, he donated two thousand dollars to the society for use as they saw fit.[36] Obviously thoroughly enjoying his travels, George described them to C. Richard Robins, adding, "Never, *never* say die!"[37]

Sutton was negotiating in June 1971 with Wood Hannah of the Frame House Gallery in Louisville, Kentucky, concerning the production of reproductions of some paintings. He was particularly concerned about what the reproductions would be called, noting that "they will not be prints. The word *prints*, as used by reputable galleries the world over, means a certain thing. The phrase *good reproductions* is not derogatory. If you do market reproductions of my work, please call each item a reproduction, not a print."[38]

The spring of 1972 brought excited preparations for two major trips late in the year. George was asked to be one of the leaders on a tour to the Amazon sponsored by the Oklahoma Zoological Society in October, and he was invited by the National Science Foundation to accompany an expedition to the Antarctic. The October trip to the Amazon was largely a pleasant cruise, exciting for the diversity of new birds. Unfortunately, George returned exhausted and with a bronchial infection. He could not make the Antarctic trip.[39]

In late December George established the first record of a Snow Bunting for the state. His exuberance is evident in his description to Eleanor Kirkpatrick: "Listen to this: Yesterday three lads from out of state went to our Westheimer Field to see Smith's Longspurs, came back with a wild tale of having seen a Snow Bunting (no less), so I got the little gun (the big one's gone to the Antarctic with Dave Parmelee) and went after the rare bird. . . . and got it. It's the first Snow Bunting for the state. It's a real arctic species, and its presence here clearly proves that we've been having cold weather."[40]

What George did not mention was that one of the "three lads" was Ted Parker, who was destined to become one of the foremost birders in the world as a result of his ability to recognize birds by their calls and songs. He also did not mention that they had climbed over a fence at the airport to shoot the bird and were escorted off the property by a policeman—with the bird and without a ticket.[41]

At the end of spring semester in 1973 George returned to Colima, Mexico, adding White-throated Magpie-Jay, Wagler's Chachalaca, and Chestnut-sided Shrike-Vireo to his growing portfolio of Mexican bird portraits. The chachalaca provided excitement. Someone had found a live chachalaca and brought it to George to draw. He had it wrapped up and immobile until three dogs at the hacienda sniffed at it. The bird became terrified, burst its bonds, and wrestled free, scattering paints, brushes, and water jar. George and the dogs all raced around the yard chasing the chachalaca, the dogs yelping, the chachalaca squawking, and George yelling. The finished painting is placid, with no dogs in sight.[42]

The fall of 1973 brought yet another honor, though as George put it, a somewhat "farcical" one: he received a letter from Kentucky Governor Wendell H. Ford naming him a "Kentucky Colonel and a member of the Governor's staff." The honor came about through the beneficence of Wood Hannah. In his letter of response to Governor Ford, George suggested that as a Kentucky Colonel he "should make better and better bird drawings from now on."[43]

Those who attended the annual Arthur Allen Award dinner at Cornell on September 28, 1974, heard a statement from George, who could not attend, that he and Sewall Pettingill were endowing the Louis Agassiz Fuertes Lectureship in honor of George's mentor.[44]

The American Ornithologists' Union held its ninety-second annual meeting at the University of Oklahoma in October 1974. George did not want it there, but he was powerless in opposing it, and in the end he was the "host of honor," being feted left and right. The cover of the *Auklet* (the irregular and irreverent parody of the AOU's *Auk*) proclaimed that the meeting was being held at "George Suttonland, Oklahoma." One of the highlights of the meeting was a special art show titled "The Fuertes-Sutton Tradition in American Bird Painting." George was hailed once again as the most prominent of Fuertes's immediate successors, and the exhibit assembled in his honor included works of nine artists who had benefited directly from George's guidance: Robert Verity Clem, Albert Earl Gilbert, H. Albert Hochbaum, John Langford, Donald L. Malick, Robert M. Mengel, David F. Parmelee, Orville O. Rice, and Don R. Eckelberry.[45]

One of the social highlights of the meeting was a trip to the Oklahoma City Zoo for ground breaking ceremonies for "Amazonia," the George Miksch Sutton Tropical American Rain Forest Exhibit. I attended that ground-breaking and it was one of the most spectacular of such events. After dignitaries had been introduced and George's contributions dutifully acknowledged, the master of ceremonies introduced "Senorita *Priodontes giganteus*" to do the actual ground breaking. At the moment of her introduction, a huge crane lifted a wooden crate from its base to release a giant armadillo from South America. The armadillo immediately dug in, almost disappearing beneath the Oklahoma soil before it could be corralled.

Two years after the Oklahoma AOU meeting George wrote to his friend Joe Hickey, once again revealing deep frustrations from his years in Michigan: "AOU meetings have depressed me, some of them badly. The recent meeting in Norman, held wholly against my wishes, was almost more than I could endure. . . . The Ann Arbor experience . . . seems to have closed my 'career' as an ornithologist. I decided—in the spring and early summer of 1952, while making the drawings for Tom Burleigh's *Georgia Birds*—that I was merely an admirer and lover of birds, not an ornithologist in the AOU sense of the word."[46]

Even the AOU celebration and the recognition it brought both to George and to the university still brought no signs of an effort to replace the old bird range with a safe modern facility. There had been talk for years, but only talk. In January 1969 the bird range had been burglarized. George had long realized how vulnerable the collection was and had gone to the administration with a plan to give paintings for sizable donations toward construction of a new museum. The administration balked at the plan, seeking instead a single donor who would provide the funds needed. They acknowledged the state of the facility. Stovall Museum Director Bruce Bell was later to describe it as "a mishmash of inadequate and often deteriorating buildings including old wooden military barracks, a former stable, a converted gun shed and vehicle garages."[47] George decided to send his most valuable specimens to a museum that could guarantee their safety. His dean, Carl Riggs, asked if there was not something that could be done to keep the collection at OU. George responded:

> For some time (several years in fact) I have been so concerned over the problem of a museum for this campus that I have not done many things that I know I should have done—things that I know I can do well. I have devoted myself to concern . . . and that's no way to produce.
>
> With your help I am now going to stick to painting and writing and we'll see if I don't produce something worth mentioning. . . . For me to get bogged down with worry about my collection and paintings and about a museum for our campus is a mistake.[48]

Nonetheless, George continued to press his case. He had no success. He blamed himself to some extent, noting in a 1974 letter to his friend Chris Anthony of Oklahoma City: "Twenty years ago I should have started a real drive myself for the right sort of Bird Range here. I kept mentioning such a thing, but didn't organize it and get it going."[49]

It was time to do something. George had been considering possible repositories for his specimens and finally settled on the new Delaware Museum of Natural History in Greenville, Delaware. He packed box after box, several thousand specimens, for shipment to Delaware. Although he had some regrets, he told Chris Anthony that his "principal feeling [was] one of gratitude for having found a really safe place for them all." John du Pont personally brought his executive jet to Oklahoma to take the specimens to their new home.[50]

In January 1975 George traveled to Colima, Mexico, in an effort to add to his collection of Mexican bird paintings. While he succeeded in getting some drawings, he became ill and could not finish them at the time.[51] A few months later his *Portraits of Mexican Birds* appeared, including a sumptuous collection of fifty paintings spanning the period 1938 to 1973. George was understandably pleased with the book, the more so because his friends John and Eleanor Kirkpatrick were discussing plans with him for a new gallery to exhibit the originals in Oklahoma City.

George traveled to Mexico again in early February 1976, this time leading a group of twenty members of the Oklahoma Zoological Society to the Rancho del Cielo. They had a great time, and George was at his best as host and "tour leader."[52]

In 1978 the Kirkpatrick Center, a museum complex developed by his friend John Kirkpatrick, opened in Oklahoma City. A major feature of the center was a special gallery displaying many of George's finest paintings. John Kirkpatrick had acquired paintings over the years, simultaneously supporting George's and student research.

March of 1980 brought a letter from OU President William S. Banowski announcing his decision to remain at OU, touting how support for university endeavors had grown, and noting a $12 million expansion of the university library. The letter also mentioned specific goals for the future, including new facilities for baseball and gymnastics teams, a music building, and a pharmacy building. George kept the letter—and annotated it: "no museum mentioned." Clearly he was disappointed. His dreamed of museum was nowhere on the horizon.[53]

Other events pleased George and revealed the depth of appreciation for his efforts. In 1980 he was named to the Oklahoma Writers Hall of Fame.[54] On November 8, 1980, the city of Norman honored George by establishing the George M. Sutton Urban Wilderness Area. This 160-acre site in northeastern Norman, widely known as "Hospital Lake," includes a stream and a diversity of habitats. It was a site George often visited alone or with his classes.[55]

The University of Oklahoma College of Fine Arts School of Music hosted a "Dedication Concert" by the piano faculty on February 28, 1981, to honor George, who had donated a concert grand piano to their program. His donation was to honor his mother for her gift of music to him. OU President William Banowski, with funds from the OU Associates, had matched George's gift with a second concert grand piano.[56]

Even in ill health, George reached out to those who reached out to him—sometimes to strangers who had questions or needs that appealed to him. When I was editor of the *Wilson Bulletin* Luis Baptista submitted a fine article on variation in the Mexican woodpeckers of the genus *Piculus*. Luis had illustrated the manuscript with original artwork he had done. While Luis had submitted a well-written manuscript, the artwork was only adequate. Because of his expertise with Mexican birds and his abilities as an art critic and teacher, I sent the manuscript to George to review. He agreed with the quality of the scientific work but felt the artwork did not do justice to the subject. Luis's work captured George's enthusiasm, and the two began corresponding. In the end George painted the frontispiece for the article—vignettes of five woodpecker heads—one of his last artistic efforts.[57]

In 1981 George was approached by fellow Oklahoman Anne Small and asked to write a foreword for her book on decorative bird carving. George had never addressed bird carving as a subject in his writing and had never been a carver. But he knew birds, and this was an art form that he admired. His foreword to the book brings us full circle—back to George's boyhood, his Uncle Frank's farm in southern Minnesota, and the big dictionary with its illustrations of birds that he had learned from so long ago. It crosses the years, reminiscing—a blizzard on Southampton Island, an encounter with an abstract artist, his own quest for accuracy—not the tedious counting of feathers but the illusion of a real live bird brought about by the understanding of the marriage of form and function, color and line.[58]

A month before his death George wrote to the Board of Directors of the Prairie Raptor Center, a fledgling organization determined to build a research center near Tulsa for the study of birds of prey. He had been nurturing the organization since at least 1980.[59] George praised the board's leadership and offered strong encouragement:

It will be advantageous to have a dedicated group working on Oklahoma's raptors and on reestablishing some of Oklahoma's former resident birds of prey as breeding birds in the state. I feel confident you should be successful in releasing our national bird the Bald Eagle in the state as well as the White-tailed Kite and the former native Swallow-tailed Kite.

I sincerely hope that the Center will receive support from the Tulsa community and the state in general so that the Center can function on a worldwide as well as a local basis. For not only are the birds of prey in Oklahoma of great importance and worthy of attention, but also are those raptors in many other areas of the world.[60]

George Sutton spent the last thirty years of his life in Oklahoma, longer than he had lived at any other location. It was home. And those around him at the university, in the city of Norman, and throughout Oklahoma were in some sense family. They were generous to him; he was generous to them. George was never an affluent man, but he was frugal and supported causes in which he believed. He was an integral part of the university and Norman and Oklahoma City communities, involved with everything from the Cleveland County Bird Club and Oklahoma Ornithological Society to the university's football, wrestling, and music programs and the Oklahoma City Zoo. He was loyal to his Oklahoma community, who were loyal to and appreciative of him.

On March 3, 1981, the city council and mayor of Oklahoma City passed a resolution dedicating the Galapagos Islands exhibit at the Oklahoma City Zoo in honor of George. George spoke to the Oklahoma Zoological Society on the occasion of the dedication. Reflecting on the fullness of his own life, he quoted from the fourth century B.C. Greek dramatist Menander of Athens:

> I hold him happiest . . .
> Who, before going quickly whence he came,
> Hath looked ungrieving on these majesties:
> The world-wide sun, the stars, water and clouds,
> And fire. Hast thou a hundred years to live
> Or but the briefest space, these thou canst always see.
> Thou wilt not ever see a greater thing."[61]

In December 1981 the OU School of Music decided to honor George with a series of chamber music concerts on Sunday afternoons. George was very pleased.[62]

CHAPTER 13

Teacher, Conservationist, Philanthropist

You felt the enthusiasm he took everywhere.

GARY D. SCHNELL, *George Miksch Sutton the Educator*

lthough George Sutton is best known to most of us as a bird artist and ornithologist, he was also a dedicated teacher and mentor.[1] His success as both a scientist and an artist came as a result of the depth and breadth of his knowledge, great abilities to see and understand interrelationships and patterns in nature, and an inquisitiveness that never let up. His focused, careful observations, rigorous follow-through, and meticulous compiling, note taking, and documentation led to the truth he sought in all that he did. George's success as a teacher was a function of these same qualities—tempered with patience and a sincere desire to be of service. It also included a positive, one-on-one approach with students, focusing on the good, demanding the best. Although he has been described as a very private person, he excelled at one-on-one relationships in which he played the role of teacher—he drew his students in with a vortex of enthusiasm, insight, and his ability to interject his personal experiences into a lesson.

Kay Oring, a graduate student in Home Economics at OU, took ornithology under George and described well the depth of his understanding of birds, his high expectations of students, and his ability to seize the moment to share that understanding in such a way that students were not only motivated to learn but anxious for the next learning experience:

> He was a walking encyclopedia. Every bird we saw brought forth an impromptu lecture. Doc would rattle off the Latin name, order, family, genus, species, nearest relatives, world distribution, Oklahoma sightings, and specimens in the Oklahoma collection. All of this information was to be learned for the quiz in class the next day. We'd be tramping across a plowed field, the red Oklahoma clay clinging to our boots. Doc would be striding ahead calling attention to a Scissortail Flycatcher overhead and a Mourning Dove calling. Suddenly he'd stoop over, pick up something and announce 'feather quiz.' Right there we'd have to identify not only the species but also the body part from which the feather came.[2]

William E. Southern, who studied with Sutton during 1956–57, noted that "He was always available to 'his' students and it seemed amazing that he got anything else done."[3] Even in a crowded lecture hall the relationship often seemed to the listener to be one-on-one. George was a raconteur whose stories enthralled any audience, turning science into an adventure and bringing art to life.

George Sutton would have ranked among the finest of naturalists of the nineteenth-century school of science. His work was basic, based on keen observation and understanding of interrelationships of birds and their environments. Although he did not use the modern shroud of statistics and his work was not experimentally based, no one can deny George's very significant contributions to twentieth-century ornithology: during his lifetime he was at the top of his genre in art and science. Would that more modern ornithologists would incorporate *with* their use of statistics the kind of drive, skills, and insight that George possessed. He had an appreciation of large samples and instilled in his students the caveat of understanding the biology and limits of data before interpreting their statistics.

My experience of this was in 1968, when I visited him to examine specimens in his care, and he generously took me into his home. After dinner each evening we had long discussions about the future of ornithology, bird art, and our own families—I was the proud father of two young sons. We also discussed at length the work I was doing on geographic variation in Downy and Hairy woodpeckers and the regression and multivariate statistics I was using to ferret out answers to questions. George was fascinated by the power of the statistics to identify and describe patterns and potential relationships. He appreciated statistics as the tools—the guideposts—that they are, and added the insight of his personal experiences with the birds, aiding my interpretation of the patterns I had seen.

George's early deliberate efforts to be a teacher were when he was about eight years old and while his family still lived in Nebraska. His prime student was his sister Dorothy, who always looked up to him, and of course, his lessons focused on birds.[4] His first formal teaching came at Bethany during 1917 and 1918, when he taught "Preparatory English."[5] Then in 1925, while employed at the Carnegie Museum, George apparently taught ornithology at the University of Pittsburgh.[6] He taught occasional seminar courses and mentored students at Cornell University (1931–43) and the University of Michigan (1947–51). George had written to Van Tyne that he wanted a position at Michigan but that he was not interested in teaching. Yet at Michigan he taught the special skill of drawing birds from life to such students as Bill Lunk, Dave Parmelee, and Dale Zimmerman.[7]

Although his duties at Cornell and the University of Michigan were primarily curatorial, George had a profound influence on many students with whom he came into contact. Prominent ornithologists and artists Robert M. Mengel and H. Albert Hochbaum were both undergraduates at Cornell when they first met George and fell under his tutelage. Hochbaum's son, George Sutton Hochbaum, noted that his father had entered Cornell as an undergraduate student in agriculture but that "George Sutton, one of his professors, persuaded him to expand his interest areas to include science, art, and ornithology."[8] After that, birds occupied most of Hochbaum's time.

One of George's joys as a scientist was the collection of bird specimens that he had amassed over the years, and he was a teacher—both formally and informally—of the values and techniques associated with this. When George led a field trip he often took his shotgun along and took the opportunity to collect important specimens. He did so with permission of landowners and with discretion. Sometimes students did not quite approve, and exchanges among students enlivened the class. One summer at the OU Biological Station George had two women in their fifties take his ornithology course. Teague Self, his former department head at the University of Oklahoma, described their interactions:

> Ruby had come up from Florida to attend his course. Helen was from the
> college at Tahlequah, OK. . . . Ruby—a true bird lover—opposed Sutton's
> willingness to kill birds because he never recorded a bird without having

it in hand. Helen didn't give a hoot—just being interested in learning about birds. George was compiling a check list of Okla birds—so when he saw a new bird he would say 'I have to take that bird.' Sutton would get his gun ready and Ruby would say 'Oh God bless its soul.' Helen would say 'Ruby shut your God damn mouth—if George wants the bird, George gets it.' And thus the fight went on. George would come to us & say 'I don't know if I can keep them apart, but they fire up the class work!' "[9]

His feelings for the collection were expressed in a letter to Mengel: "It might be argued that I spend far too much time on this reshaping, and degreasing, etc., but what about the old adage of doing well whatever one doeth, etc.? I'm damn proud of my collection, and this is partly because I know of the sincere effort which I have put into it. I derive great satisfaction, too, out of seeing the students use it as they do—carefully and intelligently."[10]

George's skill at preparing bird study skins was legendary. He was swift, and the specimens he prepared were works of art—neat and uniform, well-rounded body, with every feather in place and the tail spread perfectly to display its pattern and for examination of molt. Among those who saw his specimens and then sought and received George's guidance in the preparation of bird study skins was Dr. Max Minor Peet, a prominent neurosurgeon at the University of Michigan Medical School. A distinguished amateur ornithologist, Peet had already amassed one of the finest private collections of bird skins in North America, but he was so impressed with George's specimens that he wanted to be shown the preparation techniques. He made an offer that George quickly accepted. If George would give him a lesson in bird skinning, Dr. Peet would allow George to attend one of his brain operations! George agreed. On the appointed day George was fitted with a white surgical gown and simply introduced to those in the operating room as "Dr. Sutton." The patient was a young woman and the operation was bloody. The cutting, the sawing of the skull, and the bleeding shook George. He feared he was going to faint but stuck it out. "Never again!" he told friends. He had no doubt that the woman had died.

A few days later, George called Dr. Peet and in the course of their conversation, commented: "Too bad about that woman, wasn't it?" Dr. Peet responded indignantly: "What do you mean, too bad? She went shopping today." He then explained that unlike abdominal or thoracic surgery, brain surgery usually has a short recovery period.[11]

Other students who acknowledged benefiting from George's guidance at Michigan include Andrew J. Berger, Jean and Richard Graber, Kenneth Prescott, Paul Slud, and Dwain Warner. During the spring of 1950 the Grabers collected many specimens in Kansas, sending them to George at Michigan, where they would later be used for the Grabers' thesis research. With each shipment George responded with praise for the care with which specimens had been prepared and delight at receipt of particular specimens. Each response also included pointers for dealing with problem specimens, packing specimens for shipment, and recommendations for future collecting efforts. He always focused on the positive but managed to get in advice for improvement. The advice is so salient and so thorough that I have found it useful for my own specimen preparation and teaching. Although George never taught a formal course at Michigan, Berger told him: "You undoubtedly taught me more and had a greater influence over my scientific development than any other professor in my career. . . . Your influence was the greatest, and most wide-ranging."[12]

Evidence of George's magnetism as a teacher can be seen in the movements of students from Cornell to Michigan or from Michigan to Oklahoma to continue working with him. Although George's work at Michigan was primarily as an illustrator, curator, and researcher, occasionally he lectured to visiting classes. It was through such a lecture at the University of Michigan Biological Station, provided for a class from Carlton College brought there by Sewall Pettingill, that George first met Jean and Richard Graber. They later saw him on the main campus in Ann Arbor and he immediately recognized them. George had a knack for remembering names. The Grabers were working at the University of Michigan Museum of Zoology and came to be good friends of his. As a result of their friendship, George facilitated a job for the Grabers working for George Lowery and Bob Newman at Louisiana State University doing fieldwork on the birds of San Luis Potosí, Mexico. The project lasted for about a year but, according to the Grabers, was never finished.

When George left Michigan for Oklahoma the Grabers cast their lot with him and became his graduate students. Richard Graber told me that George was a very good teacher, but noted that he "wouldn't say that he was organized in the way that Sewall Pettingill was"—an interesting contrast from one who knew both as teachers. I knew both well, but not formally as teachers, and I would have guessed as much; Sewall was more staid and methodical, George more casual, personal, and anecdotal. It was George who had the greater ability to seize the moment to teach when a special opportunity arose. I learned from many of George's students that he did not use detailed notes. He knew his subject, and his lectures were a pleasure because of the personal anecdotes provided. Richard Graber described him as "a gentle guide as a major professor and in all other tasks. . . . He was an eager listener, and though I'm sure he was often too busy to chat, I don't recall ever having felt that way. Doc must have had infinite patience with us students." George was known for involving his students in class, demanding it, making certain that each student had grasped a concept before moving on.[13]

His formal teaching duties began in earnest at the University of Oklahoma Biological Station during the summer of 1951, and he often taught ornithology at the station. At least during one summer school class in field ornithology, George opened his class each day by reading one of the intriguing short stories of Saki (H. H. Munro). The intent, of course, was to improve his students' powers of observation. "Expect the unexpected" was a mantra. So was "Pay attention to details."

David Parmelee, a student with whom George worked both at Michigan and at the University of Oklahoma, described three important lessons of fieldwork that George had instilled in him: The first was that personal safety always came first. The second was to get into the field "as often as humanly possible." And the third was the understanding that field data often come in bits and pieces, and the challenge is in pulling all the pieces together. Among the courses George taught at the University of Oklahoma were Birds of the World, Oklahoma Avifauna, Beginning Ornithology, Ornithology, and Scientific Writing.[14]

Among George's Oklahoma students were many who went on to careers in ornithology, bird art, and popular nature writing. While several completed graduate degrees with George (see appendix), many were inspired to scientific careers by his undergraduate courses. Among such students not already mentioned were J. David Ligon, John Janovy, Warren Pulich, and Kay Oring. Others with interests in biology other than ornithology, or in music, art, athletics, or elsewhere, found richness in George's teaching. Students were brought along, made members of expeditions either physically or vicariously in his classes and impromptu teaching moments.

Exams in George's classes were often innovative and demanding. When Bill Southern, Charles Ely, Hugh Land, and Donald Baepler took George's class on birds of the world they faced a day-long final that included identification of New Zealand birds they had not previously seen. The exam had three stages: first they had to attempt to place each bird in its proper order or family by *feeling it* through the tissue paper in which it was wrapped. Next the specimens were unwrapped, and students were asked to identify each based on what they knew of New Zealand birds. Finally they were given a new book on New Zealand birds and were allowed to use it to identify each to species or subspecies.[15]

George was both financially and psychologically supportive of students. He continually gave or loaned students money when he found them in financial difficulty. Some of those working in exotic places, such as Paul Slud, received financial support through sale of specimens to George. But they received much more than cash for those specimens. To Paul, a student at Michigan before and after George left for Oklahoma, George wrote: "Tell me of your work as it progresses, and if telling me your troubles does any good (or if you feel better simply sharing them), shoot ahead. . . . Just make the time count; and never lose sight of that snow-capped peak ahead, the peak of achievement. It's a chilly looking place at times, but getting there is worthwhile, believe me."[16]

George always seemed to have the right words of encouragement, guidance, and inspiration—and was particularly generous in praising good writing. Indeed a collection of his comments could provide valuable insight and inspiration to any prospective writer. Laurie MacIvor, who was a student at OU, recalled his words of approval and encouragement of her writing: "Write alightly, but do so nightly, for writing enlights thee."[17]

While Slud was in the field in Central America, George wrote: "In your knowledge of words and their relationships you have real power, and don't forget that. You could, if you would, write in such a way as to make the world more wonderful for many persons. You might do it through merely calling to their attention that which they have been missing. You might do it through shocking them into awareness of their lethargy and complacency."[18] And in a later letter:

> I hope you are meeting some interesting people and above all I hope you are setting down (perhaps in a notebook) a lot of impressions-—statements you can draw upon one day when you feel like writing all this up. Perhaps you are spending a little time each week writing. You have so much talent along that line that I'd hate to think you were keeping mum simply because of doubting that you had a contribution to make to knowledge or literature. Had it ever occurred to you that even a record of *groping* could be of value to other human beings? I'd say such a record, especially if it could be kept honest, might be of inestimable worth. So do some of your groping on paper—and let the words fly their own courses.

I'd mighty like to hear from you. Be assured of my interest. Let me know if there's some way in which I can help.[19]

Seven years later he again wrote Slud to encourage his writing, also providing insight into the breadth of his own reading:

> Whatever you do in your further studies, I hope you will bear in mind that excellence of writing and style of expression are much to be sought after. By this I do not mean "originality" comparable to that of Bruce Goff in modern architecture (or of Roy Harris in music, or of W. H. Auden in poetry) but some sort of proof that you have worked out your own way of saying things, a way that represents your true self. You've thought all this out on your own, of course; but I say what I say in the hope that it may strengthen some of your convictions.[20]

George taught a broad audience of Oklahomans through the *Bulletin of the Oklahoma Ornithological Society*, providing guidance to the rankest amateur and encouraging careful note taking, use of the ornithological literature, and concise writing. Above all, he taught Oklahoma Ornithological Society members to be "bird *watchers*," not merely "birders." He taught them to observe behavior, to ask questions, and to seek answers. One highly effective teaching device was publication of his own observations in the *Bulletin*. At first his articles were given good, succinct titles that told the reader what the article was about. But then in 1972 he began taking a different approach, using titles written as a question: "May an Adult Canyon Wren Become Flightless during Late Summer?" "When Does the Female Cardinal Start Singing in Spring?" "How Often Does the Brown Creeper Sing in Oklahoma?"[21]

Often George did not have the answer for his questions, merely some observations that sparked them. Readers were drawn in by questions that might never have occurred to them. They had to know the answer, and they began seeking answers and asking their own questions.

Among George's students were many aspiring bird artists who never sat in a classroom with him but rather sat at his elbow as he painted or sketched, or merely exchanged letters and artwork by mail. George was forever indebted to the kindness of Fuertes, and he repaid that kindness over and over as he mentored young artists. He once commented to Roger Tory Peterson: "As I watch them, considering what they have done, and see them achieving, I sense what immortality must be."[22] Among those George mentored were Robert Verity Clem, William Dilger, Donald Richard Eckelberry, Albert Earl Gilbert, Hugh C. Land, Robert M.

Mengel, Don Malick, Richard Grossenheider, John P. O'Neill, Roger Tory Peterson, Diane Pierce, and Dale Zimmerman, all of whom went on to be recognized as among the finest of today's bird artists. The Sutton influence—the Fuertes influence through Sutton—is clear in some of the work of each.

George's students of bird art were young and old, some destined to fame, some to failure, but he truly enjoyed working with those who responded to his efforts. For example, in December 1979, he wrote to his friends Chris and Guy Anthony of a young man who had come to his house the night before with a sheaf of pictures he had painted: "Honestly, my dear friends, the pictures were awful. The background washes were muddy, the drawing was off, etc., etc., but there was something truly wonderful about the light that shone from the youngster's eyes when he began to see how the faults could be corrected. I gave him some sound advice: Be content with trying easier subject matter for a while. Some of what he had attempted to do was beyond what even I might tackle in watercolor! He likes acrylic—a medium I've never even tried."[23]

A distinct parallel to his own studies with Fuertes was the early training Sutton gave to Don Malick. Malick had always had an interest in birds, having first been drawn to bird art by Audubon's *Birds of America* and then been absolutely captured by the work of Fuertes. His early efforts were labored, but he had good models. Following Malick's high school graduation, his seventh and eighth grade teacher, Mary Curran (whom he called "a real saint of a woman"), wrote to George Sutton on his behalf, paving the way for a year-long "correspondence course" in bird painting with Sutton. Malick traveled to the University of Michigan to meet Sutton in 1948. He spent two weeks with George at the university's field station. Malick wrote to Don Radovich that he had "Fuertes' star pupil (!) as my 'tutor'—and I was in seventh heaven." Albert Earl Gilbert, Robert Verity Clem, Robert M. Mengel, John O'Neill, and Orville Rice were others who developed artistic skills in part through correspondence with George.[24]

Moving on from his teaching to examine his role as a conservationist, we see George Miksch Sutton straddling radically different eras. Throughout his life he was the kind of scientist some call a "shotgun ornithologist." He once wrote: "An ornithologist sometimes finds it hard to know just how it is that he loves birds. Most of the time he wants no one, no one at all, to harm them. Then again, feeling that it is his duty to learn all he can about them, he wants desperately to kill them."[25] His awareness of the contradiction is likewise clear in how he once signed a

Christmas letter to his friend C. Richard Robins: "Merry Christmas from that old scoundrel & reprobate G. Sutton, who loves and kills birds."[26]

He enjoyed days in the field collecting birds perhaps as much as any other endeavor. He was an expert marksman, prepared study skins that stand out in any collection as truly works of art, and almost always encouraged others to collect or salvage specimens. When Richard and Jean Graber were collecting specimens in Kansas in 1950, he told them to "bear down on the *Corvus cryptoleucus* [Chihuahuan Raven]," but then added, "if you find the breeding population is very small, maybe you'd better not collect specimens for fear of extirpation."[27]

The collecting habit never died. One day as I was walking with George from the Stovall Museum to his home for lunch we found a fresh road-killed Yellow-billed Cuckoo. I picked it up and examined it, and he asked, "Do you know how to prepare a study skin?" I did, and he said, "Good, this will make a fine specimen." While he prepared lunch, I was set to work skinning the cuckoo. Within a few minutes I was in trouble because of a tear in the skin. George patiently guided me through the problem and showed me a few tricks to improve my study skin preparation abilities.

At the beginning of the twenty-first century there are few collectors of birds, and those who do collect specimens are often the subject of derision and harsh criticism, including from professional colleagues. How can a hunter and collector of birds be a conservationist?

The foundations of effective conservation, of course, are knowledge and understanding. Today we have quality binoculars, spotting scopes, cameras, and field guides that help us observe and document the distribution and lives of birds. Thus some types of collecting are no longer justified. But a century ago quality optics and field guides were wishful thinking. Field guides with their artwork, range maps, and descriptions of identifying characteristics and variation within and among species were made possible by carefully documented museum specimens. Study skins were important tools in teaching ornithology and in providing models for artists.

We continue to use specimens for such purposes but have now learned they have other values too. They reveal intimate details not readily observed in the field, such as the pectinate claws of nightjars, Barn Owls, herons, and egrets; subtle differences in plumage between sexes or age groups; and patterns in the timing and sequence of molt. Specimens are also reservoirs of DNA that can help us understand relationships among birds. They are reservoirs of feathers that can be analyzed for the trace minerals that can reveal a bird's origin. They are reservoirs of tissues that can allow us to trace historical and geographic patterns of environmental contamination. The list of uses for study skins of birds goes on, and new uses are regularly found. Not only was George Sutton aware of the many uses of specimens; he also recognized that through such uses, study skins play important roles in conservation.

Having a bird in the hand allowed George to understand its plumage, its soft-part colors, its dimensions and anatomical details—all things that contributed to the quality of his illustrations. He then used his art to support conservation causes. George's artwork commonly appeared in *Pennsylvania Game News* when he was employed by the Pennsylvania Game Commission and even later when he was at Cornell. Among his first publications as Pennsylvania state ornithologist was a booklet he wrote and illustrated on protecting birds.[28]

Major issues during his years with the Pennsylvania Game Commission included the perception of the role of raptors in nature and the indiscriminate killing of hawks and owls. George studied raptor food habits, wrote eloquently in their defense, was involved in the efforts to create the Hawk Mountain Sanctuary, and leant his artwork for various raptor conservation uses then and later. For example, in 1940, he provided illustrations for *Common Hawks of North America*, a pamphlet produced by Rosalie Edge and Ellsworth D. Lumley of the Emergency Conservation Committee. A Cooper's Hawk painting was used on the cover of a brochure about the Witmer Stone Wildlife Sanctuary at Cape May, New Jersey. In 1973 he wrote again in defense of predators for the Oklahoma Zoological Society.[29]

George's interest in raptor conservation never waned. In 1977 he responded to an article on Golden Eagles that had been published in *True* magazine, lambasting the magazine for using information that was outdated and in error. He wrote: "The article . . . one might have expected to read in a magazine 50 years ago, but the publication of such pictures and text today is an effrontery to intelligence and decency. Golden Eagles may occasionally kill a lamb; but the all-important fact is that their daily fare is jack rabbits which would, if not controlled in some such natural, continuing, and never-failing way, eat the grass from under the sheep's faces."[30]

George was always ready to assist in raising funds for conservation or raising awareness of conservation issues, often using his artwork effectively as a conservation tool. As we have seen, he provided a painting of a Red-headed Woodpecker for the 1940 National Wildlife Federation conservation stamp set (plate 20). He provided the cover illustration for a bulletin on bird mortality from DDT spraying associated with the Dutch elm disease program in Michigan. And he allowed his artwork to be reproduced for sale to support bird research and conservation in Mexico and for efforts of the Cornell Laboratory of Ornithology and National Audubon Society (discussed later in this chapter).[31]

Many of George's publications, although including details of birds collected, also carry a conservation message. For example, in late December 1949 he documented the winter presence of Rose-throated Becards along the lower Rio Grande in Texas by collecting three specimens. He described them in the *Auk*, ending his publication by noting that the area where the birds were found was being cleared. To assure a future for Rose-throated Becards in the Rio Grande Valley he described their nest-site requirements and recommended protection of appropriate habitat.[32]

High Arctic, *At a Bend in a Mexican River*, and *Portraits of Mexican Birds* also raised awareness of Arctic and Mexican ecosystems. His Mexican books were a major stimulus in the move toward purchasing land for Rancho del Cielo. George was especially active in trying to secure Rancho del Cielo and in 1970 lobbied Mexican authorities and his friends on both sides of the border to take action. His pleas were reasoned and respectful, focusing on the positive, yet imparting the sense of urgency that was needed. For example, in a letter to the Board of Regents of the University of Tamaulipas he wrote:

> It has come to my attention that the wonderful cloud forest surrounding an area known as the Rancho del Cielo, above the lovely Río Sabinas, and not far from the hill village of Gómez Farías, southwestern Tamaulipas, is in grave danger of being destroyed. It is not clear to me whether those who may destroy the trees are after lumber primarily, or whether their purpose is merely to clear the land. In either case, the destruction of the forest would be a calamity.
>
> I know the area well, for I have visited it personally and several of my students have studied its wildlife. It is a truly wonderful area, a sort of northward-reaching finger of the true tropics. Many of its forms of life are at the very northernmost tip of their range. If the trees are felled, all of this wonderful life will go too. Furthermore, if the root systems of the trees no longer have a chance to hold the soil in place, erosion will set in, the Río Sabinas will become murky, and the whole face of nature will change.
>
> The University of Tamaulipas, as one of Mexico's leading centers of learning, should be fully aware of what may happen to this important

area. The Board of Regents should take action now in such a way as to assure protection for the woodland and its wild inhabitants. The right moves should not be delayed, for the destruction of woodland can take place quickly and such destruction can be irremediable.

I foresee that the able faculty of the University of Tamaulipas will be using the area for significant research. I hope that I may be able to participate in this research, for I love the Rancho del Cielo area and will do everything within my power to keep it from being harmed.[33]

George also wrote to many of his colleagues, sending them a copy of his letter to the Board of Regents and adding:

The Rancho del Cielo cloud forest in southwestern Tamaulipas, Mexico, is sorely threatened by the agrarians, who may swoop in, fell the timber, clear the land, and send the soil (via the Sabinas) to the sea. I have been in direct touch with those who are trying to save the area. I have sent money ($2000). The suggestion has been made that each of us write a letter giving our various angles on the value of preserving the place as it is, and send the letter to . . . William H. Walton, President of Texas Southmost College. Dr. Walton will, in turn, send the letters to a leading Mexico City attorney (Mr. Juan F. Zorilla), who will see to it that they are presented to the Board of Regents. . . . Mr. Zorilla is, himself, a member of the Board of Regents. . . . The plea should be on behalf of the forest as a tremendously valuable *Mexican* asset that may be put to important scientific use by the University of Tamaulipas. . . . Let us stress the wonderful value of the area *to the Mexicans.*[34]

By 1971 Texas Southmost College, through the efforts of Professor Barbara Warburton and the tenacity of John Hunter of Brownsville, had established a biological station at Rancho del Cielo. George was a strong supporter of the effort, obtaining funds from various sources, including the sale of his artwork for the purchase of land. Ultimately he was a major benefactor in the establishment of the seventeen-hundred-acre ecological preserve. In a letter to C. Richard Robins he took pride in his efforts and touched on the problems: "I had one thousand sent from one fund, another thousand from another fund, and recently I sent a personal thousand, this to be used in obtaining 700 additional hectares—a buffer area between the cloud forest and the damned agrarians. I'm really proud of the way in which people have collaborated in this. We've had the services of a good Mexican lawyer, title to land has been properly cleared, and so forth."[35] It was another four years, however, before the deal for the land was consummated in the spring of 1975 and Rancho del Cielo was safe.[36]

In addition to his strong efforts on behalf of raptors and Rancho del Cielo, George had a lifelong passion for the protection of wetlands. His view of some of the problems was aired vehemently in a letter to John and Eleanor Kirkpatrick:

> I am opposed almost per se to more impoundments in Oklahoma, especially large ones. The Corps of Engineers charges ahead in the name of "more employment" and "more recreational facilities," arguing for more and more impoundments, and they get away with it a lot of the time, even as the military gets away with almost anything in the name of "national defense." All we need hear is the threat of Russia (or Ecuador or Iceland) and into our pockets we dig for more and more money with which to build officers' clubs. You know very well that I'm partly right in this. It really amuses me, as well as rubs me the wrong way. I was *in* the military, remember.[37]

For his various conservation efforts, George was honored by the National Wildlife Federation in 1965 as their "Conservation Teacher of the Year." He was also posthumously honored by the Southwestern Association of Naturalists when they established their George Miksch Sutton Award for Conservation Research.[38]

George Sutton's role as a philanthropist seems an unlikely one, as he was never a wealthy man by economic standards. But his needs were small, his lifestyle was modest, and he was very generous. Robert Mengel described his generosity as being at a level that "verged on the spectacular."[39] Sutton's philanthropy was far ranging and often unnoticed; he supported the things he believed in—often in ways requiring creative efforts that provided tax deductions for others while yielding no personal benefit to him. Although George rarely sold a painting or drawing, he often donated paintings for good causes. The Internal Revenue Service noted that these were essentially products made from nothing, so George could get no tax deduction beyond the cost of paints, paper, and brushes.

Hence what he often did was to find a buyer for a painting at a price that would provide the funds needed for a particular project. He would then ask the buyer to make a contribution in that amount to the organization in question. Thus George was able to arrange for charitable contributions by using his art; he never had to pay income tax on money earned by his paintings; and the buyer was able to take a tax deduction for the contribution. As an example, when he did the color plate of woodpecker heads to accompany Luis Baptista's *Wilson Bulletin* article (see chapter 12), he wrote to Luis concerning the plate: "If you'd like to own this, let me know. You can pay for it with a check made out to the Oklahoma Ornithological Society's *Bulletin* Fund. The amount you pay will be up to you."[40]

On March 24, 1952, George, Robert M. Mengel, Ernest P. Edwards, and others incorporated the Foundation for Neotropical Research, a nonprofit foundation dedicated to the "overall purposes of stimulation, integration, and subsidization of biological research and conservation in the vast region of the New World tropics." Their intent was that this foundation would create an alliance of "scientists, conservationists, and explorers, drawn from all the nations concerned, cooperating and working together in a manner to promote the best results to all."

To raise capital for the foundation, George contributed publication rights to four of his more than eighty life-sized portraits of Mexican birds. These were reproduced as collotypes in limited edition series of five hundred each. George signed the first one hundred of each set so that they might bring a higher price.[41] Unfortunately the prints did not sell well, and later George was averse to getting involved with such efforts. When it was suggested that prints of his work be sold to raise funds for the George Miksch Sutton Scholarship Fund, he wrote to Bob Furman: "I don't want another flop such as the Foundation for Neotropical Research flop was."[42]

Sutton never forgot his alma mater, Bethany College, often contributing to various college funding campaigns. He was one of the leaders in the campaign to build the Robert Richardson Hall of Science on campus and also helped with costs of construction for the Beta Theta Pi fraternity house there.[43]

The science of ornithology has especially benefited from George's generosity through his support of the Louis Agassiz Fuertes grant for ornithological research, which is given annually to a student by the Wilson Ornithological Society. George initiated the grant in 1947 during his tenure as president of the Wilson Society, and at a time in 1949 when his personal finances left a little to be desired, he wrote to his uncle, Milton Fuller: "I can almost see the bottom of the pile, and that means unwonted penuriousness with regard to trips, Christmas presents, concerts, etc. [but] the Fuertes Grants are continuing and will continue, if they are the last thing I do." Such was his devotion to his mentor, to students, and to the Wilson Ornithological Society.[44]

George also contributed substantially to ornithology through his donation of artwork to illustrate journals and books and his monetary contributions and fund-raising efforts for the publication of artwork. He provided the cover illustrations for several journals—a Northern Cardinal for the *Cardinal*, journal of the Sewickley Valley (Pennsylvania) Audubon Society; a Western Burrowing Owl for *Nebraska Bird Review* (1938–52, 1968 to present), and two different Wilson's Warbler drawings for the *Wilson Bulletin* (1924–62, 1963 to present).

In commenting on the Burrowing Owl provided for *Nebraska Bird Review*, editor Myron Swenk noted: "As Dr. Sutton has at different times expressed to your Editor, he retains a warm regard for Nebraska, having lived in the state and studied its birds during the early part of his ornithological career." Early indeed; he had left the state by the age of eight.[45]

George's first color plate in the *Wilson Bulletin*, an American Avocet, appeared in 1926, and by 1987 twenty-six of his paintings had appeared as color plates in the journal. This is nearly four times the number of plates contributed by any other author (Don Eckelberry contributed seven).[46] In March 1929, *Wilson Bulletin* editor T. C. Stephens commented on George's plate of a group of Wood Storks that accompanied an article on birds of the Everglades. He noted George's generosity in allowing use of the plate and also that the club's income did not otherwise permit extravagance. He had solicited funds from some members and gone ahead with the plate, then through his editorial mentioned another Sutton plate that was available and solicited further funds, hoping to build an endowment that would allow frequent use of color plates. In September 1929 a Sutton plate illustrating Harris's Sparrow plumages was used in the journal, the editor noting that "this one page of color costs almost as much as the other sixty-four pages of a regular issue." He went on to add that George was "rapidly taking a place in the front row of American bird artists."[47]

George's dream of establishing a fund to assure publication of a color plate in every issue of the *Wilson Bulletin* began in the 1920s and culminated with his contribution of twenty thousand dollars in 1973 to establish the "Sutton Color Plate Fund."[48] As treasurer of the Wilson Ornithological Society when the Color Plate Fund was first established, I was intimately involved in negotiations for the gift. One of the first manuscripts submitted in 1974, after I became editor of the *Wilson Bulletin* was from George: a short note on the behavior of a Northern Mockingbird in his yard. Both reviewers recommended against publication, and I agreed that the manuscript was anecdotal and included minimal new information: something appropriate for a state journal but probably not for the *Wilson Bulletin*. How was I to tell the man who had just donated twenty thousand dollars to the society that his brief note was not up to journal standards? I rejected the manuscript, fearing the response I might get. By return mail, however, I received the most wonderful letter from Doc, agreeing with the reviewers and thanking me for keeping him from making a fool of himself.[49] A few months later when I informed George that the interest on the endowment was proving inadequate to assure a color plate in each issue, George donated another ten thousand dollars to the fund.[50]

During the late 1940s through the 1950s, George was involved with the Audubon Screen Tours, traveling across America to recount his adventures to the far north, Mexico, and Iceland. He loved an audience, and they loved him. Not only did he raise the environmental consciousness of the nation through his screen tour programs, he also sometimes provided the audience. In 1956 he wrote to Bob Furman: "Enclosed find my personal cheque . . . to pay for 20 student tickets for the Audubon Screen Tours 1956–57. . . . From each of our ten schools two students are to be recipients of these 'student tickets.' We are working out a way whereby all travel to Oklahoma City together by school bus. . . . Eventually I'd like to have these tickets be a true reward of merit of some sort. Right now it is all just beginning."[51]

Shortly after arriving in Oklahoma George made the acquaintance of Dr. Robert Furman of the University of Oklahoma Medical Center in Oklahoma City. This seems to have come about as a result of the Furman's involvement with the Oklahoma City Audubon Society and the medical center chapter of Sigma Xi, the science honorary society. George gave lectures in Oklahoma City for both groups. Bob and his wife Mary Frances Furman often arranged dinner with George before such engagements and introduced him to new supporters. In 1956 Furman established the George Miksch Sutton Research Fund through the Oklahoma Medical Research Foundation. Actually two research funds were set up, one for Mexican research that did not bear Sutton's name, and the other for any other research needs that George might have. Money deposited in the funds came from the sale of paintings and prints, from contributions from various admirers, and from Sutton himself.

The accounts were to be used for George's and his students' research. Some contributions were in lieu of payment for paintings; others were gifts; and in addition, George had payments for his Audubon Screen Tour lectures and other speaking engagements deposited directly.[52] At least some of the contributions seem to have come anonymously from Furman; receipts for the donations indicated that they had been made by "Red Red Rose."[53] Furman also provided George with medical advice, medical supplies for his and his students' field expeditions, and medical assistance for George's father. Over the years George's link to Robert Furman in Oklahoma City not only led to support for his own and his students' research, but also to further links with John and Eleanor Kirkpatrick and with the Oklahoma City Zoo.

In addition to his support of conservation, George regularly sold paintings or provided paintings for auction to raise funds for causes he deemed important. In 1962 when OU zoology professor Harriet Harvey died he did a special showing of his Icelandic film and donated four paintings to be auctioned by the University of Oklahoma Foundation to raise funds for a memorial scholarship fund in her name. Three of the paintings were erroneously listed in a letter to prospective bidders as: "Long-tailed Zaegers at Play" "Sabine's Skull," and the "Black-bellied Pluver"—presumably mistaken transcriptions of a telephone conversation about jaegers, Sabine's Gull, and the plover.[54]

Similarly, in 1966 when OU history professor Donnell M. Owings was killed in an automobile accident, George donated nine of the paintings he had done during his trips to Mexico in 1938–39 to raise funds to help create a memorial scholarship fund in Owings's name.[55]

In May 1969 George donated a thousand dollars from personal funds and another thousand from his research account to the Museum of Zoology at Louisiana State University (LSU) for the purchase of seventeen hundred Guatemalan bird skins from Hugh Land's widow, Margaret, no doubt helping her and her three children through a difficult time. He believed that the collection would be best cared for and of most use to the Neotropical ornithology program at LSU (see chapter 12 for more about Hugh Land). In a letter to Bob Furman, George wrote: "The very thought of Hugh; of the way he worked while he was here; of the way his widow Margaret is carrying on, makes me proud, very proud. It's a wonderful way to feel, truly it is."[56]

George donated another thousand dollars from his research fund in September 1969 to the Pan American Section of the International Committee for Bird Preservation to support the publication of Land's *Birds of Guatemala*.[57] A month later he provided funds for fieldwork by Stewart MacDonald and David Parmelee on Bathurst Island and one thousand dollars each toward the publication of color plates in the *Wilson Bulletin* and toward publication of the Cornell Lab's *Living Bird*. This set of contributions came because George was convinced that the funds he had been saving would never be large enough to be of significant help in building a museum. He noted that such donations would be "bread cast upon the waters" that would be more fruitful.[58] A few months later he sold ten or more drawings to benefit a juvenile shelter in Norman.[59]

Through the 1970s George contributed frequently to the Oklahoma City Zoo, allowing for enlargement of the cage for the Andean Condors, for development of a Galapagos exhibit, and for a new Neotropical exhibit.[60] In January 1972 Sutton found a hawk-eagle, White Hawk, Roadside Hawk, two Aplomado Falcons, a Plumbeous Kite, and three Crane Hawks at an animal dealer's business in Chickasha, Oklahoma. Partly to help the birds and partly to help the Oklahoma City Zoo, he donated funds to the zoo for their purchase.[61]

The university where he worked for so long was also on the receiving end of his donations. In December 1972 George contributed two hundred dollars to the OU Alumni Development Fund for their wrestling program, including the National Wrestling Hall of Fame and the university's "Take Down Club."[62] George endowed a lecture series in zoology at the University of Oklahoma, bringing outstanding biologists to campus each year. He delighted in sending personal invitations to friends to attend "his" lecture series.[63]

In May 1975 George requested help from friends and former students in suggesting worthy causes for his support. Among his own suggestions were making the Wilson Ornithological Society's Fuertes grants larger, "perhaps much larger," and an annual scholarship for fieldwork at Rancho del Cielo Biological Station. He identified some previous beneficiaries of his philanthropy: the Wilson Ornithological Society Color Plate Fund (then $25,000, ultimately $30,000); a lectureship at the University of Oklahoma ($20,000); the Fuertes Lectureship at Cornell University ($20,000); much of the $14,000 contributed to the Harvey Memorial Scholarship at the University of Oklahoma; $3,000 toward the Stoddard Scholarship at the University of Georgia; a biology laboratory at Bethany College in Bethany, West Virginia; about $12,000 to the Oklahoma City Community Foundation; and the Oklahoma Bald Eagle Project ($1,500).[64]

In May 1979 George donated two thousand dollars to the University of Oklahoma Foundation: one thousand to cover insurance costs while his artwork was being stored at the Museum of Art on campus, and one thousand to the Stovall Museum in recognition of the staff's many kindnesses in driving him about during his illness. A few weeks later he received a rather unusual request for artwork. Perry Gresham, a past president of George's alma mater, Bethany College, and a founder of the Institute for the Study of Aging at Bethany, had written an inspirational book titled *With Wings as Eagles*. It seemed only appropriate that an eagle should grace its cover, and George was the obvious source for such an illustration. The Golden Eagle that George painted for Audubon was used on the dust jacket.[65]

In 1981 George allowed his painting of Mountain Trogons to be put up for auction to raise funds for a new main building for the George Lynn Cross Academy in Norman. It brought in seventeen thousand dollars.[66] George was honored by the inauguration of the George Miksch Sutton Faculty Chamber Music Series in the spring of 1982, established with his assistance to benefit the School of Music Scholarship Fund.[67] Although he was by then ill and weak, in 1982 George responded to the Oklahoma Wildlife Federation's need to raise funds for their work. He allowed them to use his painting of a flock of Canada Geese (titled "Downwind") to produce prints for sale to raise funds for the organization. In spite of frailty and the effort to finish his last book, George signed one hundred of the prints to raise their value to the organization.[68] Right to the end, he was giving.

CHAPTER 14

From Illustration to Fine Art

*The man who did those drawings turned them out
all right. But he put no imagination into them at all.
They are completely without that spark which is so
characteristic of Audubon. I can't bear to have my
children look at anything so dull.*

A CERTAIN LADY

Bird art is not as straightforward an endeavor as it may
seem. All his many honors and widespread recognition
notwithstanding, George Sutton continually faced indif-
ference or worse when it came to his artwork. "My own sister Evie, Art
Editor for the American Book Company, merely tolerates my work,
thinking that photographs are just as good if not better," George told
Bob Furman.[1] In the same letter he told of a certain lady's dismissive
remarks made when unaware that the man to whom she was speaking
was the very artist who had painted the birds illustrating the *World Book
Encyclopedia* she refused to buy.[2]

George was a prolific artist with a repertoire that included such media
as pencil sketches in field notes, quick watercolor sketches to record flesh
colors of birds in the field, polished pencil and ink drawings, wash drawings, watercolors, and oils. His portrayal of his subjects varied to suit
needs and included cartoonlike characters, decorative art, field
guide–type illustrations, portraits of birds in their habitats, and portraits
of habitats with their birds. He demanded accuracy in his own art and in

the art of others, both in the birds presented and in the details of their habitat, though he sometimes failed.

In order to prepare 168 pen-and-ink sketches to represent all the bird families of the world in Van Tyne and Berger's *Fundamentals of Ornithology*, George had to rely on specimens, photographs, and imagination for many birds. In the second edition of the text he includes an artist's preface, identifying the materials and experience (or lack thereof) he had called upon for specific drawings. In the first edition of the text his Mexican Trogon is endowed with three toes facing forward instead of two. This he corrected for the second edition.[3]

In a letter to Albert Earl Gilbert in 1979, George expressed frustration with his efforts in painting some of the Mexican birds, especially the Russet-crowned Motmot: "These latest Colima things are very complex. I have tried doing whole backgrounds—not exactly scenic, but habitat. The Russet-crowned Motmot, for example, is in a tangle of vines with a shadowy arroyo as background. I've been working at the picture literally for months, trying to get it right and lord help me, I may just have to tear it up. How very simple a bird and twig *with no background* are!"[4]

George stressed accuracy as he mentored young artists, providing guidance but often leaving other artists to discover for themselves how to achieve that accuracy. As might be expected, his own early art was crude, then it emulated that of his mentor, Fuertes. By the 1920s it had begun to take on characteristics that were uniquely Sutton's. Such is the pattern of growth in most artists.[5]

In Gus Swanson's opinion, George's year on Southampton seemed to have been an epiphany for his art.[6] Perhaps it was the total immersion, the lack of interruptions from other duties, and the lack of specific direction from others for each piece. Through the Carnegie Museum phase and later, through his time with the Pennsylvania Game Commission, George had received an increasing number of commissions for illustrations— art that was done to order rather than because of personal inspiration. In his assessment of the previous fifty years of American bird art George acknowledges this constraint.[7]

Changes in George's art over time are obvious and can be seen best in paintings or drawings of the same species done at widely different times. For example, his Ivory-billed Woodpecker done for Bailey's *The Birds of Florida* before he had seen the species (plate 23) is crude and inaccurate, showing a sharply pointed bill, excessive white, and slicked-down plumage, quite a contrast to paintings done in the late 1930s after he had studied the Ivory-bill and sketched it from life (plate 13). George's drawing of a Wilson's Warbler that appeared on the cover of the *Wilson Bulletin* for the first time in 1926 is a heavy, frozen profile, less alive than his two Wilson's Warblers that have graced the journal's covers since 1963 (fig. 14.1).

Negatives of Sutton's early period were the degree of roundness to the head, lack of texture in the plumage, and the generic or exaggerated pointedness of the bill of some birds (for example, the Common Terns in plate 7).[8] Another aspect that he lamented was the way he sometimes indicated feathers with hatch marks (fig. 14.2).[9] But his work was also beginning to show a masterful touch: his ability to create with few lines pen-and-ink portraits that could be reduced to small size and yet remain useful in representing species (fig. 14.3).[10]

George's work with oils was essentially limited to his years in Pennsylvania and at Cornell. He much preferred the immediacy and flexibility of watercolor, a medium in which he could capture the soft textures of downy plumage with incredible skill. His few oils, however, were well received. That of the Northern Goshawk stems from a period when the species had invaded Pennsylvania in numbers (plate 24). This dark

14.1. *Two Sutton drawings of Wilson's Warbler that have appeared on the covers of the* Wilson Bulletin. *The first (left) appeared in 1926 and was replaced by a new drawing in 1963 (right). When the journal's name was changed to the* Wilson Journal of Ornithology *in 2006, the cover changed as well, incorporating new art on the cover but retaining a small image of the 1926 Sutton drawing on the cover and the 1963 drawing on the masthead on the first page of the journal.*

A YEAR'S PROGRAM FOR

BIRD PROTECTION

HAIRY WOODPECKER
Valuable Destroyer of Wood Borers
BULLETIN No. 7
By GEORGE MIKSCH SUTTON, Chief, Educational Service
BOARD OF GAME COMMISSIONERS
Commonwealth of Pennsylvania

14.2. Sutton drawing of a Hairy Woodpecker that appeared on the cover of his 1925 publication A Year's Program for Bird Protection. *Note the lack of feather detail and the use of hatch marks to indicate feathers and shading. This was a technique sometimes used by Fuertes but of which George later came to disapprove.*

picture, suggesting the bird's forest habitat, perhaps also expresses the dark attitudes of the time toward this bird that kills other birds. However, during his years as Pennsylvania state ornithologist and well into his tenure at the University of Oklahoma, George's finished bird portraits typically featured a dark background, focusing on and accentuating his birds. In contrast his Mexican birds, done between 1938 and the 1970s, typically include perched birds against a white background, lending a bright airiness to the portraits.

The most dramatic change in George's artistic style came when he was seventy and is seen in his series of arctic portraits, which explore the beauty of the landscape and place birds, muskoxen, and other northern wildlife within the context of arctic vastness (plate 25). Fellow artist and former student Robert M. Mengel referred to these as "truly remarkable,"

adding that they "caused some of his more prosaic followers to conclude
. . . that he had 'flipped his lid and gone 'modern'!"[11] Roger Tory Peterson
suggested that George had gone through at least three well-defined periods of transition since his youth, although he did not characterize these.[12]

To look at a single medium: if we consider watercolor, three easily dis-
cernible stages in the development of George's work would be an initial

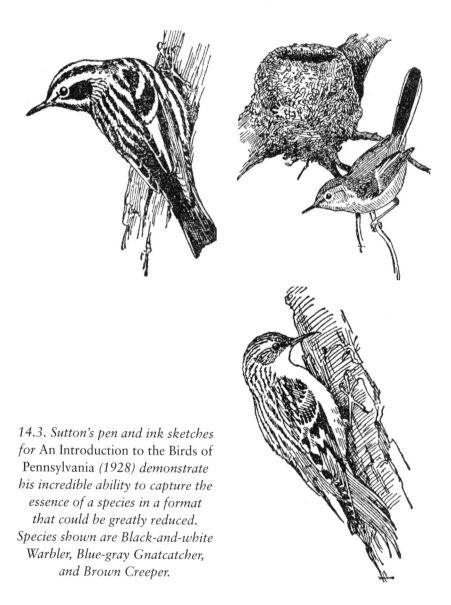

*14.3. Sutton's pen and ink sketches
for* An Introduction to the Birds of
Pennsylvania *(1928) demonstrate
his incredible ability to capture the
essence of a species in a format
that could be greatly reduced.
Species shown are Black-and-white
Warbler, Blue-gray Gnatcatcher,
and Brown Creeper.*

period of providing feather detail, followed by a gradual trend to no feather detail but use of simple brush strokes to provide the impression of feathers, and finally his shift in focus from depicting almost exclusively the bird to showing the habitat with a bird included. The latter was the most dramatic change, clearly providing a greater feeling of space and reflecting the oneness of the bird with its environment. Was this final shift a function of a greater understanding of the intimacy of the relationship of birds and their environment? Was it a function of the subject matter, the vast open expanses of the Arctic? Or was it a function of something more mundane, such as a less agile hand or failing eyesight? To suggest the latter is not at all intended to detract from the quality of the work. Indeed many would place the *High Arctic* work as the culmination of George's quest for understanding of birds and their world. Perhaps the truth includes the influence of all these factors.

George's frontispiece for Leon A. Hausman's *Birds of Prey of Northeastern North America* is a departure from traditional bird portraiture. He shows an adult Red-tailed Hawk soaring over partially forested hills, but interestingly, the bird's wings extend beyond the boundaries of the painting, as if the bird were flying out of the scene and off the page.[13]

Roger Tory Peterson felt that George had an especially good feeling for feather texture and facial expressions, characteristics for which understanding might be expected to come with the preparation of birds as scientific specimens and the close study of living birds. George considered a bird's eyes as most important to the success of a painting and usually began with the head and eyes. As Peterson noted, "If the eyes have life, the rest of the bird should have life."[14]

George always emphasized the use of living models, not only of birds or other animals but also of the plants that provide essential structure to bird habitats. He was not, however, averse to borrowing compositional ideas from other artists. A case in point is a painting he did of a pair of Canada Warblers on a blooming rhododendron branch. This he published in the *Cardinal*. Bayard Christy, its editor, referred to this painting as a "paraphrase of Audubon," whose ideas he considered romantic and theatrical, often giving an "inappropriate" and sometimes "grotesque" impression. Sutton's rendition of the same bird and flowering tree Christy saw as a "gentle, sympathetic, and literal presentment," providing "justification of the intended plagiarism."[15]

All his life George Sutton agonized over the question of whether bird art qualifies as art. Certainly he considered himself an artist from early in his career, but he was often not considered an artist by artists who were not bird artists. In an article in the *Living Bird* he commented that at the University of Oklahoma "any show that is not abstractionist is retrospective, any painting that is not abstract is no art at all." Thus he was caught up in an age-old dichotomy within the visual arts—that between "illustrators" and "fine artists."[16]

In a letter to Helen Van Tyne George noted that "Homer St. Gaudens' chief criticism of bird-artists as a whole is that they are 'museum men rather than real artists.'"[17] He pondered the question "what is it about 'bird art' that has special appeal" in a letter to his friends John and Eleanor Kirkpatrick:

> Is a good bird picture effective and meaningful because it makes clear what is beautiful about us, or does it, in a way, become part of nature and therefore have a right to command respect as deep as that felt for the thing it represents? Poor representations of birds bother me, of course; yet it is thinkable that, when an artist is completely sincere, and interested in stressing that which he feels to be a bird's most important quality, he has a right to stress airiness, or gaudiness, or fluffiness, or what not, to the exclusion of, or at the expense of, all other qualities. Carry this idea far enough and lo, you have an abstraction.
>
> Am I getting there? Is a glimmer of light breaking through?[18]

Certainly George sold his work to illustrate a number of books, and the key to his success in selling it was his faithfulness to reality. He *was* an illustrator. He also provided illustrations for popular magazines such as *Outdoor Life, Pennsylvania Game News, Sportsman Magazine,* and *Woman's Home Companion.* But what is it that makes a painting "art" as opposed to "illustration"? Artist Don Eckelberry believed that art has nothing to do with visual appearances, suggesting that "it is not what is seen but *what is felt* in what is seen that counts: in other words, not sight but insight." Arthur Singer similarly referred to his painting as an "emotional experience that might later become an illustration through reworking to show specific things. Guy Coheleach suggests that an illustrator may copy a photo, whereas an artist creates a painting from his own knowledge of the bird. By such measures most of George's work was clearly art. But was it "fine art"? Having achieved recognition as a great bird illustrator by his forties, George sought recognition as a fine artist and often lamented the lack of recognition as such.[19]

George Sutton's drawings of birds evolved from simple drawings, in which he used hatched lines to represent body plumage, to detailed drawings of feathers and finally to an economy of line and an increasing reliance on light to leave one with the impression of feathers, although the details of feathers were not actually there. As we have seen he favored watercolor, using both transparent and opaque colors, but not acrylics. Although Roger Tory Peterson urged him to use an airbrush for his backgrounds, George distrusted the technique.[20]

George commented on Audubon many times, changing his opinions of Audubon's work as his own art matured, and adding a new perspective on the frontier artist. In an early exchange with Fuertes, George had expressed a negative view of Audubon's work and was chided by Fuertes for having done so. This certainly gave him a different perspective, yet he never completely embraced Audubon's work as either art or science, perhaps driven by his own struggles for recognition as both an artist and a scientist. In 1950 he was hard at work on an article about Audubon to be published in *Audubon Magazine* when he wrote to his sister Dorothy suggesting that editors and readers might not like his article, because he was going to be critical of Audubon. In the end the article seems balanced, with George making a reasonable argument that Audubon sought to put drama into his work and, in so doing, sometimes put his birds in poses that were biologically unrealistic.

Earlier he had written to longtime friends Bob and Mary Frances Furman about Audubon: "What a stormy, imaginative, fear-ridden person he was! And there were those who really seemed to hate him. No part of his life was simple. He never went anywhere without having to lug along ibises, wild pigeons, snakes, alligators, seedlings, and the like, a bit as if he were everybody's messenger boy. What a simple life Alexander Wilson's was—by comparison."[21] George must have been at a low ebb, adding: "I have my own serious doubts as to how good an 'artist' I am. So the end result is that I now turn out virtually nothing. Does it boil down to a conviction *resident in me* that I'm really no good? Perhaps it does."[22] The Furmans said nothing of this apparent despair but came to their friend's aid, purchasing two of George's hawk paintings.

Although George appreciated abstract art and commented that he particularly enjoyed a Picasso show in New York, he found frustration in abstract art too. The frustration grew out of his own lack of acceptance by fine artists as anything but a bird illustrator. This is a theme that has been voiced repeatedly by wildlife artists of all kinds, and a pivotal component of the debate over what constitutes fine art. Perhaps a distinction is the purpose for which a painting is created. If it is created for identification or to show a specific behavior or plumage or soft-part color or pattern, then it is likely to be called an illustration. If it is created to provoke an emotional response, to set a mood, to capture a feeling, perhaps the work will be considered fine art. Even Audubon was derided by the art critics of his day.

At least in George's case, and perhaps in others, it seems to me that another component of the conundrum is a human one—the alliances that the bird artist makes. Graduate students are told that if they want to be considered professionals, they must belong to and be active in professional organizations. George believed that, but he chose to belong only to professional *scientific* organizations—he listed not a single art organization on his résumé, although clearly he interacted with the art faculty at Cornell and in Oklahoma. He is also listed in "Who Was Who in American Art." In April 1963 he put on a show of his bird paintings in the gallery of the fine arts department at the University of Oklahoma, at their invitation, for their "Focus on Fine Arts Month." In this, perhaps he did achieve his dream. In response to the invitation to show his work, George wrote to his friends the Kirkpatricks that the fine arts hierarchy "must not be so all-fired opposed to my sort of bird-art after all!"[23]

There was another side to Sutton's art as well. Art was not just illustration or an emotional expression; it was a source of enjoyment, at times even entertainment. George used his art to please. He prepared the invitation to Sewall Pettingill's wedding reception (fig. 14.4) and fanciful

14.4 *The Common Tern drawing George prepared for the invitations to Sewall and Eleanor Pettingill's wedding reception. Courtesy of Olin Sewall Pettingill, Jr.*

place cards for each of the attendees (fig. 14.5). Tragically, the reception never took place because the bride's father died that day.[24]

For the Pettingill children he put together a small booklet illustrating the letters of the alphabet with drawings of animals and gave it the title *Uncle George's Zoo*. This was not given as a gift, but "on loan"; it ultimately made the rounds of several families. In the book he inscribed the name of each of those to whom it had been sent. I have been unable to locate the book but know of its existence from several "readers" and found a photocopy of it (fig. 14.6).[25] Besides the Pettingill children it circulated to George's nephew Mark Swartz, Michigan friend Bill Lunk's son Ed, bird field guide author and artist Roger Tory Peterson's son Tory Coulter Peterson, and others. George seems to have kept the book on the move for many years. In a 1950 letter to his family he told Evie: "If Mark has learned his alphabet through the Zoo book by now, please return it to me. There are so many young folks coming along in this country now that I want it to make the proper rounds. There's a young Hickey lady [wife of ornithologist Joe Hickey] out in Madison who's probably next on the list. Then a namesake in Manitoba has never seen it (one George Sutton Hochbaum, no less). And there are others."[26]

At times George tagged quick, fanciful sketches onto letters as a means of expressing himself. One appended to a letter of November 20, 1957, to

MISS BRÜNNICH'S MURRE, OF COPPERTHWAITE-ON-TYNE'S ELECT, CARRIES A SHY CORSAGE OF KIPPERED HERRING

14.5. One of the place cards (this one a murre) drawn by Sutton for Sewall and Eleanor Pettingill's wedding reception. Each guest was represented by a different bird. The reception was canceled when Eleanor's father died. Courtesy of Olin Sewall Pettingill, Jr.

Bob Furman, is a postscript noting that the "Boat-tailed Grackles are doing fine."[27]

George enjoyed his own art even when it was not just right. An example of such lightness crops up in his ironic comments as he was trying to draw a Connecticut Warbler to illustrate Sewall Pettingill's *Guide to Bird Finding East of the Mississippi*.[28] He made three stabs at it before he got what he considered an acceptable drawing. Sewall mentioned to me that he had a few Sutton drawings in his files, and he pulled out several. The

14.6. *A composite of illustrations from* Uncle George's Zoo, *an unpublished children's alphabet book that George created and sent on loan to numerous friends. The name of each recipient was added to the cover of the book. From a photocopy courtesy of the Sutton archives, Western History Collection, University of Oklahoma.*

Connecticut Warbler file yielded all three drawings; Sewall quickly said George had had difficulty with the warbler, that the one used was clearly marked, and that he should have thrown out the other two long ago.

Each drawing is lightly annotated in pencil in George's handwriting. The first note says: "First try by chiclet." The next says: "Second try by spearmint." What in the world did these annotations mean? Then it was clear. The third drawing—used as an illustration on page 377 of Sewall's book—was labeled "Third try by gum!" Sewall had never noticed the penciled comments. When my photographs of the three drawings proved overexposed and I asked to borrow the drawings, Sewall sent them to me as a gift. But he had erased "Third try by gum!" and written over it: "Final." Apparently he never appreciated the humor.

A wonderfully unexpected Sutton piece crossed my path quite by chance. Following a presentation about him before the Oktibbeha Audubon Society in Starkville, Mississippi, my hometown at the time, I asked for questions and was rewarded when Grace Bull, a longtime friend and Audubon member, raised her hand and said, "We have some Sutton artwork."

Suspecting it would be one of the beautiful prints from *At a Bend in a Mexican River*, I was surprised to learn that it was something Sutton had painted for the father of Grace's husband, Gifford. Harry Gifford Bull had been Sutton's physician in Ithaca, New York, during the late 1930s and early 1940s. Dr. Bull was also an amateur naturalist and poet and sometimes shared his work with Sutton. During a visit in 1940 Dr. Bull showed George a poem he had copied from the back of a magazine—an anonymously authored poetic prayer of St. Francis of Assisi:

> Dear father, hear and bless
> Thy beasts and singing birds
> And guard with tenderness
> Small things that have no words.

George so enjoyed it that he asked if Dr. Bull would print a copy of the poem for him, to which the doctor agreed, if George would illustrate the margins of Bull's own copy. With the help of a local high school teacher, Bull printed the poem on 8½ by 11-inch watercolor paper, and George illustrated it with tiny watercolor figures of birds, squirrels, turtles, and other animals—an exquisite and unique piece (plate 26).

Although George is obviously known best for his portraits of birds, he also showed considerable technical skill, keen powers of observation, and biological insight with other subjects. A 1927 drawing of a weasel at play (fig. 14.7) demonstrates his ability to capture the animal's action.[29] His illustrations of walrus, lemming, and various fish during his year on Southampton provided aesthetically pleasing and scientifically useful documentation of their color and form. A lizard caught at the Rancho Rinconada was briefly anesthetized with carbon tetrachloride so that George could paint it in the role of prey in his painting of a Gray Hawk.[30] Struck by its colors as it basked in the sun, George opportunistically painted a Yarrow's spiny lizard in Mexico in 1949 and later provided a color plate of a collared lizard for the cover of *Reptiles of Oklahoma* and a vignette of a fox squirrel that was used as the frontispiece for *Mammals of Oklahoma* (plate 27).[31]

Growing sophistication in any artist's skill may be identifiable in a chronological review, but it may not be a linear progression. It is worth revisiting the fact that one of Sutton's greatest gifts was his ability to capture the essence of the living bird in tiny black-and-white sketches. He did this early on, in his first book, *An Introduction to the Birds of*

14.7. *A weasel George kept in his office while he was state ornithologist for Pennsylvania. Two weasels sent to the Pennsylvania Game Commission were to be employed for an educational film. One became an office pet, and George sketched it from life, playing with string. From his article "Stoat," published in* Nature Magazine *in 1942.*

Pennsylvania, demonstrating an economy of line and space while adding immeasurably to the printed word. Such sketches were in great demand because they enlivened a text at modest cost.

Work of this kind should not, however, be considered to involve minimal artistic effort. George often agonized over such sketches, making repeated efforts to get them exactly right.[32] He considered some of the drawings he did for Van Tyne and Berger's *Fundamentals of Ornithology* to be among the finest of his pen-and-ink work and wanted some of these to be preserved as examples of his style "at its best," even though some of the strongest were done from photographs rather than from living birds. The drawing of a Vulturine Guineafowl was his self-proclaimed "*tour de force*" of the series—a special challenge because of its spots. He wrote to his family that he "just about went daffy with guinea spots. This probably sounds like a variety of the hives, but the spots were real spots and the guinea was a real guinea. The plumage of this blasted fowl is minutely spotted, as all know, but what most folks don't realize is that the spots are amazingly uniform and laid out in the most wonderful geometric pattern." In 1975 he noted "even *today*, my eyes have a tendency to 'swim around a bit' when I contemplate those dozens of tiny spots."[33]

As a critic of bird art, Sutton was usually generous, but at times he could cut to the bone with insight from his deep knowledge and understanding of birds as well as of art. In his introduction to Anne Small's *Masters of Decorative Bird Carving* he takes a swipe at Picasso. To the Kirkpatricks he commented: "Picasso didn't want to draw a bird nicely. He wanted to make a caustic comment, through it, on bird art in general."[34] At a bird art show in Wausau, Wisconsin, ornithologist Jay Buckelew got a special tour of the exhibit with Sutton, during the course of which they stopped in front of a painting of an American Woodcock. Jay commented favorably, but Sutton disagreed. The painting doubtless evoked memories of his time at Fuertes's side listening to advice Fuertes had received from his mentor, Abbott Thayer, about the nature of camouflage. George noted: "You can see the woodcock."[35]

CHAPTER 15

Ovenbird and Golden Eagle

A very little time shall pass—
A White-crowned Sparrow's song or two, a rustle in
the grass—

GEORGE MIKSCH SUTTON, ". . . Forever and Ever, Amen"

In the spring of 1982 George was busy working on an article to accompany his painting of a stub-tailed young Yellow-billed Cuckoo for the inaugural issue of the Cornell Laboratory's new magazine, the *Living Bird Quarterly*.[1] As summer came on, only months before his death, George Sutton knew the end was near.[2] On June 11 he wrote to his former student Lewis Oring: "I am nearly incapacitated as a result of surgery, cobalt treatments, etc. after returning from Mexico in 1978. But I keep busy with the OOS Bulletin and a book that may or may not be published."[3]

On September 13 he wrote to John and Eleanor Kirkpatrick to tell them that he was advising some friends not to visit him. He could not bear having them remember him in his weakened condition. He also commented that Roger Vandiver of the Stovall Museum staff had prepared a clay sculpture portrait of him and that he considered it "by far the best portrait . . . that's ever been done."[4]

He wrote in late September to congratulate his friend, artist Albert Earl Gilbert, on "the great way" Gilbert's career had developed, but noting, "I am very weak and hardly know what keeps me going. I am trying to finish another book." And in thanking Oring for a reprint, he added: "Reading is not easy for me, for I don't read well lying down and sitting

166

is uncomfortable for me. The cobalt treatments have left the lower part of my body in really bad shape. I can hardly walk—can you believe it?"[5]

George was concerned about his current book project, an effort that he was not up to illustrating with his artwork. Instead he opted for quality photographs, which he solicited from former students and friends. He wanted this book, *Birds Worth Watching*, to be different.[6] In October he wrote to Oring: "My book is intended to be homespun, so to speak. This you will perceive before you've finished with the first paragraph."[7]

Aware that he was not likely to live to see *Birds Worth Watching* in print, he entered into a contract with the University of Oklahoma Press to assure its publication and recruited his good friend John Shackford to handle the details of obtaining the best of photographs to illustrate it. John fully lived up to George's confidence in him.[8]

In early November George entered the nursing home for the last time. He lamented his inability to be of use to others. Allan Ross arranged to bring musicians to George's room to provide him with a special concert.[9]

On November 19, George signed a statement directing Mike McCarty and Bill Johnson to retrieve his paintings from the safe in the Stovall Museum and to divide them as they saw fit, among themselves and his sister Dorothy.[10] These were a parting gift to his only family and to the two men who had seen him through his last crises.

Warren Harden discovered a late fall Ovenbird in his yard in Norman on November 30. The next day he captured it and immediately thought of George. The two had often exchanged surprises. He placed the live bird in a paper bag and went to the nursing home. As Warren walked into the room, George opened his eyes and said a soft hello. Warren said: "Doc, I have something to show you."

Warren gently removed the Ovenbird from the bag and held it close with a careful grip on its legs so that George could appreciate the fresh beauty of the bird's plumage. George raised his right arm toward the bird and marveled: "That's one of the most beautiful faces I have ever seen. Just imagine painting a bird and being able to capture the beauty of a face like that on paper." George could see little from the window of his room at the nursing home; the Ovenbird was probably the last live bird he saw.[11]

Three days later George asked his doctor how long he would last if he quit taking medication and food. Three days, he was told. He began his final fast and died quietly at 7:21 on the evening of December 7, 1982. The cause of death listed on his death certificate: congestive heart failure, complicated by prostate cancer. Bill Johnson took care of necessary final arrangements; Doc's sister Dorothy, herself in a nursing home in Topeka, was unable to assist. Two days later George was cremated.

It was fitting that the month that he died, an Acorn Woodpecker he had painted on a foggy morning in Mexico in 1938 graced the cover of *Bird Watcher's Digest* and that inside the magazine he offered sage advice as a scientist to those reporting hybrid warblers such as Sutton's Warbler: "The limits of variation within such a species as *Dendroica dominica* [Yellow-throated Warbler] are ill-defined to say the least, and to call a variant (even an obvious one) a hybrid may be a bad mistake." Thus his life ended as he had lived it, sharing his art and his science, bridging the divide between amateurs and professionals who studied birds.[12]

Although at the very end he had been incapacitated, George's final months and weeks had been as he had wanted. He had been aware of his condition and life was a gift he wished to share to the end. His strong convictions and desires are expressed in a poem he had apparently written in the final months:

Living and Dying

Let me die working—
Still tackling plans unfinished, tasks undone.
Clear to its end, swift may my race be run;
No lagging steps, no faltering, no shirking.
Let me die working!

Let me die thinking—
Let me fare forth still with an open mind,
Fresh secrets to unfold, new truths to find;
No soul undimmed, alert, no questions blinking.
Let me die thinking.

Let me die giving—
The substance of life for life's enriching;
Time, things and self to heaven converging
No selfish thought . . . loving, redeeming, living.
Let me die giving![13]

Governor George Nigh of Oklahoma and Mayor William S. Morgan of Norman, through separate proclamations, set aside March 20, 1983, as "George Miksch Sutton Day." The Norman community celebrated George's life in many ways. Special art exhibits honoring George were on display at the Stovall Museum and in the University of Oklahoma library. A memorial concert held in Holmberg Hall on the campus was sponsored by University President William S. Banowsky and his wife and the OU School of Music. George would have been pleased—and quick to add that the concert was also a tribute to his mother, Lola, who had given him the gift of music and for whom, as noted, he had donated a grand piano to the music program at the university.[14]

Following George's own instructions given to his sister Dorothy, a small group of George's closest friends from Norman traveled toward the Black Mesa country on Friday, June 17, 1983, for an informal and very special remembrance of George.[15] The group included Warren Harden, his son Wade, John Shackford, Roger Vandiver, Mike McCarty, and Bill Johnson. Bill had kept George's ashes and he carried them with him. The party birded along the way at several places on Friday, camped en route, and arrived at the Black Mesa early on Saturday morning. They set up their tents and birded in the Black Mesa country much of the morning, finding Say's Phoebe, Tree Swallow, Mississippi Kite and others—each bird bringing back memories of past trips with George.[16]

About eleven o'clock that morning they went toward the Rainier ranch, along the way adding more birds to the day's list: Brown Thrasher, Greater Roadrunner, Wild Turkey. As they neared the ranch they looked up on the cliffs to the west, and there was a Golden Eagle. It appeared above the cliffs and seemed to be putting on a special show for them. Near the Rainier ranch they went up a small side canyon and parked, then walked up the canyon perhaps a hundred yards to a big juniper at the foot of the mesa. They all gathered around and sat.

Warren Harden started by saying that they were all there to honor George. They agreed that the best way to do this was for each to tell what he or she wanted to say about George. Bill was last to speak. The words came from the heart, everyone present telling what was at once the same story yet also each individual's story. Woven through them all was the message that George had pursued friendship with each person. They did not pursue the friendship; he did. All their lives had been changed as a result. After contributing his own memories Bill opened the container of ashes and spread them around the large juniper. George always wanted to make a contribution; his last contribution would be to nourish a tree providing shelter for the birds he loved. Two ravens circled high in the morning sky, calling to each other with their hoarse notes, as ravens do. Bill read Sutton's poem ". . . Forever and Ever, Amen."[17]

The party had lunch with the Rainers. On Sunday morning they all went home. Depending on how one looks at it, the memorial gathering for George had taken an hour or it had lasted three days.

John Shackford was true to his word. With the help of many of George's friends and the university press, *Birds Worth Watching* came out in 1986. It provides a fine starting point for new graduate students. Not only does the book offer dozens of ideas for projects; it also offers inspiration, encouragement, and guidance for any who would study nature. George teaches us to open our eyes—to observe. The first step of the scientific method is to observe. Hypothesis formulation and testing and experimental design all come later—following careful observation.[18]

In addition to *Birds Worth Watching*, George's legacy included several unpublished manuscripts to help keep the *Bulletin of the Oklahoma Ornithological Society* on track. Since his death there have been ten articles in the journal by George Miksch Sutton: four in 1984, two in 1985, two in 1986, one in 1988, and one in 1990. He had also written an article for *Living Bird Quarterly* and the foreword to a birding guide for the Tulsa Audubon Society, both of which would be published after his death. In 1992 *Sooner Magazine* published a previously unpublished article of George's on drawing birds from life.[19]

Throughout his life George had had a particular interest in birds of prey, and as we have seen there had been many occasions when he had generously supported conservation efforts focused on them. He had been acutely aware of the declining numbers of Bald Eagles in the state and had supported efforts to protect them and a new Prairie Raptor Research Center that was being established near Tulsa in late 1982. The center was later incorporated as the South Prairie Raptor Research Center. Efforts to build it had begun before George's death, and the founding board of directors included many of his close friends. In the spring of 1983 talk began of changing the center's name to honor him. Warren Harden wrote to George's sister Dorothy in May 1984: "Many of us, including Steve [Sherrod], have been directly and positively influenced in our lives by George Sutton and his philosophy, thusly our desire to commemorate 'Doc' by using his name in our title."[20] The center became the George Miksch Sutton Avian Research Center.

The Omniplex at the Kirkpatrick Center dedicated a new exhibit on bird migration to George in 1983. He had contributed his expertise during the development of the exhibit, focusing on Oklahoma's migrants and complementing the display of his paintings in the Kirkpatrick Center. The exhibit was a computer-based interactive display including large backlit transparencies of Oklahoma migrants, recordings of the songs of each species, and life history information that was available at the touch of a button. The final phase of the project included a woodcarving of an Arctic Tern and a display about the annual migration of that species from the Arctic to the Antarctic.[21]

In 1984 the Wilson Ornithological Society established the George Miksch Sutton Award for Ornithological Art, in recognition of George's many contributions to the society and in furtherance of his lifelong support of bird art. The award is given for art that would be suitable as a color plate in the *Wilson Bulletin* and is limited to artists who do not make their living painting birds and whose work has not been featured in such magazines as *Audubon* or *National Wildlife*.[22]

The University of Oklahoma inaugurated the Sutton Music Series in 1992 to honor George and his longtime support of the music program.[23] The zoology building on campus was renamed Sutton Hall in his honor.

Months or perhaps years before he died, George wrote another poem about death—in a sense, his own epitaph: ". . . Forever and Ever, Amen." His sister Dorothy sent it to Les Line, editor of *Audubon* magazine, after George's death, and it was published as a memorial in *Audubon* in 1985. The poem embodies George's beliefs and his love for all nature.

. . . Forever and Ever, Amen

A very little time shall pass—
A White-crowned Sparrow's song or two, a rustle in the grass—
Ere I shall die: ere that which now is grief and sense of loss
And emptiness unbearable shall vanish
As curved reflections vanish with the shattering of a glass.

By the wind I shall be scattered
Up and down the land,
By strong waves strewn along the farthest shore;
No part of the dear world shall I not reach and, reaching, understand,
No thing that I have loved shall I not love the more.

No leaf of sedge nor cattail blade shall push
Up from the dark mud toward the open sky
But I shall be there, in the tender tip,
Experiencing the steady surge of growing.
No drop of water shall move upward, cell by cell,
No sunlight fall on any opening fern,
No breeze send waves across the yellowing grain,

But I shall be there, intimately learning
All that all things know and, knowing all, discerning
The full significance of suffering and pain.

No bird of passage shall fly north or south
Breasting the stiff wind or pushing through the fog,
But I shall be there, feeling the deep urge
That drives it otherwise at summer's ending,
And otherwhere once more with spring's return;
Ever so thoroughly I shall learn
The signs a bird must travel by,
The many ways in which a bird can die.

Day after day, season after season, brown in summer, white in winter,
'knowing the fierce drive of hunger,
With the slender weasel I shall hunt, and with the rabbit die—
I at the place where the sharp white teeth
Pierce the skin and the tearing hurts,
I, too, shivering while the hot blood spurts.

No vainly croaking, vainly struggling frog shall feel
The water snake's inexorable jaws
Moving over and round it, slowly engulfing it
But I shall be there struggling too, and crying
An anguished, futile protest against dying.

With the snake too I shall die:
Clutched by sharp talons, borne swiftly upward from the shallow creek,

I shall look down bewildered and surprised
By this new aspect of a familiar place.
Writhing, twisting, striking at the claws which hold me fast
I shall feel the hooked beak closing on my neck at last.

With the hawk, too, I shall die:
I shall feel the hot sting of shot, the loss of power, the sudden collapse,
The falling downward through unsupporting space,
The last swift rush of air past my face.[24]

Dorothy survived George by more than thirteen years. Very bizarrely, a notice of her death was published in the June 1994 issue of the *Scissortail*, the newsletter of the Oklahoma Ornithological Society. She died a year later, on June 7, 1995, at the age of ninety-three. Like George, she died thinking of others, asking that memorial contributions be made to the Children's Hour Preschool of Topeka. She also planned for her memorial service, asking that live plants be purchased that could be transplanted to the Aldersgate Village grounds for all to enjoy. She had lived at Aldersgate Village for her last nine years.[25]

George's epitaph from *Audubon* was brought to bear again in 1995 to remember another Oklahoman. Friends of Trudy Rigney, who had died in the blast at the Alfred P. Murrah Federal Building in Oklahoma City, heard the lines while gathered to toss dirt around a tree planted in her memory. Trudy had been close to finishing a degree at the University of Oklahoma; George would have approved.[26]

On February 23, 1996, the University of Oklahoma broke ground for the Sam Noble Oklahoma Museum of Natural History. At last a donor had made the dream possible. Certainly George had played a major role in creating a "museum climate" in the community.[27] Perhaps there was a collective twinge of regret that the community had failed him in the one thing he so wanted. He would have been so proud of it ("I shall be there, intimately learning . . . "). It would become everything George had dreamed of for the University of Oklahoma.

In 2000 a bust of George Miksch Sutton created by Karen Eisenhouser was installed in the Bizzell Library at the University of Oklahoma. George has been memorialized and remembered in many ways, but his student, colleague, and fellow ornithologist and artist Robert M. Mengel summed up collective feelings in a letter to Sewall Pettingill: "Our friend was a multi-faceted man and an extremely private one, hence enigmatic to many. If not most. But—my God—the energy, and the unfailing goodness."[28]

Appendix

GRADUATE STUDENTS MENTORED
BY GEORGE MIKSCH SUTTON

Unless otherwise indicated, Sutton chaired each student's graduate committee. There were other graduate students on whose committees he served and countless undergraduates whose careers benefited from his efforts.

Loetscher, Fredrick W. 1941. Ornithology of the Mexican state of Veracruz, with an annotated list of the birds. Ph.D. dissertation. Cornell University, Ithaca, New York. (Loetscher was under the direction of Arthur Allen from 1935 to 1939 and under Sutton from 1939 to 1941.)

Berger, Andrew J. 1950. The comparative functional morphology of the pelvic appendage in three subfamilies of Cuculiformes. Ph.D. dissertation, University of Michigan, Ann Arbor. (Sutton served as a member of Berger's six-member committee; Alfred H. Stockard, chair.)

Prescott, Kenneth Wade. 1950. A life history study of the Scarlet Tanager (*Piranga olivacea*). Ph.D. dissertation, University of Michigan, Ann Arbor. (Sutton served as a member of Prescott's six-member committee; Josselyn Van Tyne, chair.)

Graber, Richard Rex. 1955. Taxonomic and adaptive features of the juvenal plumage in North American sparrows. Ph.D. dissertation, University of Oklahoma, Norman.

Baepler, Donald Henry. 1956. Comparative dominance behavior in certain fringillid birds. M.S. thesis, University of Oklahoma, Norman.

Ely, Charles Adelbert. 1957. Comparative nesting success of certain south-central Oklahoma birds. M.S. thesis, University of Oklahoma, Norman.

Johnson, John Christopher, Jr. 1957. Habitat preferences among representative wintering and breeding birds of the central Oklahoma forest-prairie ecotone. Ph.D. dissertation, University of Oklahoma, Norman.

175

Graber, Jean Weber. 1957. A bioecological study of the Black-capped Vireo, *Vireo atricapillus*. Ph.D. dissertation, University of Oklahoma, Norman.

Parmelee, David Freeland. 1957. The annual avian breeding cycle at high latitudes in the Canadian Arctic. Ph.D. dissertation, University of Oklahoma, Norman.

Baepler, Donald Henry. 1960. The avifauna of the Soloma region in Huerhuetenango, Guatemala. Ph.D. dissertation, University of Oklahoma, Norman.

Ely, Charles Adelbert. 1960. The avifauna of southeastern Coahuila, Mexico. Ph.D. dissertation, University of Oklahoma, Norman.

Land, Hugh Colman. 1960. Ornithological investigations in eastern Guatemala. Ph.D. dissertation, University of Oklahoma, Norman.

Oring, Lewis Warren. 1962. Ecology and behavior of certain ducks during the post-nuptial molt. M.S. thesis, University of Oklahoma, Norman.

Janovy, John, Jr. 1965. Epidemiology of malaria in certain birds of the Cheyenne Bottoms, Barton County, Kansas. Ph.D. dissertation, University of Oklahoma, Norman. (Sutton served as a committee member; Teague Self, chair.)

Oring, Lewis Warren. 1966. Breeding biology and molts of the Gadwall, *Anas strepera* Linnaeus. Ph.D. dissertation, University of Oklahoma, Norman.

Nighswonger, Paul Floyd. 1969. A study of viable seeds in a selection of birds' nests. Ph.D. dissertation, University of Oklahoma, Norman. (Sutton served as a committee member; Elroy L. Rice, chair.)

James, Frances C. 1970. Geographic size variation in birds and its relationship to climate. Ph.D. dissertation, University of Arkansas. (Sutton served as a committee member; Douglas James, chair.)

McHenry, Merril G. 1971. Breeding and post-breeding movements of Blue-winged Teal (*Anas discors*) in southwestern Manitoba. Ph.D. dissertation, University of Oklahoma, Norman.

Trainer, John Ezra, Jr. 1971. An ultrastructural investigation of body wall components in *Porocephalus crotali* (Pentastomida). Ph.D. dissertation, University of Oklahoma, Norman. (Sutton served as a committee member.)

Notes

MAJOR COLLECTIONS CONSULTED

Sutton archives: George Miksch Sutton archives, Western History Collection, University of Oklahoma, Norman, Oklahoma.

Van Tyne Library: George Miksch Sutton–Josselyn Van Tyne correspondence, Van Tyne Library, Museum of Zoology, University of Michigan, Ann Arbor, Michigan.

Kroch Library: George Miksch Sutton–Arthur A. Allen correspondence, Rare and Manuscript Collections, Carl A. Kroch Library, Cornell University Library, Ithaca, New York.

Wetmore Papers: Alexander Wetmore Papers, 1898–1976, Record Unit 7006, Smithsonian Institution Archives, Washington, D.C.

PREFACE

1. George Miksch Sutton to Robert W. Storer, September 21, 1974, and George Miksch Sutton to Andrew J. Berger, November 25, 1974, both in Sutton archives, Western History Collection, University of Oklahoma, Norman, Oklahoma (hereafter cited as Sutton archives).

2. George Miksch Sutton to Fred Haecker, October 13, 1947, Sutton archives.

3. The George Miksch Sutton–Josselyn Van Tyne correspondence is in the Van Tyne Library, Museum of Zoology, University of Michigan, Ann Arbor (hereafter cited as Van Tyne Library), and was made available to me by Janet Hinshaw.

4. George Miksch Sutton to John and Eleanor Kirkpatrick, September 20, 1964, courtesy of John Kirkpatrick; P. Teilhard de Chardin, *The Phenomenon of Man* (New York: Harper & Row, 1959), 52.

5. G. M. Sutton, *Bird Student* (Austin: University of Texas Press, 1980); O. S. Pettingill, Jr., *My Way to Ornithology* (Norman: University of Oklahoma Press, 1992).

6. George Miksch Sutton to Robert W. Storer, December 14, 1970, Sutton archives.

CHAPTER 1. FAMILY TIES

1. Dorothy Miksch Sutton Fuller interviews by Jerome A. Jackson, Topeka, Kansas, November 8, 1991, and May 9, 1992; Greta Nordstrom interviews by Jerome A. Jackson, Mediapolis, Iowa, August 17, 1997, and September 7, 2002; most dates and names are from family records viewed at the time of the interviews.

2. Sutton, *Bird Student*, 27; George spells his grandfather's name "Critten," although family records spell it "Critton," the same as his great grandmother's family name.

3. Greta Nordstrom interview, August 17, 1997.

4. Records courtesy of Clinton J. Holloway, Disciples of Christ Historical Society.

5. Sutton, *Bird Student*, 53.

6. H. T. Sutton, *The Temptation of the Man Unpurchasable* (Bethany, Nebr.: H. E. Wetherell Company, undated, ca. 1906).

7. H. T. Sutton, "From My Window," *Overland Monthly* 53 (1909): 423; for other examples, see H. T. Sutton's poems "The 'Soddy,'" *Overland Monthly* 54 (1909): 576; "Communion, a Feast of Rebels," *Christian Century* 53 (July 29, 1936): 1032; and "Luke 16:20," *Christian Century* 53 (March 4, 1936): 360.

8. G. M. Sutton, *Bird Student*, 14.

9. R. M. Virtue, *A History of Gnadenhutten* (Gnadenhutten, Ohio: Ross M. Virtue, 1976).

10. Marriage, death, and birth records courtesy of David D. Danneberger, pastor of the Moravian Church, Gnadenhutten, Ohio.

11. Sutton, *Bird Student*, 14; Dorothy Miksch Sutton Fuller interview, November 8, 1991.

12. Anonymous, *Cotner Collegian* (Bethany, Nebr.: Cotner College, 1906).

13. A. Watkins, *History of Nebraska*, vol. 3 (Lincoln, Nebr.: Western Publishing and Engraving Company, 1913).

14. Records courtesy of Clinton J. Holloway, Disciples of Christ Historical Society.

15. George Miksch Sutton to Ross Anthony, December 5, 1979, Sutton archives.

16. Harry Trumbull Sutton to the Editor, *State Journal*, Lincoln, Nebraska.

17. Greta Nordstrom interview, August 17, 1997.

18. Ibid.

19. George Miksch Sutton to Dick [Frederick M.] Gaige, July 28, 1937, Van Tyne Library.

20. Dorothy Miksch Sutton Fuller interview, November 8, 1991.

21. Ibid.; H. S. Gregg, *At Break of Day* (Indiana, Pa.: Park Press, 1937).

22. Records courtesy of Clinton J. Holloway, Disciples of Christ Historical Society.

23. Ibid.; records at Penny Farms, Florida.

CHAPTER 2. GROWING UP

1. Some recollections, including the perspective in the epigraph, are in G. M. Sutton, unpublished manuscript in box 18, Sutton archives.

2. Sutton, *Bird Student*, 3–5.

3. George Miksch Sutton to family, February 19, 1950, Sutton archives.

4. G. M. Sutton, *Birds in the Wilderness: Adventures of an Ornithologist* (New York: Macmillan Company, 1936), 1–2.

5. F. M. Chapman, *Bird Life* (New York: D. Appleton and Company, 1901).

6. Sutton, *Bird Student*, 5–6.

7. G. M. Sutton, *An Introduction to the Birds of Pennsylvania* (Harrisburg, Pa.: J. Horace McFarland Company, 1928).

8. Sutton, *Bird Student*, 11.

9. Sutton, *Bird Student*, 10.

10. Ibid., 9; G. M. Sutton, "David Clark Hilton," *Auk* 64 (1947): 179–80.

11. Sutton, *Bird Student*, 17.

12. Ibid., 19.

13. F. M. Bailey, *Handbook of Birds of the Western United States* (New York: Houghton Mifflin, 1902).

14. Sutton, *Bird Student*, 19.

15. Sutton, *Bird Student*, 22.

16. Sutton, *Bird Student*, 23.

17. Sutton, *Bird Student*, 27.

18. G. M. Sutton, "Little Black Rail in Illinois," *Auk* 43 (1926): 233.

19. Sutton, *Bird Student*, 25.

20. G. M. Sutton, "Birdnesting under Difficulties," *Atlantic Monthly* 143 (1929): 810–13; Sutton, *Birds in the Wilderness*, 8–16.

21. G. M. Sutton, "An Adventure with a Turkey Vulture," *Read* 19, no. 18 (1970): 16–21.

22. G. M. Sutton, "The Turkey Vulture's Ability to Carry Food in Its Beak," *Auk* 53 (1936): 76.

23. G. M. Sutton, "A Pet Road-Runner," *Bird-Lore* 15 (1913): 324–26.

24. A. H. Walter (editorial comment), *Bird-Lore* 15 (1913): 326.

25. G. M. Sutton, "The Interesting Road-Runner," *Oologist* 31 (1914): 141–42.

26. G. M. Sutton, "Notes on the Road-Runner at Fort Worth, Texas," *Wilson Bulletin* 34 (1922): 2–20.

27. Sutton, *Birds in the Wilderness*, 2–3.

28. Sutton, *Bird Student*, 23.

CHAPTER 3. BETHANY, WEST VIRGINIA

1. His observations about the town of Bethany are from Sutton, *Bird Student*, 44.

2. George Miksch Sutton to Mr. and Mrs. John E. Kirkpatrick, January 13, 1961, courtesy of John E. Kirkpatrick; Sutton, *Bird Student*, 46; drawing courtesy of Bethany College archives, Bethany, West Virginia. Note that the drawing shown, while from the college herd records, does not indicate that this particular drawing was one done by Sutton.

3. G. M. Suttard [*sic*], "A Trip to Waynesburg, Pa.," *Oologist* 32 (1915): 14–18.

4. Anonymous, *The Bethanian* (Bethany, W.Va.: Bethany College, 1914–19).

5. John Wiens to Jerome A. Jackson, February 20, 2005.

6. G. M. Sutton, "Suggestive Methods of Bird-Study: Pet Road Runners,' *Bird-Lore* 17 (1915): 57–61.

7. M. F. Boynton, *Louis Agassiz Fuertes His Life Briefly Told and His Correspondence Edited* (New York: Oxford University Press, 1956), 238.

8. Louis Agassiz Fuertes to George Miksch Sutton, January 21, 1916, in G. M. Sutton, *To a Young Bird Artist: Letters from Louis Agassiz Fuertes to George Miksch Sutton* (Norman: University of Oklahoma Press, 1979), 48.

9. Boynton, *Louis Agassiz Fuertes*, 228; R. M. Peck, *A Celebration of Birds: The Life and Art of Louis Agassiz Fuertes* (New York: Walker and Company, 1982), 95.

10. George Miksch Sutton to Robert Arbib, December 3, 1975, Sutton archives.

11. Dorothy Miksch Sutton Fuller interview, November 8, 1991.

12. Anonymous, *The Bethanian*.

13. Sutton, *Bird Student*, 72.

14. Ibid.; Dorothy Miksch Sutton Fuller interview, November 8, 1991.

15. Sutton, *Bird Student*, 72–74.

16. Ibid., 76–79; *The Catalogue of Birds in the British Museum* included twenty-seven volumes published between 1874 and 1895 under the authorship of several different ornithologists.

17. Sutton, *To a Young Bird Artist*, 113–14; Sutton, *Bird Student*, 82.

18. Sutton, *Bird Student*, 83; "A Deplorable Situation at Bethany," *Christian Oracle* (East Liverpool, Ohio) 4, no. 18 (May 2, 1919): 2; "College Boys Strike," *Baltimore Sun*, June 1, 1919; R. J. Cobb, "The Mood of Bethany: 1919–1940," unpublished manuscript (April 1991), Bethany College archives; W. K. Woolery, *Bethany Years* (Huntington, W. Va.: Standard Printing and Publishing Company, 1941); numerous undated anonymously authored hand-bills, news clippings, and other documents in the Bethany College archives made available courtesy of R. Jeanne Cobb, archivist, Bethany College Library.

19. Sutton, *Bird Student*, 121; John Wiens to Jerome A. Jackson, February 21, 2005.

20. Dorothy Miksch Sutton Fuller interview, November 8, 1991; Albert R. Buckelew, Jr., and R. Jeanne Cobb interviews by Jerome A. Jackson, Bethany College, April 10, 1996. The painting of a pair of Hooded Mergansers in flight appeared on the cover of the December 1927 issue of *Outdoor Life* magazine.

21. Dorothy Miksch Sutton Fuller interview, November 8, 1991; Albert R. Buckelew, Jr., and R. Jeanne Cobb interviews, April 10, 1996; G. M. Larrimore, in a 1930 clipping from an unidentified newspaper in Wheeling, West Virginia, had also spelled George's middle name "Miske," and President Cramblett had likely used this article in the Bethany College archives as he pre-pared his remarks for the occasion.

22. Dorothy Miksch Sutton Fuller interview, November 8, 1991.

23. W. E. C. Todd, *Birds of Western Pennsylvania* (Pittsburgh: Carnegie Museum, 1940); George Miksch Sutton to Mr. and Mrs. C. E. Addy, May 25, 1976, Sutton archives.

24. George Miksch Sutton to Ed Addy, June 24, 1982, Sutton archives.

CHAPTER 4. PITTSBURGH AND CARNEGIE

1. This was his first experience of city living; his opinion of cities is from Sutton, *Bird Student*, 78.

2. Sutton, *Bird Student*, 110.

3. Rudyerd Boulton was later active in the Wilson Ornithological Club, a founder of the Eastern Bird Banding Association, an author of children's books, and the illustrator of R. B. Sturgis, *Field Book of Birds of the Panama Canal Zone* (New York: G. P. Putnam's Sons, 1928).

4. G. M. Sutton, "Bayard Henderson Christy," *Auk* 61 (1944): 178–79.

5. G. M. Sutton, "John Bonner Semple," *Auk* 67 (1950):429–30.

6. Sutton, *Birds in the Wilderness*, 45–57; W. E. C. Todd, *Birds of the Labrador Peninsula and Adjacent Areas* (Toronto: University of Toronto Press, 1963), 31–34.

7. W. E. C. Todd and M. A. Carriker, Jr., "The Birds of the Santa Marta Region of Colombia: A Study in Altitudinal Distribution," *Annals of the Carnegie Museum* 14 (1922); W. E. C. Todd, "A Revision of the Genus *Eupsychortyx*," *Auk* 37 (1920): 189–220.

8. Sutton, *Bird Student*, 109; T. S. Palmer, "Thirty-Eighth Stated Meeting of the American Ornithologists' Union," *Auk* 38 (1921): 89–105; Sutton, *To a Young Bird Artist*, 122.

9. Sutton, *To a Young Bird Artist*, 125–26; H. Harris, "Examples of Recent American Bird Art," *Condor* 28 (1926): 191–206.

10. G. M. Sutton, "Some Remarks on the Facial Expression of Birds," *Wilson Bulletin* 34 (1922): 141–47.

11. G. M. Sutton, "Notes on the Road-Runner at Fort Worth, Texas," *Wilson Bulletin* 34 (1922): 3–20; G. M. Sutton, Bird Leaflet no. 1 (Pittsburgh: Carnegie Museum, 1922); Sutton, *Bird Student*, 120.

12. R. M. Barnes, *The American Oologists' Exchange Price List of North American Bird Eggs* (Lacon, Ill.: R. Magoon Barnes, 1922), 89.

13. George Miksch Sutton to T. Walter Weiseman, October 9, 1922, Sutton archives.

14. W. L. Dawson, *The Birds of California*, 4 vols. (San Diego: South Moulton Company, 1923).

15. See, for example, G. M. Sutton, "The Season: Pittsburgh Region," *Bird Lore* 25 (1923): 132, and "The Season: Pittsburgh Region," *Bird Lore* 25 (1923):193–95.

16. H. H. Bailey, *The Birds of Florida* (Baltimore, Md.: Williams & Wilkins Company, 1925).

17. George Miksch Sutton to Arthur A. Allen, August 22, 1928, Rare and Manuscript Collections, Carl A. Kroch Library, Cornell University Library, Ithaca, New York (hereafter cited as Kroch Library); "Among the Authors," *Audubon* 43 (1941): 219.

18. George Miksch Sutton scholastic record, courtesy of Office of the Registrar, University of Pittsburgh.

19. Sutton, *Bird Student*, 123–34; G. M. Sutton, "The Blue Goose Expedition," *Cardinal* 1, no. 3(1924): 16–18.

20. Sutton, *Bird Student*, 135–43; G. M. Sutton, "Visit to a Wood Ibis

Colony," *Bird-Lore* 26 (1924): 391–95; G. M. Sutton, "An Expedition to Cape Sable," *Cardinal* 1, no. 4 (1924): 14–16; E. G. Holt and G. M. Sutton, "Notes on Birds Observed in Southern Florida," *Annals of the Carnegie Museum* 16, nos. 3–4 (1926): 409–30.

21. T. S. Palmer, "The Forty-Second Stated Meeting of the American Ornithologists' Union," *Auk* 42(1925): 105–15.

22. Sutton, *Bird Student*, 144.

CHAPTER 5. ELOISE

1. Pettingill, *My Way to Ornithology*, 165; Olin Sewall Pettingill, Jr., interview by Jerome A. Jackson, Fort Worth, Texas, November 6, 1991.

2. Pettingill, *My Way to Ornithology*.

3. Sutton, *Bird Student*, 110.

4. Olin Sewall Pettingill, Jr., interview, November 6, 1991.

5. Dorothy Miksch Sutton Fuller to Olin Sewall Pettingill, Jr., October 15, 1984, courtesy of Olin Sewall Pettingill, Jr.

6. Dorothy Miksch Sutton Fuller interview, May 9, 1992.

7. Greta Nordstrom interviews, August 17, 1997, and September 7, 2002.

8. George Miksch Sutton to George E. Gifford, Jr., May 17, 1973, Sutton archives.

9. George Miksch Sutton to a friend who prefers to remain anonymous, January 1947.

CHAPTER 6. PENNSYLVANIA STATE ORNITHOLOGIST

1. Todd's perspective on the fascination of Pennsylvania's birds is from his *Birds of Western Pennsylvania* 3.

2. S. E. Gordon, "Introduction," pp. 4–5 in G. M. Sutton, *A Year's Program for Bird Protection*, Bulletin no. 7 (Harrisburg: Pennsylvania Board of Game Commissioners, 1925).

3. C. Richard Robins to Jerome A. Jackson, February 19, 1992 (Beck was a business partner of Robins's father); Sutton, *Bird Student*.

4. "G. M. Sutton Honored; Awarded Degree," *Bethany Collegian* 42, no. 9 (February 4, 1925): 1.

5. "Specimens Received for Biology Dep't.," *Bethany Collegian* 42, no. 9 (February 4, 1925): 1.

6. G. M. Sutton, "A Natural Zoological Garden in Western Pennsylvania: Pymatuning Swamp," *Wild Life Magazine* 3 (1925): 4–5; G. M. Sutton, "The Birds of Pymatuning Swamp and Conneaut Lake, Crawford County, Pennsylvania," *Annals of the Carnegie Museum* 18 (1928): 19–239.

7. Sutton, *A Year's Program for Bird Protection*.

8. T. C. Stephens, "Publications Reviewed," *Wilson Bulletin* 37 (1925): 108–11.

9. G. M. Sutton, "The Ruffed Grouse Situation in Pennsylvania," *Cardinal* 1, no. 5 (1925): 17–19; G. M. Sutton, "The Ruffed Grouse Situation in

Pennsylvania," *Wild Life Magazine* (Greenville, Pa.) 3 (January–February, 1925); G. M. Sutton, "The Present Status of the Ruffed Grouse in Pennsylvania," *American Midland Naturalist* 9 (1925): 373–78.

10. Sutton, *Bird Student*, 147; I have not been able to locate a copy of this dictionary, published by the John C. Winston Company, apparently in 1925; W. A. DuPuy, *Our Bird Friends and Foes* (Philadelphia: John C. Winston Company, 1925).

11. L. Jones, "Editorial," *Wilson Bulletin* 28 (1916): 31–32.

12. Sutton, *Bird Student*, 173.

13. G. M. Sutton, *Birds Worth Watching* (Norman: University of Oklahoma Press, 1986); Sutton, *Bird Student*, 153; G. M. Sutton, "Loon Banded in Pennsylvania Killed in Ontario, *Canadian Field-Naturalist* 41 (1927): 139.

14. Sutton, *Bird Student*, 154–68; Todd, *Birds of the Labrador Peninsula*, 35–37.

15. Sutton, *To a Young Bird Artist*, 145.

16. J. D. Scott, "Art Genius of the Bird World," *Coronet* 37 (February 1955): 49–54; George Miksch Sutton to Robert W. Storer, August 15, 1955, Van Tyne Library.

17. T. W. Burgess, *The Burgess Seashore Book for Children* (Boston: Little, Brown, and Company, 1929).

18. See G. M. Sutton, "Notes on the Nesting of the Goshawk in Potter County, Pennsylvania," *Wilson Bulletin* 37 (1925): 193–99; G. M. Sutton, "A Fair Deal for the Hawks and Owls," *Outdoor America* (January 1928): 30–31, 51.

19. G. M. Sutton, *An Introduction to the Birds of Pennsylvania* (Harrisburg, Pa.: J. Horace McFarland Company, Mount Pleasant Press, 1928).

20. W. S[tone], "Sutton's '*Introduction to the Birds of Pennsylvania*,'" *Auk* 46 (1929): 133.

21. Arthur A. Allen to George Miksch Sutton, August 31, 1928, Kroch Library; Todd, *Birds of the Labrador Peninsula*, 37–38; G. M. Sutton, *Iceland Summer* (Norman: University of Oklahoma Press, 1961), viii.

22. George Miksch Sutton to Arthur A. Allen, August 22, 1928, Kroch Library.

23. Arthur A. Allen to George Miksch Sutton, August 31, 1928, Kroch Library.

24. George Miksch Sutton to Arthur A. Allen, September 6, 1928, Kroch Library.

25. George Miksch Sutton to Arthur A. Allen, October 1, 1928, and February 19, 1929, Kroch Library.

26. Sutton, *Bird Student*, 186–87.

27. George M. Sutton to Dorothy M. Sutton, spring 1929, courtesy of Dorothy M. Sutton Fuller and Tom J. Cade.

CHAPTER 7. SOUTHAMPTON ISLAND

1. Sutton's explanation about the island's name is from G. M. Sutton, *Eskimo Year* (New York: Macmillan, 1934), 1.

2. G. M. Sutton, *The Exploration of Southampton Island, Hudson Bay*, part 1, sections 1, 2, 3, Memoirs of the Carnegie Museum 12 (1932): 1–75; Sutton, *Eskimo Year*.

3. D. Parmelee, "Foreword to the Second Edition," in Sutton, *Eskimo Year*, vii.

4. G. M. Sutton, "Quaint Folk, the Eskimos," *Atlantic Monthly* 150 (1932): 57–63; G. M. Sutton, "Quaint Folk, the Eskimos," *Readers Digest* 21, no. 125 (September 1932): 5–7.

5. Sutton, *Bird Student*, 191.

6. Sutton, *Eskimo Year*, 9.

7. G. M. Sutton, unpublished journals from his trip to Southampton Island, 1929–30, Sutton archives (hereafter cited as Southampton Island journal entry, with date).

8. Sutton, Southampton Island journal entry, October 18, 1929.

9. Ibid.

10. George Miksch Sutton to Arthur A. Allen, August 16, 1929, Kroch Library.

11. KDKA; news clippings; Sutton archives.

12. Sutton, multiple Southampton Island journal entries, 1929, Sutton archives.

13. Anonymous (Announcement of Sutton trip to Southampton Island), *Auk* 46 (1929): 584.

14. Sutton, Southampton Island journal entry, October 20, 1929.

15. Sutton, Southampton Island journal entry, December 15, 1929.

16. Ibid.; Sutton, *Bird Student*, 200.

17. Sutton, Southampton Island journal entry, November 21, 1929.

18. Sutton, *Eskimo Year*, 144.

19. Sutton, Southampton Island journal entry, April 6, 1930.

20. G. M. Sutton, "Easter Warfare," in *Eskimo Year*, 247–51; Sutton, Southampton Island journal entries, April 9–30, 1930. A komatik is a long Inuit sledge, and komatik races are fun contests that also hone the survival skills of people who live in a hostile environment. Ellipsis points after "if Jack wouldn't turn . . ." indicate an undecipherable word; the meaning seems to be that he would change demeanor and shift allegiances when his friends were present.

21. Sutton, *Eskimo Year*, 317–21.

22. G. M. Sutton, *The Exploration of Southampton Island, Hudson Bay*, part 1, and part 2: Zoology, section 2, *The Birds of Southampton Island*, Memoirs of the Carnegie Museum 12 (1932): 1–275.

23. C. P. Alexander, "Diptera Collected on Southampton Island by George Miksch Sutton: Trichoceridae and Tipulidae," part 2, section 4, article 2 in Sutton, *Exploration of Southampton Island*, Memoirs of the Carnegie Museum 12 (1934): 3–10, plate 25.

24. O. E. Jennings, "Bryophyta (Bryophytes) of Southampton Island," part 3, article 3 in Sutton, *Exploration of Southampton Island*, Memoirs of the Carnegie Museum 12 (1936): 7–16, plate 30.

25. G. M. Sutton letter to Andrew J. Berger, December 6, 1967, courtesy of Andrew J. Berger.

26. "Mushrooms of Southampton Island from Water-color Sketches made by Dr. George Miksch Sutton during August, 1930" (plate), in O. E. Jennings, "Algae and Fungi of Southampton Island," part 3, article 1 in Sutton, *Exploration of Southampton Island*, Memoirs of the Carnegie Museum 12 (1936): 1–4, plate 29; Sutton, *Eskimo Year*.

27. Sutton, *Bird Student*, 201.

CHAPTER 8. CORNELL

1. Sutton, *Bird Student*, 201.

2. Sutton, *Bird Student*, 201–8.

3. Olin Sewall Pettingill, Jr., interview, November 6, 1991; see also G. M. Sutton and O. S. Pettingill, Jr., "Good Lantern Slides of Birds," *Wilson Bulletin* 50 (1938): 170–75.

4. Olin Sewall Pettingill, Jr., interview, November 6, 1991; Sutton, *Bird Student*, 206.

5. Sutton, *Bird Student*, 209–16.

6. Sutton, *Birds in the Wilderness*, 123.

7. G. M. Sutton, Excerpts from his letter of July 5, 1931, *Pennsylvania Game News* 2, no. 17 (1931): 4.

8. "Rare Eggs," *Time*, July 27, 1931.

9. Transcripts and dissertation materials from Cornell University, Sutton archives.

10. T. S. Roberts, *The Birds of Minnesota* (Minneapolis: University of Minnesota Press, 1932).

11. Walter Breckenridge interview by Jerome A. Jackson, Minneapolis, October 12, 1995; Gustav A. Swanson to Jerome Jackson, April 23, 1992.

12. Gustav A. Swanson to Jerome Jackson, April 23, 1992.

13. T. S. Palmer, "The Fiftieth Stated Meeting of the American Ornithologists' Union, October 17–20, 1932," *Auk* 50 (1932): 64–79.

14. Anonymous, Exhibition of Bird Art Held in Connection with the 50th Meeting of the American Ornithologists' Union, Chateau Frontenac Hotel, Quebec, Canada, 8–21 October 1932 (Quebec: American Ornithologists' Union, 1932).

15. G. M. Sutton, "Fifty Years of Progress in American Bird-Art," pp. 181–97 in F. M. Chapman and T. S. Palmer, eds., *Fifty Years' Progress of American Ornithology 1883–1933* (Lancaster, Pa.: American Ornithologists' Union, 1933).

16. With Van Tyne correspondence in archives at Van Tyne Library.

17. George Miksch Sutton to Josselyn Van Tyne, June 21, 1934, Van Tyne Library.

18. A. Petretti, *Petretti's Coca-Cola Collectibles Price Guide*, 10th edition (Dubuque, Iowa: Antique Trader Books, 1997), 530.

19. Sutton, *Bird Student*, second plate following p. 64.

20. P. A. Johnsgard, *Baby Bird Portraits by George Miksch Sutton* (Norman: University of Oklahoma Press, 1998).

21. G. S. Hochbaum, "Introduction," in H. A. Hochbaum, G. S. Hochbaum, Jack A. Barrie, and Glenn D. Chambers, eds., *Wings Over the Prairie* (Winnipeg, Canada: Tamos Books, 1994), 10.

22. Harry C. House to Steve K. Sherrod, June 2, 2001; courtesy of Steve K. Sherrod.

23. J. Van Tyne to G. M. Sutton, March 30, 1933, Van Tyne Library.

24. J. Van Tyne to G. M. Sutton, March 31, 1933; Van Tyne Library.

25. G. M. Sutton to J. Van Tyne, April 1933 (no specific date given); Van Tyne Library; J. Van Tyne and G. M. Sutton, *The Birds of Brewster County, Texas*, University of Michigan Museum of Zoology, Miscellaneous Publication no. 37 (1937).

26. G. M. Sutton to J. Van Tyne, April 18, 1934, Van Tyne Library; G. M. Sutton, "An Egg of the Marbled Murrelet," *Auk* 58 (1941): 580–81.

27. Albert J. Buckelew to Jerome A. Jackson, March 13, 2005.

28. J. Van Tyne to G. M. Sutton, September 10, 1934, Van Tyne Library.

29. G. M. Sutton to J. Van Tyne, October 2, 1934, Van Tyne Library.

30. G. M. Sutton, "Kints," in *Birds in the Wilderness*.

31. H. C. Oberholser, *The Bird Life of Louisiana*, Bulletin no. 28 (Baton Rouge: Louisiana Department of Conservation, 1938); J. T. Tanner, *The Ivory-billed Woodpecker*, Research Report no. 1 (New York: National Audubon Society, 1942).

32. There are two Sutton Ivory-billed Woodpecker paintings in the collection of the Cornell Laboratory of Ornithology, including the one reproduced here as plate 13, which also appears on the cover of the phonograph record by P. P. Kellogg, *Florida Bird Songs*, (Ithaca, N.Y.: Cornell Laboratory of Ornithology, 1969); Paul Kellogg to George Miksch Sutton, January 7, 1969, Sutton archives.

33. "Birds Sing Despite Dust; Scientists Fight Storms to Study Them. Expedition Finds Ivory-billed Woodpecker, Thought Extinct, Deep in Huge Louisiana Swamp," *Science Service*, April 26, 1935.

34. G. M. Sutton and J. Van Tyne, *A New Red-tailed Hawk from Texas*, Occasional Papers of the Museum of Zoology, University of Michigan 321 (1935): 1–6; G. M. Sutton to J. Van Tyne, November 1, 1934, Van Tyne Library.

35. Sutton and Van Tyne, "A New Red-tailed Hawk."

36. G. M. Sutton to Helen Van Tyne, August 25, 1935, Van Tyne Library.

37. G. M. Sutton to J. Van Tyne, September 15, 1935, Van Tyne Library.

38. A. A. Allen, *American Bird Biographies* (Ithaca, N.Y.: Comstock Publishing Company, 1934); A. A. Allen, *The Golden Plover and Other Birds* (Ithaca, N.Y.: Comstock Publishing Company, 1939).

39. A. R. Brand, *Songs of Wild Birds* (New York: Thomas Nelson and Sons, 1934); A. R. Brand, *More Songs of Wild Birds* (New York: Thomas Nelson and Sons, 1936).

40. R. B. Vale, *Wings, Fur and Shot* (Harrisburg, Pa.: Stackpole Sons, 1936); R. B. Vale, *How to Hunt American Game* (Harrisburg, Pa.: Stackpole Company, 1946).

41. Sutton, *Birds in the Wilderness*.

42. E. G. Palmer, "Lines to the Hummingbird," *Woman's Home Companion* 63, no. 7 (1936): 7.

43. T. S. Palmer, "The Fifty-Fourth Stated Meeting of the American Ornithologists' Union," *Auk* 54 (1937): 117–26.

44. "Sudden's 'Birds of the Wilderness,'" *Auklet* 1, no. 2 (1936): 19–21.

45. P. H. Falk, *Who Was Who in American Art, 1564–1975* (Madison, Connecticut: Sound View Press, 1999).

46. George Miksch Sutton to Dean Amadon, April 3, 1977, Sutton archives.

47. G. M. Sutton, *Mexican Birds: First Impressions* (Norman: University of Oklahoma Press, 1951); A. J. Van Rossem, "A New Race of Sharp-shinned Hawk from Mexico," Auk 56 (1939): 127–28, frontispiece by Sutton facing p. 127.

48. T. C. Stephens, "Editorial," *Wilson Bulletin* 50 (1938): 138.

49. J. Delacour, ed., *Proceedings, IXᵐᵉ Congrès Ornithologique International* (Rouen, France 1938); color plate of *Trogon ambiguus ambiguus* Gould, *L'Oiseau* 9 (1939): facing p. 161; the same Coppery-tailed Trogon painting appears in Sutton, *Mexican Birds*, as plate 11; also on the dust jacket of J. E. Holloway, *Dictionary of Birds of the United States* (Portland, Ore.: Timber Press, 2003).

50. Sutton, *Mexican Birds*, 94.

51. O. S. Pettingill, Jr., "Proceedings of the Wilson Ornithological Club," *Wilson Bulletin* 51 (1939): 51–67.

52. George Miksch Sutton to Helen Van Tyne, November 29, 1938, Van Tyne Library.

53. G. M. Sutton to J. Van Tyne, December 28, 1938, Van Tyne Library.

54. J. Van Tyne to G. M. Sutton, December 30, 1938, Van Tyne Library.

55. G. M. Sutton and T. D. Burleigh, "Birds of Las Vigas, Veracruz," *Auk* 57 (1940): 234–43; G. M. Sutton and T. D. Burleigh, "Birds of Valles, San Luis Potosí, Mexico," *Condor* 42 (1940): 259–62.

56. K. Haller, "A New Wood Warbler from West Virginia," *Cardinal* 5 (1940):49–52; G. M. Sutton to J. Van Tyne, September 2, 1939, Van Tyne Library; "New Bird: *Dendroica potomac* Haller," *Time* 35 (February 26, 1940): 48; "Ornithologist Discovers New Bird Species: *Dendroica potomac*, or Sutton's Warbler," *Hobbies* 45 (May 1940): 105; "Discover New Warbler," *Pennsylvania Game News* 10, no. 12 (1940): 19.

57. M. Brooks, "George Sutton and His Warbler," *Audubon* 47 (1945): 145–50; C. W. Carlson, "The Sutton's Warbler: A Critical Review and Summation of Current Data," *Atlantic Naturalist* 34 (1981): 1–11; D. Morse, *American Warblers* (Cambridge, Mass.: Harvard University Press, 1989); American Ornithologists' Union, *Check-List of North American Birds* (Washington, D.C.: American Ornithologists' Union, 1998), 702; G. M. Sutton, "Is Sutton's Warbler a Valid Species?" *Cardinal* 5 (1942): 151–54.

58. R. T. Peterson, *Wildlife in Color* (Boston: Houghton Mifflin Company, 1951), 35.

59. Todd, *Birds of Western Pennsylvania*, 1940.

60. *World Book Encyclopedia* (Chicago: World Book, 1942); "Birds and Flowers," *Nature Magazine* 35 (1942): 341.

61. George Miksch Sutton to Milton Fuller, January 30, 1941, Sutton archives.

62. George Miksch Sutton to Alexander Wetmore, February 27, 1940, and Alexander Wetmore to George Miksch Sutton, March 1, 1940, both in box 67, Record Unit 7006, Alexander Wetmore Papers, 1898–1976, Smithsonian Institution Archives, Washington, D.C. (hereafter cited as Wetmore Papers).

63. Brochure describing "A New Lecture: Bird Magic in Mexico," Wetmore Papers.

64. T. H. Manning, "Remarks on the Physiography, Eskimo, and Mammals of Southampton Island," *Canadian Geographical Journal* 24 (1942): 17–33.

65. G. M. Sutton to George Breiding, May 27, 1942, courtesy of George Breiding.

66. G. M. Sutton, "The Wildlife Gallery, Following Audubon's Trail," *Audubon Magazine* 44 (1942): 226–29.

67. George Miksch Sutton to Arthur A. Allen, August 7, 1942, Kroch Library.

68. Arthur A. Allen to George Miksch Sutton, August 12, 1942, Kroch Library.

69. George Miksch Sutton to Arthur A. Allen, August 14, 1942, Kroch Library.

70. Arthur A. Allen to F. B. Hutt, August 18, 1942, Kroch Library.

71. F. B. Hutt to George Miksch Sutton, August 21, 1942, Kroch Library.

72. George Miksch Sutton to Arthur A. Allen, August 22, 1942, Kroch Library.

CHAPTER 9. WORLD WAR II

1. George Miksch Sutton to George Breiding, March 3, 1942, courtesy of George Breiding.

2. G. M. Sutton letters to J. Van Tyne, March 17, 23, and April 8, 1942, Van Tyne Library.

3. George Miksch Sutton to George Breiding, May 27, 1942, courtesy of George Breiding.

4. G. M. Sutton to J. Van Tyne, June 10, September 7, 21, 30, October 2, and November 4, 12, 1942, Van Tyne Library.

5. Olin Sewall Pettingill, Jr., interview, November 6, 1991; G. M. Sutton, "World War II," unpublished manuscript, Sutton archives.

6. G. M. Sutton to J. Van Tyne, November 10, 12, and December 1, 1942, Van Tyne Library.

7. Sutton, "World War II" manuscript; George Miksch Sutton to Dorothy Miksch Sutton, January 4 and February 17, 1943, Sutton archives.

8. Sutton, "World War II" manuscript; G. M. Sutton and O. S. Pettingill, Jr., "Yellow Rail in Rice County, Minnesota," *Auk* 61 (1944): 474–75.

9. Walter Breckenridge interview, October 12, 1995.

10. G. M. Sutton, "A Bird Painter Goes to Hollywood," unpublished manuscript, Sutton archives; G. J. Siegel, "Hollywood's Army: The First Motion Picture Unit, US Army Air Forces. Culver City, California," http://www.militarymuseum.org/1stmpu.html.

11. George Miksch Sutton to Dorothy Miksch Sutton, September 12, 1943, Sutton archives.

12. G. M. Sutton to J. Van Tyne, October 7, 1943, Van Tyne Library.

13. G. M. Sutton, "At a Bend in a Mexican River," *Audubon Magazine* 46 (1944): 258–66, 344–51; 47 (1945): 35–40, 107–12, 173–78, 239–42.

14. Nicholas Collias interview by Jerome A. Jackson, October 27, 1995.

15. Sutton, "World War II" manuscript; E. Stefansson, "A Short Account of the Stefansson Collection," *Polar Notes* (Dartmouth College Library, Hanover, New Hampshire), no. 1 (1959): 5–12; George Miksch Sutton to Dorothy Miksch Sutton, December 3, 1943, Sutton archives.

16. G. M. Sutton to J. Van Tyne, March 28, 1944, Van Tyne Library.

17. George Miksch Sutton to Alexander Wetmore, April 13, 1944, box 67, Wetmore Papers.

18. J. Kieran, *Footnotes on Nature* (Garden City, N.Y.: Doubleday, 1947), 193–96.

19. G. M. Sutton, "Behavior of Birds during a Florida Hurricane," *Auk* 62 (1945): 603–6.

20. G. M. Sutton, "A Visit to Merritt's Island," unpublished manuscript, Sutton archives.

21. Sutton, "World War II" manuscript; and see his *Auk* articles: G. M. Sutton, "The Bronzed Grackle as a Species," *Auk* 62 (1945): 170; "Autumnal Duelling among Mockingbirds," *Auk* 62 (1945): 301; "Arkansas Kingbird in Southeastern Florida," *Auk* 62 (1945): 462; and "Behavior of Birds during a Florida Hurricane," *Auk* 62 (1945): 603–6.

22. G. M. Sutton, "Notes on the Winter Bird-Life of Fairbanks, Alaska," *Condor* 47 (1945): 264–67.

23. G. M. Sutton and R. S. Wilson, "Notes on the Winter Birds of Attu," *Condor* 48 (1946): 83–91.

24. George Miksch Sutton to R. M. Mengel, June 23, 1945, courtesy of Marion Jenkinson Mengel.

25. Frank McCamey interview by Jerome A. Jackson, October 27, 1995.

26. Anonymous (untitled news item), *Pennsylvania Game News* 14, no. 9 (1943): 24; Sutton, "World War II" manuscript. George was not alone; my father similarly contracted undulant fever while stationed at Fort Benning, Georgia, during the war.

27. Anonymous (biographical sketch of G. M. Sutton as a new life member of the Wilson Ornithological Society), *Wilson Bulletin* 55 (1943): 215; M. G. Brooks, "Report of the Secretary for 1943," *Wilson Bulletin* 56 (1944): 63; "Report of the Secretary for 1944," *Wilson Bulletin* 57 (1945): 143; "Report of the Secretary for 1945," *Wilson Bulletin* 58 (1946): 66; "Proceedings of the Twenty-Eighth Annual Meeting," *Wilson Bulletin* 59 (1947): 59–67.

CHAPTER 10. THE MICHIGAN YEARS

1. The observation about tigers is in R. B. Payne, "Ornithology at the University of Michigan Museum of Zoology: An Historical Account," pp. 1–58 in W. E. Davis, Jr., and J. A. Jackson, *Contributions to the History of North*

American Ornithology, vol. 2, Memoirs of the Nuttall Ornithological Club no. 13 (Cambridge, Mass.: Nuttall Ornithological Club).

2. G. M. Sutton to J. Van Tyne, November 7, 1931, and J. Van Tyne to G. M. Sutton, November 9, 1931, Van Tyne Library.

3. [G. M. Sutton], "Cranbrook Institute of Science Proposed Research Project No. ___," unsigned, undated research proposal to the Cranbrook Institute of Science for work to be done during the summer of 1934, Van Tyne Library.

4. G. M. Sutton to J. Van Tyne, April 22, 1934, Van Tyne Library.

5. G. M. Sutton, *The Juvenal Plumage and Postjuvenal Molt in Several Species of Michigan Sparrows,* Cranbrook Institute of Science Bulletin no. 3 (1935): 36 pp.

6. G. M. Sutton, "Tribulations of a Sparrow Rancher," *Audubon Magazine* 50 (1948): 286–95; J. V. Coevering, *Real Boys and Girls Go Birding* (Philadelphia: J. B. Lippincott Company, 1939), 65–71.

7. G. M. Sutton, "The Nesting Fringillids of the Edwin S. George Reserve, Southeastern Michigan," parts 1–7, serialized as follows: parts 1, 2, 3, 4, *Jack-Pine Warbler* 37 (1959): 2–11, 37–50, 77–101, 127–51; parts 5, 6, 7, *Jack-Pine Warbler* 38 (1960): 2–15, 46–65, 124–39.

8. Johnsgard, *Baby Bird Portraits.*

9. George Miksch Sutton to Robert M. Mengel, January 18, 1946, courtesy of Marion Jenkinson.

10. G. M. Sutton to J. Van Tyne, May 2, 1946; O. S. Pettingill, Jr., and N. R. Whitney, Jr., *Birds of the Black Hills,* Special Publication no. 1 (Ithaca, N.Y.: Cornell Laboratory of Ornithology, 1965).

11. G. M. Sutton to J. Van Tyne, May 16, 1946; Harold F. Mayfield to Jerome A. Jackson, February 8, 1992.

12. R. M. Mengel, *The Birds of Kentucky,* Ornithological Monographs no. 3 (Lawrence, Kans.: American Ornithologists' Union 1965).

13. G. M. Sutton to J. Van Tyne, April 4, 1946, Van Tyne Library.

14. G. M. Sutton to J. Van Tyne, October 3, 1946, Van Tyne Library.

15. Undated curriculum vitae, Sutton archives; R. Payne, *The History of Ornithology at the University of Michigan* (Ann Arbor: University of Michigan Museum of Zoology, 2000); George Miksch Sutton to family, May 1, 1949, Sutton archives; George Miksch Sutton to family, October 22, 1950, Sutton archives.

16. George Miksch Sutton to family, September 11, 1949, Sutton archives.

17. Harold Mayfield to Jerome A. Jackson, February 8, 1992.

18. George Miksch Sutton to Dorothy Miksch Sutton, May 5, 1949, Sutton archives.

19. Harold F. Mayfield to Jerome A. Jackson, February 8, 1992; Payne, "Ornithology at the University of Michigan Museum," in Davis and Jackson, *Contributions.*

20. Harold F. Mayfield to Jerome A. Jackson, February 8, 1992.

21. Ernest P. Edwards to Jerome A. Jackson, October 5, 1994. Edwards, Lea, and Boehm had spent the spring in Mexico and met Sutton in Tamaulipas in late May or early June, worked a few days, then drove directly to the Black

Hills to assist Pettingill. George set up the tableau, and Lea took the photo using a delayed shutter release.

22. J. B. Young, "Proceedings of the Twenty-Ninth Annual Meeting," *Wilson Bulletin* 60 (1948): 62–71.

23. G. M. Sutton and H. H. Spencer, "Observations at a Nighthawk's Nest," *Bird-Banding* 20 (1949): 141–49; George Miksch Sutton to Haven Spencer, March 9, 1982, Sutton archives.

24. George Miksch Sutton to Alexander Wetmore, August 16, 1948, box 67, Wetmore Papers.

25. George Miksch Sutton to Alexander Wetmore, September 30, 1948, box 67, Wetmore Papers.

26. George Miksch Sutton to Ben B. Coffey, November 5, 1948, courtesy of Lula Coffey.

27. George Miksch Sutton to family, October 12, 1949, Sutton archives.

28. George Miksch Sutton to Dorothy Miksch Sutton, May 5, 1949, Sutton archives.

29. George Miksch Sutton to family, August 20 and September 11, 1949, Sutton archives.

30. George Miksch Sutton to family, September 11, 1949, Sutton archives.

31. George Miksch Sutton to family, September 18 and October 12, 1949, Sutton archives.

32. George Miksch Sutton to family, October 27, 1949, Sutton archives.

33. George Miksch Sutton to Milton Fuller, November 22, 1949, Sutton archives.

34. George Miksch Sutton to family, December 11, 1949, Sutton archives.

35. George Miksch Sutton to Richard and Jean Graber, February 20, 1950, and George Miksch Sutton to family, February 26, 1950, both in Sutton archives.

36. George Miksch Sutton to family, May 28, 1950, Sutton archives.

37. George Miksch Sutton to family, March 3, 1950, Sutton archives. Having myself worked under Hall's direction in the 1960s, I think Sutton recognized the divergence between them.

38. George Miksch Sutton to family, March 12, 1950, Sutton archives.

39. George Miksch Sutton to family, March 19, 1950, Sutton archives.

40. George Miksch Sutton to family, April 2, 1950, Sutton archives.

41. George Miksch Sutton to family, April 16, 1950, Sutton archives.

42. George Miksch Sutton to family, May 28, 1950, Sutton archives.

43. George Miksch Sutton to family, December 10, 1950, Sutton archives.

44. Sutton to family, May 28, 1950.

45. George Miksch Sutton to family, August 6, 1950, Sutton archives.

46. George Miksch Sutton to Paul Slud, July 26, 1955, Sutton archives.

47. Stefansson, "Short Account of the Stefansson Collection."

48. G. M. Sutton, "David Clark Hilton," *Wilson Bulletin* 63 (1951): 218.

49. George Miksch Sutton to "Folksies" [family], December 31, 1950, Sutton archives.

50. L. J. Lear, *Rachel Carson: Witness for Nature* (New York: Henry Holt and Company, 1997), 195.

51. Robert W. Storer to George Miksch Sutton, August 1, 1951, Van Tyne Library.
52. George Miksch Sutton to family, November 20, 1949, Sutton archives.
53. George Miksch Sutton to family, December 16, 1951, Sutton archives.
54. G. M. Sutton, "Three Pine Grosbeaks," *Living Bird* 17 (1979): 5–6 + color plate.
55. George Miksch Sutton to family, April 30, 1952, Sutton archives.
56. J. Van Tyne to G. M. Sutton, August 15, 1952, Van Tyne Library.
57. G. M. Sutton to J. Van Tyne, August 20, 1952, Van Tyne Library.
58. George Miksch Sutton to family, September 2 and 6, 1952, Sutton archives.
59. S. L. Olson, "In Memoriam: Pierce Brodkorb, 1908–1992," *Auk* 110 (1993): 911–15.
60. George Miksch Sutton to family, January 7, 1951, Sutton archives.
61. H. Brandt, *Arizona and Its Bird Life* (Cleveland, Ohio: Bird Research Foundation, 1951); T. C. Stanwell-Fletcher, *The Tundra World* (Boston: Little, Brown and Company, 1952); Sutton, *Mexican Birds*; J. Van Tyne and A. J. Berger, *Fundamentals of Ornithology* (New York: John Wiley & Sons, 1959).
62. Richard Graber to Jerome A. Jackson, April 6, 1992.

CHAPTER 11. VISITING OKLAHOMA

1. M. M. Nice, *The Birds of Oklahoma*, rev. edition, Biological Survey 3, no. 1 (Norman: University of Oklahoma, 1931).
2. G. M. Sutton, "Notes on the Birds of the Western Panhandle of Oklahoma," *Annals of the Carnegie Museum* 24 (1934): 1–50.
3. Ibid., 2.
4. Ibid.
5. G. M. Sutton, *Oklahoma Birds* (Norman: University of Oklahoma Press, 1967), xvii. The chapter epigraph is from his description in this book of the allure of the Black Mesa country, which kept drawing him back to the state, xxi.
6. G. M. Sutton, "The Mississippi Kite in Spring," *Condor* 41 (1939): 41–53.
7. G. M. Sutton, "The Mississippi Kite," *Oologist* 56 (1939): 92.
8. R. M. Barnes, [Untitled editorial comments], *Oologist* 56 (1939): 92.
9. G. M. Sutton, "Some Findings of the Semple Oklahoma Expedition," *Auk* 55 (1938): 501–8.
10. M. Stephenson, "Did Sutton Get State's Rare Birds?" *Tulsa World*, May 16, 1937.
11. Ibid.
12. G. M. Sutton to J. Van Tyne, June 15, 1937, Van Tyne Library.
13. G. M. Sutton to J. Van Tyne, April 7, 1944, Van Tyne Library.

CHAPTER 12. AN OKLAHOMA INSTITUTION

1. The optimistic view in the epigraph is from G. M. Sutton, "The Future of Ornithology in Oklahoma," *Oklahoma Quarterly* 2 (1953): 20–22, 30.
2. Sutton, *Mexican Birds*.

3. Nice, *Birds of Oklahoma*; G. M. Sutton, "On the History of the Cleveland County Bird Club," undated manuscript, Sutton archives.

4. T. D. Burleigh, *Georgia Birds* (Norman: University of Oklahoma Press, 1958).

5. George Miksch Sutton to family, March 24, 1952, Sutton archives.

6. George Miksch Sutton to Phillips B. Street, November 17, 1958, courtesy of Phillips B. Street.

7. V. Stefansson, *Encyclopedia Arctica* (Ann Arbor, Mich.: University Microfilms, 1974), 27 microfilm reels.

8. George Miksch Sutton to Lewis W. Oring, February 3, 1981, courtesy of Lewis W. Oring.

9. G. M. Sutton and D. F. Parmelee, "Breeding of the Snowy Owl in Southeastern Baffin Island," *Condor* 58 (1956): 273–82; George Miksch Sutton to Paul S. Martin, October 2, 1953, Sutton archives.

10. George Miksch Sutton to Paul Slud, July 26, 1955; Sutton archives.

11. W. Eugene Hollon, *A History of the Stovall Museum of Science and History, University of Oklahoma* (Norman: Stovall Museum of Science and History, University of Oklahoma, 1956), 19–20.

12. G. M. Sutton, *Iceland Summer* (Norman: University of Oklahoma Press, 1961).

13. Advertisement for Audubon Screen Tour program "Iceland Summer," Sutton archives; winners of the Burroughs Medal for nature writing are listed at http://www.johnburroughs.org/jb_assoc/medlbk.htm.

14. George Miksch Sutton to Robert H. Furman, November 9, 1967, courtesy of Robert H. Furman.

15. Sutton, *Iceland Summer*; Finnur Gudmundsson to George Miksch Sutton, June 15, 1959, and George Miksch Sutton to Finnur Gudmundsson, August 11, 1959, both in Sutton archives; announcement of the award from Dr. Kristjan Eldjarn, president of Iceland, came via Ambassador Gudmundur I. Gundmundsson to George Miksch Sutton, June 26, 1972.

16. Stefansson, *Encyclopedia Arctica* microfilm reels.

17. George Miksch Sutton to Lewis W. Oring, February 3, 1981, courtesy of Lewis W. Oring.

18. George Miksch Sutton to Jean Graber, November 20, 1958, and to Richard and Jean Graber, May 25, 1959, courtesy of Richard and Jean Graber.

19. Sutton, "Nesting Fringillids of the Edwin S. George Reserve," parts 1–7, *Jack-Pine Warbler* 37–38.

20. Anonymous, "Sutton Escapes Injury in Fire," (Transcript, Norman, Oklahoma, October 9, 1963), 2; George Miksch Sutton to Mrs. John E. Kirkpatrick, October 17, 1963, courtesy of John E. Kirkpatrick; George Miksch Sutton to C. Richard Robins, February 12, 1964, courtesy of C. Richard Robins.

21. George Miksch Sutton to Dean Amadon, February 23, 1967, Sutton archives.

22. R. L. Osborn, "Dr. Sutton Reaps 2 Honors," *Oklahoma Daily* (University of Oklahoma), November 3, 1967, 22; "Allen Award Won by OU Professor," *Daily Oklahoman*, August 27, 1969, 21.

23. G. M. Sutton, "Footprint Thieves," *Audubon* 69 (1967): 53–57.

24. Sutton, *Oklahoma Birds*; Mrs. George L. Bowman, Introductory remarks given for Dr. George M. Sutton, honoree, during the Oklahoma Hall of Fame Induction Ceremony, November 16, 1967, Sheraton Hall Ballroom, Sheraton Oklahoma Hotel, Oklahoma City, transcript in Sutton archives.

25. George Miksch Sutton to Zella Moorman, July 27, 1970, Sutton archives.

26. F. M. Baumgartner and A. M. Baumgartner, *Oklahoma Bird Life* (Norman: University of Oklahoma Press, 1992.

27. George Miksch Sutton to Ella Delap, January 21, 1979, Sutton archives.

28. Sutton served on the Administrative Board of the Cornell Laboratory of Ornithology from 1968 to 1974; "Former Members of the Board and Past Director," *Living Bird* 14 (1975): 304.

29. Thomas D. Burleigh to George Miksch Sutton, August 15, 1968, and George Miksch Sutton to Thomas D. Burleigh, August 29, 1968, both in Sutton archives; T. D. Burleigh, *Birds of Idaho* (Caldwell: Caxton Printers,1971).

30. George Miksch Sutton to Lewis Oring, January 3 and 21, 1969, courtesy of Lewis Oring.

31. G. M. Sutton, [Obituary of Hugh Colman Land], *Auk* 90 (1973): 964–67; Land , *Birds of Guatemala* (Wynnewood, Pa.: Livingston Publishing Company, 1970).

32. G. M. Sutton, *High Arctic* (New York: Paul S. Eriksson, 1971).

33. L. R. Mewaldt, "Proceedings of the Eighty-Seventh Stated Meeting of the American Ornithologists' Union," *Auk* 87 (1970): 136–53; invitation to the presentation of the third Arthur A. Allen Award to George Miksch Sutton, September 13, 1969, Sutton archives; "Allen Award Won by OU Professor," *Daily Oklahoman*, August 27, 1969, 21.

34. Proclamation of "George M. Sutton Day," September 13, 1969, in Oklahoma, signed by Governor Dewey Bartlett and Secretary of State John Rogers, Sutton archives.

35. George Miksch Sutton to John and Eleanor Kirkpatrick, October 19, 1970, courtesy of John E. Kirkpatrick.

36. George Miksch Sutton to John E. Kirkpatrick, March 17, 1971, courtesy of John E. Kirkpatrick.

37. George Miksch Sutton to C. Richard Robins, December 17, 1971, courtesy of C. Richard Robins.

38. George Miksch Sutton to John and Eleanor Kirkpatrick, June 28, 1971, courtesy of John and Eleanor Kirkpatrick. Sutton was negotiating with Wood Hannah but recounted the negotiating and described his concerns to the Kirkpatricks.

39. George Miksch Sutton to Eleanor and John Kirkpatrick, June 18 and 27, 1972, and George Miksch Sutton to Eleanor Kirkpatrick, December 23, 1972, courtesy of Eleanor and John Kirkpatrick.

40. George Miksch Sutton to Eleanor Kirkpatrick, December 23, 1972, courtesy of John and Eleanor Kirkpatrick.

41. Ted Parker, personal communication.

42. George Miksch Sutton to Eleanor and John Kirkpatrick, June 3, 1973, courtesy of John and Eleanor Kirkpatrick.

43. George Miksch Sutton to Governor Wendell H. Ford, November 11, 1973, and note to Eleanor and John Kirkpatrick appended to this letter, courtesy of John Kirkpatrick.

44. G. M. Sutton, transcript of announcement of Louis Agassiz Fuertes lectureship, Sutton archives; "Louis Agassiz Fuertes Lectureship Established," *Newsletter to Members*, Cornell University Laboratory of Ornithology, no. 74 (Fall 1974): 1.

45. G. E. Watson, "Proceedings of the Ninety-Second Stated Meeting of the American Ornithologists' Union," *Auk* 92 (1975): 347–68; Anonymous, *Auklet*, October 1974.

46. George Miksch Sutton to Joseph J. Hickey, June 7, 1976, courtesy of Joseph J. Hickey.

47. George Miksch Sutton to Mary Frances and Robert H. Furman, January 14, 1969, and Bruce M. Bell to Robert H. Furman, February 11, 1981, courtesy of Mary Frances and Robert H. Furman.

48. George Miksch Sutton to Carl D. Riggs, April 8, 1969, courtesy of Robert H. Furman.

49. George M. Sutton to Chris [Mrs. Guy] Anthony, April 19, 1975, Sutton archives.

50. George Miksch Sutton to Eleanor Kirkpatrick, August 25, 1975, courtesy of John and Eleanor Kirkpatrick.

51. George Miksch Sutton to John and Eleanor Kirkpatrick, February 2, 1975, courtesy of John and Eleanor Kirkpatrick.

52. George Miksch Sutton to Robert H. Furman, February 23, 1976, courtesy of Robert H. Furman.

53. William S. Banowsky to George Miksch Sutton, March 25, 1980, Sutton archives.

54. I. Coffey, "Two Writers Win Honors," Transcript, Norman, Oklahoma, November 9, 1980,

55. Robert H. Furman to George Miksch Sutton, January 10, 1980, courtesy of Robert H. Furman.

56. Program from "Dedication Concert by the Piano Faculty," February 28, 1980, courtesy of Robert H. Furman.

57. L. F. Baptista, "A Revision of the Mexican *Piculus* (Picidae) Complex," *Wilson Bulletin* 90 (1978): 159–81 + illustration by G. M. Sutton facing p. 159.

58. A. Small, *Masters of Decorative Bird Carving* (Tulsa, Okla.: Winchester Press, 1991), 13–16.

59. George Miksch Sutton to Robert H. Furman, undated note written on the announcement of "A George Miksch Sutton Lecture" dated October 15, 1980, courtesy of Robert H. Furman.

60. George Miksch Sutton to Board of Directors, Prairie Raptor Center, November 8, 1981, courtesy of Dorothy Miksch Sutton Fuller.

61. Jimmie C. Thomas to "the Friends of George M. Sutton," June 3, 1983, courtesy of John Kirkpatrick.

62. George Miksch Sutton to Allan A. Ross, December 14, 1981, Sutton archives.

CHAPTER 13. TEACHER, CONSERVATIONIST, PHILANTHROPIST

1. G. D. Schnell, "George Miksch Sutton the Educator," *Stovall Museum Newsletter* 8, no. 5 (1982): 2–3.

2. From unpublished notes written in December 1982 by Kay Oring, courtesy of Kay Oring.

3. William E. Southern to Olin Sewall Pettingill, Jr., March 28, 1983, courtesy of Olin Sewall Pettingill, Jr.

4. Sutton, *Bird Student*.

5. Anonymous, *The Bethanian* (Bethany, W. Va.: Bethany College, 1919).

6. "Among the authors," *Audubon Magazine* 43 (1941): 219.

7. Peter Stettenheim to Jerome A. Jackson, February 9, 1992.

8. G. S. Hochbaum, "Introduction," in H. A. Hochbaum, G. S. Hochbaum, Jack A. Barrie, and Glenn D. Chambers, eds., *Wings over the Prairie* (Winnipeg, Canada: Tamos Books, 1994), 10–12.

9. Teague Self to Dorothy Miksch Sutton Fuller, January 26, 1984, courtesy of Dorothy Miksch Sutton Fuller.

10. George Miksch Sutton to Robert M. Mengel, July 9, 1949; courtesy of Marion Jenkinson.

11. Harold F. Mayfield to Jerome A. Jackson, February 8, 1992.

12. See for example George Miksch Sutton to Richard and Jean Graber, February 20, 28, March 7, 28, 1950, Sutton archives; Andrew J. Berger to George Miksch Sutton, December 25, 1966, Sutton archives.

13. Richard R. Graber to Jerome A. Jackson, April 6, 1992.

14. D. F. Parmelee, *Bird Island in Antarctic Waters* (Minneapolis: University of Minnesota Press, 1980), 129.

15. William E. Southern to Olin Sewall Pettingill, Jr., March 28, 1983; courtesy of Olin Sewall Pettingill, Jr.

16. George Miksch Sutton to Paul Slud, October 17, 1955, Sutton archives.

17. L. MacIvor, "Brothers on the Wind," *ZooSounds* (Oklahoma Zoological Society) 19, no. 1 (1983): 8–9.

18. George Miksch Sutton to Paul Slud, June 9, 1950, Sutton archives.

19. George Miksch Sutton to Paul Slud, November 7, 1950, Sutton archives.

20. George Miksch Sutton to Paul Slud, January 8, 1957, Sutton archives.

21. See G. M. Sutton articles in *Bulletin of the Oklahoma Ornithological Society:* "May an Adult Canyon Wren Become Flightless during Late Summer?" vol. 7 (1974): 15; "When Does the Female Cardinal Start Singing in Spring?" vol. 8 (1975): 7–8; and "How Often Does the Brown Creeper Sing in Oklahoma?" vol. 10 (1977): 33–34.

22. R. T. Peterson, "George Miksch Sutton 1898–1982," *American Birds* 37 (1983): 135.

23. George Miksch Sutton to Mr. and Mrs. Guy Anthony, December 21, 1979, Sutton archives.

24. Don Malick to Don Radovich, courtesy of Don Radovich; Anonymous, "The Sutton Show," *Newsletter to Members*, Cornell University Laboratory of Ornithology, no. 76 (Spring 1975).

25. G. M. Sutton, "Europe," undated, unpublished manuscript, Sutton archives.

26. George Miksch Sutton to C. Richard Robins, June 12, 1972; courtesy of C. Richard Robins.

27. George Miksch Sutton to Richard and Jean Graber, March 7, 1950, Sutton archives.

28. G. M. Sutton, *A Year's Program for Bird Protection*, Bulletin no. 7 (Harrisburg, Pa.: Board of Game Commissioners, 1925).

29. R. Edge and E. D. Lumley, *Common Hawks of North America* Publication no. 81 (New York: Emergency Conservation Committee, 1940); R. H. Pough, *The Witmer Stone Wildlife Sanctuary* (New York: National Audubon Society, undated); G. M. Sutton, "In Defense of Predators," *ZooSounds* (Oklahoma Zoological Society) 9, no. 2 (1973):1.

30. George Miksch Sutton to Douglas S. Kennedy, June 13, 1977, courtesy of Robert H. Furman.

31. R. T. Peterson, *Wildlife in Color* (Boston: Houghton Mifflin Company, 1951), 35.

32. G. M. Sutton, "Rose-throated Becard, *Platypsaris aglaiae*, in the lower Rio Grande Valley of Texas," *Auk* 66 (1949): 365–66.

33. George Miksch Sutton to Board of Regents of the University of Tamaulipas, Sutton archives.

34. George Miksch Sutton to numerous colleagues, cover letter accompanying a copy of Sutton's letter to the Board of Regents of the University of Tamaulipas, Sutton archives.

35. George Miksch Sutton to C. Richard Robins, December 17, 1971, courtesy of C. Richard Robins.

36. George Miksch Sutton to Chris [Mrs. Guy] Anthony, April 19, 1975, Sutton archives.

37. George Miksch Sutton to John and Eleanor Kirkpatrick, March 13, 1971, courtesy of John and Eleanor Kirkpatrick.

38. Mention of the National Wildlife Federation Conservation Teacher of the Year Award is included in the catalog of the Leigh Yawkey Woodson Art Museum 1980 Bird Art Exhibition honoring Peter Scott and other bird artists, including Sutton; the Southwestern Association of Naturalists began awarding the George Miksch Sutton Award for Conservation Research annually for the best conservation-oriented research paper published in *Southwestern Naturalist* beginning with the 1989 volume of the journal; L. L. Janecek, "The Southwestern Association of Naturalists Minutes of the Annual Business Meeting, University of Texas at El Paso, El Paso, Texas, Friday, 19 April 1991," Southwestern Naturalist 36(1991): 680–84.

39. R. M. Mengel, "George Miksch Sutton: A Bird Artist's Bird Artist," *Living Bird Quarterly* 2 (1983): 30.

40. George Miksch Sutton to Luis Baptista, March 16, 1982, Sutton archives. In another example, when Chris Anthony wanted a drawing of two Ferruginous Pygmy Owls, George wrote: "If I can find the cause that I very

much want to support and you can donate to that cause, then perhaps the picture can change hands"; George Miksch Sutton to Chris [Mrs. Guy] Anthony, September 14, 1977, Sutton archives.

41. Papers and correspondence associated with incorporation of the Foundation for Neotropical Research, Sutton archives.

42. George Miksch Sutton to Robert H. Furman, August 21, 1981, courtesy of Robert H. Furman.

43. P. E. Gresham, "George Sutton, Nature Writer and Painter," *Beta Theta Pi* (June 1972): 464.

44. George Miksch Sutton to Milton Fuller, November 22, 1949, Sutton archives.

45. M. Swenk, "Editorial Comments," *Nebraska Bird Review* 6 (1938): inside back cover.

46. K. C. Parkes, "Colored Plates in the *Wilson Bulletin* through 1962," *Wilson Bulletin* 75 (1963): 289–94; K. C. Parkes, "Colored Plates in the *Wilson Bulletin,* 1963–1987," *Wilson Bulletin* 100 (1988): 650–58; as a matter of style, George preferred "colorplate" as one word.

47. T. C. Stephens, "Editorial," *Wilson Bulletin* 41 (1929): 39, Sutton plate facing p. 3; T. C. Stephens, "Editorial," *Wilson Bulletin* 41 (1929): 186, Sutton plate facing p. 129.

48. Council of the Wilson Ornithological Society, "The George Miksch Sutton Colorplate Fund," *Wilson Bulletin* 85 (1973): 486; Parkes, "Colored Plates in the *Wilson Bulletin, 1963–1987.*"

49. George Miksch Sutton telephone conversation with Jerome A. Jackson, October 12, 1974; George Miksch Sutton to Jerome A. Jackson, October 19, 1974; J. A. Jackson, "The Wilson Ornithological Society in the Last Third of Its First Century," *Wilson Bulletin* 100 (1988): 632–49.

50. Jerome A. Jackson to George Miksch Sutton, April 8, 1976; George Miksch Sutton to Jerome A. Jackson, April 18, 1976, July 5, 1977.

51. George Miksch Sutton to Robert H. Furman, October 19, 1956, courtesy of Robert H. Furman.

52. George Miksch Sutton to Wayne Short, January 2, 1958, courtesy of Robert H. Furman.

53. The accountant for the fund had sent a receipt thanking Furman for his personal check; the donor listed on the receipt, dated November 30, 1957, was "Red Red Rose"; found among materials sent to me by Robert H. and Mary Frances Furman.

54. George Miksch Sutton to Mrs. John E. Kirkpatrick, January 22, 1963, and R. Boyd Gunning to John E. Kirkpatrick, October 1, 1963, courtesy of John E. Kirkpatrick.

55. Dorothy Miksch Sutton Fuller interview, November 8, 1991.

56. George Miksch Sutton to Robert H. Furman, May 12, 1969, courtesy of Robert H. Furman.

57. George Miksch Sutton to Robert H. Furman, September 15, 1969, courtesy of Robert H. Furman; H. C. Land, *Birds of Guatemala* (Wynnewood, Pa.: Livingston Publishing Company, 1970).

58. George Miksch Sutton to Robert H. Furman, October 21, 1969, courtesy of Robert H. Furman.

59. Dorothy Miksch Sutton Fuller interview, November 8, 1991.

60. George Miksch Sutton to C. R. Anthony, April 19, 1971, Sutton archives.

61. George Miksch Sutton to John and Eleanor Kirkpatrick, January 24, 1972, courtesy of John Kirkpatrick.

62. George Lynn Cross to George Miksch Sutton, December 11, 1972, Sutton Archives.

63. Dorothy Miksch Sutton Fuller interview, November 8, 1991.

64. George Miksch Sutton to colleagues, May 1975, Sutton archives.

65. P. E. Gresham, *With Wings as Eagles* (Winter Park, Fla.: Anna Publishing, 1980).

66. George Miksch Sutton to Robert H. Furman, November 30, 1981, courtesy of Robert H. Furman; George Miksch Sutton to John and Eleanor Kirkpatrick, December 14, 1981, courtesy of John and Eleanor Kirkpatrick.

67. From an invitation to the inaugural concert held February 21, 1982, courtesy of Robert H. Furman.

68. George Miksch Sutton to Robert H. Furman, March 17, 1982, courtesy of Robert H. Furman.

CHAPTER 14. FROM ILLUSTRATION TO FINE ART

1. George Miksch Sutton to Robert H. Furman, undated, courtesy of Robert H. Furman.

2. Ibid.; *World Book Encyclopedia* (Chicago: World Book, 1942).

3. G. M. Sutton, "Artist's Preface," in J. Van Tyne and A. J. Berger, *Fundamentals of Ornithology* (New York: John Wiley & Sons, 1976), xi–xiii.

4. George Miksch Sutton to Albert Earl Gilbert, January 15, 1979, courtesy Western History Collection, University of Oklahoma.

5. J. P. O'Neill, "George Miksch Sutton 1898–1982," *American Birds* 37 (1983): 135.

6. Gustav A. Swanson to Jerome Jackson, April 23, 1992.

7. G. M. Sutton, "Fifty Years of Progress in American Bird-Art," pp. 181–97 in *Fifty Years' Progress of American Ornithology 1883–1933* (Lancaster, Pa.: American Ornithologists' Union, 1933).

8. Note the roundness of the head and the generic and slightly upturned bill of the Greater Yellowlegs in this Sutton illustration from T. W. Burgess, *The Burgess Seashore Book for Children* (Boston: Little, Brown, and Company, 1929), facing p. 16.

9. From the cover of Sutton, *A Year's Program for Bird Protection.*

10. G. M. Sutton, *An Introduction to the Birds of Pennsylvania* (Harrisburg, Pa.: J. Horace McFarland Company, 1928).

11. R. M. Mengel, "George Miksch Sutton 1898–1982," *American Birds* 37 (1983): 135.

12. R. T. Peterson, "The Fuertes Legacy Will Never Die," *National Wildlife* 10, no. 4 (1972): 20–24; R. Pasquier and J. Farrand, Jr., *Masterpieces of Bird Art: 700 Years of Ornithological Illustrations* (New York: Abbeville Press, 1991), 205–7.

13. L. A. Hausman, *Birds of Prey of Northeastern North America* (New Brunswick, N.J.: Rutgers University Press, 1948).

14. Quoted in J. C. Devlin and G. Naismith, *The World of Roger Tory Peterson* (New York: Times Books, 1977), 230–31.

15. Sutton's Canada Warbler painting appeared in the *Cardinal*, vol. 2, facing p. 49; Christy was referring to plate 103 of Audubon's Elephant Folio.

16. G. M. Sutton, "Is Bird Art Art?" *Living Bird* 1 (1962): 73–78.

17. George Miksch Sutton to Helen Van Tyne, July 14, 1938, Van Tyne Library.

18. George Miksch Sutton to John and Eleanor Kirkpatrick, April 4, 1963, courtesy of John Kirkpatrick.

19. A. E. Gilbert and D. Amadon, "In Memoriam: Don Richard Eckelberry, 1921–2001," *Auk* 118 (2001): 736–39; M. Wexler, "Wildlife Artists Search for an Identity," *National Wildlife* 18, no. 1 (1980): 54–63.

20. George Miksch Sutton to Mrs. Carroll W. Pieper, November 19, 1977, courtesy Leigh Yawkey Woodson Art Museum.

21. George Miksch Sutton to Robert H. and Mary Frances Furman, November 30, 1967, courtesy of Robert H. and Mary Frances Furman; G. M. Sutton, "Audubon, Pioneer American Bird Artist," *Audubon* (1951) 53: 31–37.

22. George Miksch Sutton to Robert H. and Mary Frances Furman, November 30, 1967, courtesy of Robert H. and Mary Frances Furman.

23. P. H. Falk, *Who Was Who in American Art, 1564–1975*, (Madison, Connecticut: Sound View Press, 1999); George Miksch Sutton to Mr. and Mrs. John E. Kirkpatrick, October 25, 1962, courtesy of John E. Kirkpatrick.

24. Sutton artwork from Sewall Pettingill's wedding courtesy of Olin Sewall Pettingill, Jr.

25. G. M. Sutton, *Uncle George's Zoo*, photocopy of unpublished manuscript, Sutton archives.

26. George Miksch Sutton to family, March 12, 1950, Sutton archives; the namesake was the son of waterfowl artist H. Albert Hochbaum.

27. George Miksch Sutton to Robert H. Furman, November 20, 1957, courtesy of Robert H. Furman.

28. O. S. Pettingill, Jr., *A Guide to Bird Finding East of the Mississippi* (New York: Oxford University Press, 1951).

29. G. M. Sutton, "Stoat at Play," *Nature Magazine* 10 (1927): 327.

30. G. M. Sutton, "A Painting of Yarrow's Spiny Lizard," *Southwestern Naturalist* 6 (1961): 1 + frontispiece.

31. Ibid.; R. G. Webb, *Reptiles of Oklahoma* (Norman: University of Oklahoma Press, 1970); Robert G. Webb to Jerome A. Jackson, September 22, 1992; W. Caire, J. D. Tyler, B. P. Glass, and M. A. Mares, *Mammals of Oklahoma* (Norman: University of Oklahoma Press, 1989).

32. G. M. Sutton, *An Introduction to the Birds of Pennsylvania.*

33. George Miksch Sutton to Andrew J. Berger, January 28, 1975, courtesy of Andrew J. Berger; Sutton, "Artist's Preface," in Van Tyne and Berger, *Fundamentals of Ornithology*; George Miksch Sutton to family, August 25, 1949, Sutton archives.

34. Small, *Masters of Decorative Bird Carving*, 13–16; George Miksch Sutton to Eleanor and John Kirkpatrick, courtesy of Eleanor and John Kirkpatrick.

35. Albert J. Buckelew interview, April 10, 1996. The Leigh Yawkey Woodson Art Museum in Wausau focuses on bird art and holds a special competition and show each year titled "Birds in Art."

CHAPTER 15. OVENBIRD AND GOLDEN EAGLE

1. G. M. Sutton, "Portrait of a Young Cuckoo." *Living Bird Quarterly* 1, no. 1 (1982): 16–17. The scholarly annual *Living Bird* had become a quarterly magazine more popular in nature.

2. His poem from which the epigraph is drawn was published as the birding community remembered him; G. M. Sutton, ". . . Forever and Ever, Amen," *Audubon* 87 (1985): 86–87.

3. George Miksch Sutton to Lewis W. Oring, June 11, 1982, courtesy of Lewis W. Oring.

4. George Miksch Sutton to John and Eleanor Kirkpatrick, September 13, 1982, courtesy of John and Eleanor Kirkpatrick.

5. George Miksch Sutton to Lewis W. Oring, September 30, 1982, courtesy of Lewis W. Oring.

6. Warren D. Harden interview by Jerome A. Jackson, November 1991; G. M. Sutton *Birds Worth Watching* (Norman: University of Oklahoma Press, 1986).

7. George Miksch Sutton to Lewis W. Oring, October 13, 1982, courtesy of Lewis W. Oring.

8. Bill Cason (art editor at the University of Oklahoma Press), "Recognition of John S. Shackford," unpublished script of recognition given to John Shackford at the Oklahoma Ornithological Society meeting, October 17, 1987, courtesy of Dorothy Miksch Sutton Fuller.

9. William Johnson interview by Jerome A. Jackson, November 1991.

10. William Johnson interview, November 1991.

11. W. D. Harden, unpublished, untitled manuscript dated March 18, 1983, courtesy of Warren D. Harden.

12. The Acorn Woodpecker (plate 18, this volume) had been painted on February 13, 1938, near Monterrey, Mexico, and appeared on the cover of the November–December 1982 *Bird Watcher's Digest* (vol. 5, no. 2). The comment about hybrid warblers had been in a letter to Elsa Thompson, co-publisher of *Bird Watcher's Digest*, and was included in P. Murphy, "Quick Takes," *Bird Watcher's Digest* 5, no. 2(1982): 6–7.

13. G. M. Sutton, "Living and Dying," unpublished poem courtesy of Dorothy Miksch Sutton Fuller.

14. George Nigh, "State of Oklahoma Executive Department Proclamation," March 14, 1983; Wm. S. Morgan, "A Proclamation of the Mayor of the City of Norman, Oklahoma, Proclaiming the Day of March 20, 1983, as 'George Miksch Sutton Day' in the City of Norman," issued March 15, 1983; program

for the memorial concert held in Holmberg Hall on the University of Oklahoma campus, March 20, 1983, Sutton archives.

15. Dorothy Miksch Sutton Fuller to Olin Sewall Pettingill, Jr., December 24, 1982, courtesy of Olin Sewall Pettingill, Jr.

16. William Johnson interview, November 1991; Warren Harden interview, November 1991.

17. Sutton, ". . . Forever and Ever, Amen."

18. Sutton, *Birds Worth Watching.*

19. See G. M. Sutton's articles "A Big Owl Watches the Hand that Portrays It," *Living Bird Quarterly* 2, no. 1 (1983): 14–15, reprinted in *Bulletin of the Oklahoma Ornithological Society* 23 (1990): 1–3; "Foreword," p. x in Tulsa Audubon Society, *A Guide to Birding in Oklahoma* (Tulsa: Tulsa Audubon Society, 1987); and "On Drawing Birds from Life," *Sooner Magazine* 12, new series 3 (1992): 8–12.

See also G. M. Sutton's articles in volumes 17–21 of the *Bulletin of the Oklahoma Ornithological Society*: in vol. 17 (1984) "The Red-bellied Woodpeckers Fail Again," 1–3; "Early Nesting of Blue Jay in Oklahoma," 8; "Common Grackle Nest in Tree Cavity," 15–16; and "Singing of Female Northern Cardinal in Winter," 33; in vol. 18 (1985) "European Starlings Lining Nest or Roosting Quarters in Fall," 7–8, and "Eastern Screech-Owl Eats Red Bat," 22–23; in vol. 19 (1986) "Nests of Western Kingbirds in Pines," 5–6, and "Dichromatism of the Screech Owl in Central Oklahoma," 17–20; and in vol. 21 (1988) "Some Critical Comments about Audubon's Artwork," 17–18.

20. Warren D. Harden to Dorothy Miksch Sutton Fuller, May 16, 1984, courtesy of Dorothy Miksch Sutton Fuller.

21. Jimmie C. Thomas to "the Friends of George M. Sutton," June 3, 1983, courtesy of John Kirkpatrick.

22. Anonymous, "George Miksch Sutton Award for Ornithological Art," *Wilson Bulletin* 96 (1984): 646.

23. David G. Woods to Dorothy Fuller, September 10, 1992, Sutton archives.

24. Sutton, ". . . Forever and Ever, Amen."

25. Anonymous, "Dr. Sutton's Sister Dies," *Scissortail* 44, no. 2 (1994): 21; Anonymous, [Memorial for Dorothy Miksch Sutton Fuller], Sutton archives.

26. "Motherless Boy Must Dream Alone," *Las Vegas Review-Journal*, May 1, 1995, 4A.

27. Robert M. Mengel to Olin Sewall Pettingill, Jr., January 10, 1983, courtesy of Olin Sewall Pettingill, Jr.

28. Program for the ground breaking ceremony for the Sam Noble Oklahoma Museum of Natural History.

Works by George Miksch Sutton

George Miksch Sutton was prolific indeed. This bibliography is as complete as I could make it, including his books, contributions to ornithological journals, publications in museum and other series, and publications in popular media. I fully anticipate additions and would be grateful to receive them. Except in a very few cases where noted, I have examined the original or a photocopy of each publication to confirm the bibliographic information included.

Although many of the entries are also illustrated with Sutton artwork, this bibliography does not include works authored by others and illustrated by Sutton. Some such works are listed in the separate bibliography that follows. Not included in either listing are Sutton's numerous book reviews published in the *New York Herald-Tribune* or the articles he wrote about birds published in newspapers across Pennsylvania between 1924 and 1929.

The works included herein are arranged first by year. Within each year, books or book chapters authored by Sutton appear first. Next are journal, periodical, or serial articles authored solely by Sutton. These are arranged alphabetically by the title of the journal, periodical, or serial. Works in the same publication are arranged by issue and page number sequence to retain the sequence of continued or follow-up articles. Last are multi-authored articles inserted in appropriate alphabetic position by the lead author. For these articles, Sutton's name is abbreviated as "G. M. S."

1913

"A Pet Road-Runner." *Bird-Lore* 15: 324–26.

1914

"The Interesting Road-Runner." *Oologist* 31: 141–42.

1915

(as Suttard [*sic*], G. M.) "A Trip to Waynesburg, Pa." *Oologist* 32: 14, 16, 18.
"Suggestive Methods of Bird-Study: Pet Road-Runners." *Bird-Lore* 17: 57–61.

1916

"Cape May Warbler in Virginia in Winter." *Auk* 33: 203.
"Blood Stains." *Oologist* 33: 60–61.
"Owls within Owls." *Oologist* 33: 100.

1917

"A Vulture Cardinal." *Oologist* 34: 216–17.

1918

"An Albinistic Meadowlark." *Oologist* 35: 158–59.

1919

"Night Voices." *Bird-Lore* 21: 108–10.

1920

"Annotated List of the Birds of Brooke County, W. Va." *Oologist* 37: 52–58, 64–68, 76–80.

1922

[Untitled.] Bird Leaflet no. 1. Pittsburgh, Pa.: Carnegie Museum.
"Notes on the Road-Runner at Fort Worth, Texas." *Wilson Bulletin* 34: 3–20 [black-and-white frontispiece].
"Some Remarks on the Facial Expression of Birds." *Wilson Bulletin* 34: 141–47.

1923

"The Season: Pittsburgh Region." *Bird-Lore* 25: 132.
"The Season: Pittsburgh Region." *Bird-Lore* 25: 193–95.
"The Season: Pittsburgh Region." *Bird-Lore* 25: 260.
"Field Identification of Our Winter Birds. *Bulletin of the Audubon Society of Western Pennsylvania* 1: 4–9.
"The Starling in Southwestern Pennsylvania." *Bulletin of the Audubon Society of Western Pennsylvania* 1: 38–40.
"Notes on the Nesting of the Wilson's Snipe in Crawford County, Pennsylvania." *Wilson Bulletin* 35: 191–202.

1924

"The Season: Pittsburgh region." *Bird-Lore* 26: 55–56.
"The Season: Pittsburgh Region." *Bird-Lore* 26: 122–23.
"The Season: Pittsburgh Region." *Bird-Lore* 26: 189–90.
"The Season: Pittsburgh Region." *Bird-Lore* 26: 266–67.
"The Season: Pittsburgh Region." *Bird-Lore* 26: 336–37.
"Visit to a Wood Ibis Colony." *Bird-Lore* 26: 391–95.
"The Season: Pittsburgh Region." *Bird-Lore* 26: 418–19.
"The Blue Goose Expedition." *Cardinal* 1, no. 3: 16–18.
"An Expedition to Cape Sable." *Cardinal* 1, no. 4: 14–16.

1925

"The Present Status of the Ruffed Grouse in Pennsylvania." *American Midland Naturalist* 9: 373–78.
"American Egret (*Casmerodius egretta*) and Little Blue Heron (*Florida caerulea*) in Brooke Co., W. Va." *Auk* 42: 129.

"Swimming and Diving Activity of the Spotted Sandpiper (*Actitis macularia*)." *Auk* 42: 580–81.

"The American Egret (*Casmerodius egretta*) in Eastern and Central Pennsylvania." *Auk* 42: 583–84.

"Strange Nesting-Site of the Chimney Swift (*Chaetura pelagica*)." *Auk* 42: 586–87.

"The Ruffed Grouse Situation in Pennsylvania." *Cardinal* 1, no. 5: 17–19.

A Year's Program for Bird Protection. Bulletin No. 7. Harrisburg: Pennsylvania Board of Game Commissioners.

"The Ruffed Grouse Situation in Pennsylvania." *Wild Life Magazine* (Greenville, Pa.) 3 (January–February) [not seen; cited in *Auk* 42 (1925):473].

"A Natural Zoological Garden in Western Pennsylvania: Pymatuning Swamp." *Wild Life Magazine* (Greenville, Pa.) 3 (April 1925): 4–5 [not seen; cited in *Wilson Bulletin* 37: 183].

"Notes on the Nesting of the Goshawk in Potter County, Pennsylvania." *Wilson Bulletin* 37: 193–99.

1926

"The Egret at Wildwood Lake, Dauphin County, Penna." *Auk* 43: 233.

"Little Black Rail in Illinois." *Auk* 43: 233.

"Long-eared Owl Capturing Ruffed Grouse." *Auk* 43: 236–37.

"The Egret in Clinton and Lycoming Counties, Pennsylvania." *Auk* 43: 366.

[Northern Bobwhite in Pennsylvania.] *Cardinal* 1, no. 7: 18–19.

E. G. Holt and G. M. S. "Notes on Birds Observed in Southern Florida." *Annals of the Carnegie Museum* 16, nos. 3–4: 409–30.

1927

"White Pelican in Southeastern Pennsylvania." *Auk* 44: 94.

"Madeira Petrel (*Oceanodroma castro*) in Pennsylvania." *Auk* 44: 556–57.

"Cackling Goose (*Branta canadensis minima*) in Southeastern Michigan." *Auk* 44: 559.

"Goshawk Nesting in Clarion County, Pennsylvania." *Auk* 44: 563.

"Mortality among Screech Owls of Pennsylvania." *Auk* 44: 563–64.

"Snowy Owl Killed by Automobile." *Auk* 44: 564.

"Nest-Stealing Tactics of the Starling." *Bird-Lore* 29: 251–54.

"Loon Banded in Pennsylvania Killed in Ontario." *Canadian Field-Naturalist* 41: 139.

"The Invasion of Goshawks and Snowy Owls during the Winter of 1926–1927." *Cardinal* 2: 35–41.

[Turkey Vulture nesting in Crawford County, Pennsylvania.] *Cardinal* 2: 44.

"Stoat." *Nature Magazine* 10: 327.

"A Loon Strangled by Its Fish Food." *Wilson Bulletin* 39: 39.

"Flocking, Mating, and Nest-Building Habits of the Prairie Horned Lark." *Wilson Bulletin* 39: 131–41.

"Loon Banded in Pennsylvania Killed in Ontario." *Wilson Bulletin* 39: 170–71 [reprinted from *Canadian Field-Naturalist* 41 (1927)].

"Ruffed Grouse Captured by a Screech Owl." *Wilson Bulletin* 39: 171.
"An Albino Red-tailed Hawk." *Wilson Bulletin* 39: 177.

1928

An Introduction to the Birds of Pennsylvania. Harrisburg, Pa.: J. Horace
    McFarland Company, Mount Pleasant Press, 1928.
"The Birds of Pymatuning Swamp and Conneaut Lake, Crawford County,
    Pennsylvania." *Annals of the Carnegie Museum* 18: 19–239.
"A New Swift from Venezuela." *Auk* 45: 135–36.
"Abundance of the Golden Eagle in Pennsylvania in 1927–28." *Auk* 45: 375.
"Extension of the Breeding Range of the Turkey Vulture in Pennsylvania." *Auk*
    45: 501–503.
"An Exhibit of Bird-Paintings." *Bird-Lore* 30: 114.
"The Mammals of Cook Forest." *Cardinal* 2: 76–81.
"Notes on the Flight of the Chimney Swift." *Cardinal* 2: 85–92.
[Snowy Owl invasion, kingfisher nest.] *Cardinal* 2: 104–105.
[Feature article on deer in Pennsylvania.] *New York Times*, August 26, 1928,
    VII, 12: 4 [not seen].
"A Fair Deal for the Hawks and Owls." *Outdoor America*, January, 30–31,
    51.
"Notes on a Collection of Hawks from Schuylkill County, Pennsylvania."
    Wilson Bulletin 40: 84–95.
"A Note on the Food of Young Great Horned Owls." *Wilson Bulletin* 40:
    196–97.
B. H. Christy and G. M. S. "The Summer Birds of Cook Forest." *Cardinal* 2:
    68–75.

1929

"Birdnesting under Difficulties." *Atlantic Monthly* 143: 810–13.
"White Pelican in Chester County, Pennsylvania." *Auk* 46: 104.
"Yellow-headed Blackbird in Pennsylvania." *Auk* 46: 119.
"How Can the Bird-Lover Help to Save the Hawks and Owls?" *Auk* 46:
    190–95.
"Can the Cooper's Hawk Kill a Crow?" *Auk* 46: 235–36.
"Photographing Wild Turkey Nests in Pennsylvania." *Auk* 46: 326–28.
"Insect-Catching Tactics of the Screech Owl (*Otus asio*)." *Auk* 46: 545–46.
"Bird Notes from Pymatuning Swamp." *Cardinal* 2: 121.
[Golden Eagle.] *Cardinal* 2: 129.
[Saw-whet Owl.] *Cardinal* 2: 129–30.
[Northern Shrike.] *Cardinal* 2: 130–31.
"The Summer Birds of Cook Forest." *Cardinal* 3: 68–74.
The White-Tailed Deer in Pennsylvania. Bulletin. Harrisburg: Pennsylvania
    Game Commission [not seen; Bulletin number not known].
"Tactics of the Domestic Pigeon in Evading the Duck Hawk." *Wilson Bulletin*
    41: 41–42.

"Hawks and Owls—Friends or Foes?" *Saturday Evening Post*, no. 202, November 16, 1929, 237–38.
"Does the Great Horned Owl Have a Poor Memory?" *Wilson Bulletin* 41: 247–48.
B. H. Christy and G. M. S. "The Turkey in Pennsylvania." *Cardinal* 2: 109–16.

1930

"Notes on the Northern Pileated Woodpecker in Pennsylvania." *Cardinal* 2: 207–17.
"The Nesting Wrens of Brooke County, West Virginia." *Wilson Bulletin* 42: 10–17.
"Four Eggs in the Nest of a Mourning Dove." *Wilson Bulletin* 42: 54.

1931

"The Blue Goose and Lesser Snow Goose on Southampton Island, Hudson Bay." *Auk* 48: 335–64.
"A Year on Southampton Island." *Cardinal* 3: 1–5.
"A Year at Southampton Island." *Carnegie Magazine* 4, no. 9: 269–73.
"The Harris' Sparrow's Eggs." *Carnegie Magazine* 5, no. 4: 105–106.
"Notes on Birds Observed along the West Coast of Hudson Bay." *Condor* 33: 154–59.
"The Status of the Goshawk in Pennsylvania." *Wilson Bulletin* 43: 108–13.

1932

"Quaint Folk, the Eskimos." *Atlantic Monthly* 150: 57–63.
"Notes on the Molts and Sequence of Plumages in the Old-squaw." *Auk* 49: 42–51.
"Deposition of Eggs in Time of Snow-Storm." *Auk* 49: 366–67.
"Feeding Habits of the Yellow-billed Cuckoo, *Coccyzus a. americanus* (Linnaeus)." *Cardinal* 3: 92–93.
"Notes on a Collection of Birds from Mansel Island, Hudson Bay. *Condor* 34: 41–43.
The Exploration of Southampton Island, Hudson Bay. Part 1. Section 1, Prefatory; Section 2, Introductory; Section 3, Bibliography of Part I and Part II, Section 2. Memoirs of the Carnegie Museum 12: 1–78.
The Exploration of Southampton Island, Hudson Bay. Part 2. Zoology, Section 2, *The Birds of Southampton Island*. Memoirs of the Carnegie Museum 12 (1932): 1–275 [This published account was accepted by Cornell University as Sutton's dissertation.].
J. B. Semple and G. M. S. "Nesting of the Harris's Sparrow (*Zonotrichia querula*) at Churchill, Manitoba." *Auk* 49: 166–83.
G. M. S. and W. J. Hamilton, Jr. "A New Arctic Weasel from Southampton Island, Hudson Bay." *Annals of the Carnegie Museum* 21, no. 2: 79–81.
G. M. S. and W. J. Hamilton, Jr. *The Exploration of Southampton Island, Hudson Bay*. Part 2. Zoology, Section 1, *The Mammals of Southampton Island*. Memoirs of the Carnegie Museum 12: 1–107.

"Hints on Field Bird Study." P. 6 [unnumbered] in S. G. Jewett and I. N. Gabrielson, compilers, *Pocket Field List of Birds of the Portland District*. Oregon Audubon Society.

1933

"Fifty Years of Progress in American Bird-Art." Pp. 181–97 in *Fifty Years' Progress of American Ornithology 1883–1933*. Lancaster, Pa.: American Ornithologists' Union.
"Birds of the West Virginia Panhandle." *Cardinal* 3: 101–23.
"They Stand Out from the Crowd." *Literary Digest* 116: 11.
"What Do *You* Know about Hawks?" *Pennsylvania Game News* 4, no. 9: 11, 14.

1934

Eskimo Year. New York: MacMillan.
"Notes on the Birds of the Western Panhandle of Oklahoma." *Annals of the Carnegie Museum* 24: 1–50.
"A New Bewick's Wren from the Western Panhandle of Oklahoma." *Auk* 51: 217–20.
"Little Blue Heron and American Egret in the West Virginia Panhandle." *Auk* 51: 226.
"Hudsonian Curlew in the West Virginia Panhandle." *Auk* 51: 231.
"A Double Nest of Baltimore Oriole." *Wilson Bulletin* 46: 124–25.
P. A. Taverner and G. M. S. "The Birds of Churchill, Manitoba." *Annals of the Carnegie Museum* 23: 1–83.

1935

"Note on the Breeding Range of the Black Pigeon Hawk." *Auk* 52: 79–80.
"A New Blue Jay from the Western Border of the Great Basin." *Auk* 52: 176–77.
"An Abnormally Plumaged Cardinal." *Auk* 52: 314–15.
"An Expedition to the Big Bend Country." *Cardinal* 4: 1–7.
"Spring Notes from Bethany, West Virginia." *Cardinal* 4: 50.
"An Expedition to British Columbia." *Carnegie Magazine* 8: 297–301.
The Juvenal Plumage and Postjuvenal Molt in Several Species of Michigan Sparrows. Cranbrook Institute of Science Bulletin no. 3.
"Some Aivilik Tribal Stories." *Scholastic* 25: 10–11+ [not seen].
G. M. S. and J. Van Tyne. *A New Red-tailed Hawk from Texas*. Occasional Papers of the Museum of Zoology, University of Michigan, no. 321.

1936

Birds in the Wilderness. New York: Macmillan.
"Food Capturing Tactics of the Least Bittern." *Auk* 53: 74–75.
"The Turkey Vulture's Ability to Carry Food in Its Beak." *Auk* 53: 76.
"Palm Warbler in the Northern Panhandle of West Virginia. A Correction." *Auk* 53: 89.

"Connecticut Warbler in the Northern West Virginia Panhandle." *Auk* 53: 90.
"Blue Grosbeak in the Northern Panhandle of West Virginia." *Auk* 53: 90–91.
"White-winged Crossbill on Baffin Island." *Auk* 53: 91.
"Man-o'-War Bird in Oklahoma." *Auk* 53: 438.
"Notes from Ellis and Cimarron Counties, Oklahoma." *Auk* 53: 432–35.
"Lincoln's Sparrow and Lark Sparrow in the Northern West Virginia
    Panhandle." *Auk* 53: 453–54.
The Postjuvenal Molt of the Grasshopper Sparrow. Occasional Papers of the
    Museum of Zoology, University of Michigan, no. 336: 9 pp. [color
    plate].
"The Kingbird." *Pennsylvania Game News* 7, no. 4: 17.
W. E. C. Todd and G. M. S. "Taxonomic Remarks on the Carolina Chickadee,
    Penthestes carolinensis." *Proceedings of the Biological Society of
    Washington* 49: 69–70.

1937

"Notes from Brooke County, West Virginia." *Cardinal* 4: 117–18.
"Bird Notes from the West Virginia Panhandle." *Cardinal* 4: 144.
The Juvenal Plumage and Postjuvenal Molt of the Chipping Sparrow.
    Occasional Papers of the Museum of Zoology, University of Michigan, no.
    355.
J. Van Tyne and G. M. S. *The Birds of Brewster County, Texas.* University of
    Michigan Museum of Zoology, Miscellaneous Publication no. 37 [color
    frontispiece].

1938

"An Expedition to Mexico." Pp. 367–71 in *Proceedings, IXme Congrès
    Ornithologique International*, Rouen, France, May 9–13, ed. J. Delacour.
"Breeding Birds of Tarrant County, Texas." *Annals of the Carnegie Museum*
    27: 171–206.
"Oddly Plumaged Orioles from Western Oklahoma." *Auk* 55: 1–6 [color
    plate].
"Glaucous-winged Gull in Oklahoma." *Auk* 55: 277–78.
"An Unfortunate Pine Warbler." *Auk* 55: 282, plate facing p. 282.
"Some Findings of the Semple Oklahoma Expedition." *Auk* 55: 501–508.
"The Naturalist's Debt to the Sportsman." *Pennsylvania Game News* 9, no. 1:
    6–7.
"The Door-Step Friend: The Chipping Sparrow." *Pennsylvania Game News* 9,
    no. 1: 30.
"Our Feathered Friends." *Pennsylvania Game News* 9, no. 2: 29.
J. B. Semple and G. M. S. "Hudsonian Curlew, White-faced Glossy Ibis and
    Black-bellied Plover in Oklahoma." *Auk* 55: 274–75.
G. M. S. and J. R. Arnold. "An Abnormal Blue Jay Primary." *Auk* 55: 281.
G. M. S. and O. S. Pettingill, Jr. "Good Lantern Slides of Birds." *Wilson
    Bulletin* 50: 170–75.

1939

"Parasitic Jaeger on Cayuga Lake, New York." *Auk* 56: 185–86.
"The Mississippi Kite in Spring." *Condor* 41: 41–53.
"The Mississippi Kite." *Oologist* 56: 92.
"A Rare Winter Visitor—The Rough-legged Hawk." *Pennsylvania Game News* 9, no. 10: 31.
"Our Feathered Friends." *Pennsylvania Game News* 10, no. 4: 26.
G. M. S. and T. D. Burleigh. "A New Blue Bunting from Tamaulipas." *Auk* 56: 71–72.
G. M. S. and T. D. Burleigh. "A New Screech Owl from Nuevo Leon." *Auk* 56: 174–75.
G. M. S. and T. D. Burleigh. *A List of Birds Observed on the 1938 Semple Expedition to Northeastern Mexico.* Occasional Papers of the Museum of Zoology, Louisiana State University, no. 3: 15–46.
G. M. S. and T. D. Burleigh. "A New Abeille's Grosbeak from Tamaulipas." *Proceedings of the Biological Society of Washington* 52: 145–46.

1940

"*Geococcyx californianus* (Lesson), Roadrunner." Pp. 36–51 in A. C. Bent, *Life Histories of North American Cuckoos, Goatsuckers, Hummingbirds and Their Allies.* U.S. National Museum Bulletin 176.
M. Brooks and G. M. S. "Red Crossbills Summering in the West Virginia Mountains." *Wilson Bulletin* 52: 36–37.
"Black-capped Petrel in New York." *Auk* 57: 244.
"Black Gyrfalcon in New York State." *Auk* 57: 401.
"Winter Range of the Short-billed Marsh Wren." *Auk* 57: 419.
"Drawings of Living Birds." *Bird-Lore* 42: 31–32 [plus four color plates on unnumbered pages].
G. M. S. and T. D. Burleigh. "Birds of Las Vigas, Veracruz." *Auk* 57: 234–43.
G. M. S. and T. D. Burleigh. "A New Warbling Vireo from Hidalgo." *Auk* 57: 398–400.
G. M. S. and T. D. Burleigh. "Birds of Valles, San Luis Potosi, Mexico." *Condor* 42: 259–62.
G. M. S. and T. D. Burleigh. "A New Tufted Flycatcher from Hidalgo." *Wilson Bulletin* 52: 30–31.
G. M. S. and T. D. Burleigh. "Birds of Tamazunchale, San Luis Potosi." *Wilson Bulletin* 52: 221–33.
G. M. S. and W. Montagna. "Washed Birdskins." *Wilson Bulletin* 52: 91–95.

1941

"Crousty: The Story of a Redbird." *Audubon Magazine* 43: 161–68, 270–78.
"The Road of a Naturalist. By Donald Culross Peattie." *Audubon Magazine* 43: 456–57.
"The Wildlife Gallery: Louis Fuertes, Teacher." *Audubon Magazine* 43: 521–24.

"Baltimore Oriole in Tompkins County, New York, in Winter." *Auk* 58: 411.

Hylocichla fuscescens salicicola in Tamaulipas: A Correction." *Auk* 58: 584.

The Juvenal Plumage and Postjuvenal Molt of the Vesper Sparrow. Occasional Papers of the Museum of Zoology, University of Michigan, no. 445. 10 pp. [color plate].

The Plumages and Molts of the Young Eastern Whippoorwill. Occasional Papers of the Museum of Zoology, University of Michigan, no. 446. 7 pp. [color plate].

"Expedition to Study Mexican Birds." *Scientific Monthly* 52: 283–86.

"A New Race of *Chaetura vauxi* from Tamaulipas." *Wilson Bulletin* 53: 231–33.

"Blue Goose in Tioga County, New York." *Wilson Bulletin* 53: 236.

"Wilson's Thrush in Oklahoma." *Wilson Bulletin* 53: 237.

G. M. S. and T. D. Burleigh. "Birds Recorded in the State of Hidalgo, Mexico, by the Semple Expedition of 1939." *Annals of the Carnegie Museum* 28: 169–86.

G. M. S. and T. D. Burleigh. "Some Birds Recorded in Nuevo Leon, Mexico." *Condor* 43: 158–60.

G. M. S. and E. P. Edwards. "Does the Southern Hairy Woodpecker Occur in Oklahoma?" *Wilson Bulletin* 53: 127–28.

G. M. S., A. R. Phillips, and L. L. Hargrave. "Probable Breeding of the Beautiful Bunting in the United States." *Auk* 58: 265–66.

G. M. S. and J. B. Semple. "An Egg of the Marbled Murrelet." *Auk* 58: 580–81.

1942

"The Wildlife Gallery: Louis Fuertes at Work." *Audubon Magazine* 44: 37–40.

"The Wildlife Gallery: Fuertes and the Young Bird Artist." *Audubon Magazine* 44: 82–85.

"The Wildlife Gallery: Dick Grossenheider's Mammal Drawings." *Audubon Magazine* 44: 146–49.

"The Wildlife Gallery: Following Audubon's Trail." *Audubon Magazine* 44: 226–29.

"Mexican Black Hawk in Tamaulipas: A Correction." *Auk* 59: 108.

"Turkey Vulture and Killdeer in Newfoundland Labrador." *Auk* 59: 304–305.

"Is Sutton's Warbler a Valid Species?" *Cardinal* 5: 151–54.

"Pigmy Nuthatch in Oklahoma." *Condor* 44: 36.

"Winter Range of Oklahoma's Hybrid Orioles." *Condor* 44: 79.

"A Modern Audubon in Mexico." *Natural History* 50: 116–28.

"Bat Falcon." *Wilson Bulletin* 54:2 [Color frontispiece].

"A Pensile Nest of the Red-wing." *Wilson Bulletin* 54: 255–56.

G. M. S. and T. D. Burleigh. "Birds Recorded in the Federal District and States of Puebla and Mexico by the 1939 Semple Expedition." *Auk* 59: 418–23.

G. M. S. and P. W. Gilbert. "The Brown Jay's Furcular Pouch." *Condor* 44: 160–65 [black-and-white plate].

G. M. S. and O. S. Pettingill, Jr. "Birds of the Gomez Farias Region, Southwestern Tamaulipas." *Auk* 59: 1–34.

G. M. S. and O. S. Pettingill, Jr. "The Nest of the Brown Jay." *Wilson Bulletin* 54: 213–14.
G. M. S., O. S. Pettingill, Jr., and R. B. Lea. "Notes on Birds of the Monterey District of Nuevo Leon, Mexico." *Wilson Bulletin* 54: 199–203.
G. M. S. and A. R. Phillips. "June Bird Life of the Papago Indian Reservation, Arizona." *Condor* 44: 57–65.
G. M. S. and A. R. Phillips. "The Northern Races of *Piranga flava.*" *Condor* 44: 277–79.

1943

"Hudsonian Godwit in Wayne County, New York." *Auk* 60: 108.
"Records from the Tucson Region of Arizona." *Auk* 60: 345–50.
"Bird Hunting at Ciudad Victoria." *Cardinal* 6, no. 1: 1–5.
Notes on the Behavior of Certain Captive Young Fringillids. Occasional Papers of the Museum of Zoology, University of Michigan, no. 474: 1-14.
"Catching Birds with a Paintbrush." *Popular Science* 143, no. 2: 61–64.
"The Wing Molts of Adult Loons: A Review of the Evidence." *Wilson Bulletin* 55: 145–50.
G. M. S. and O. S. Pettingill, Jr. "The Alta Mira Oriole and Its Nest." *Condor* 45: 125–32.
G. M. S. and O. S. Pettingill, Jr. "Birds of Linares and Galeana, Nuevo Leon, Mexico." *Occasional Papers of the Museum of Zoology, Louisiana State University*, no. 16: 273–91.

1944

"Foreword." Pp. i–ii (unnumbered) in M. G. Brooks, *A Checklist of West Virginia Birds*. Bulletin 316. Morgantown: Agricultural Experiment Station, West Virginia University.
"At a Bend in a Mexican River." *Audubon Magazine* 46: 258–66, 344–51.
[Bayard Henderson Christy, obituary]. *Auk* 61: 178–79.
"The Kites of the Genus *Ictinia.*" *Wilson Bulletin* 56: 3–8.
Review of *Alaska Bird Trails*, by Herbert Brandt. *Wilson Bulletin* 56: 120–21.
G. M. S. and O. S. Pettingill, Jr. "Yellow Rail in Rice County, Minnesota." *Auk* 61: 474–75.

1945

"At a Bend in a Mexican River." *Audubon Magazine* 47: 35–40, 107–12, 173–78, 239–42.
"The Bronzed Grackle as a Species." *Auk* 62: 170.
"Autumnal Dueling among Mockingbirds." *Auk* 62: 301.
"Arkansas Kingbird in Southeastern Florida." *Auk* 62: 462.
"Behavior of Birds during a Florida Hurricane." *Auk* 62: 603–606.
"Notes on the Winter Bird-Life of Fairbanks, Alaska." *Condor* 47: 264–67.
Review of *Birds of Kentucky*, by Jesse Dade Figgins. *Wilson Bulletin* 57: 265–67.

1946

"Great Blue Heron Swallows Large Snake." *Auk* 63: 97.

"A Baby Florida Sandhill Crane." *Auk* 63: 100–101.

"To the Members of the Wilson Ornithological Club." *Wilson Bulletin* 58: 116.

"Wing-Flashing in the Mockingbird." *Wilson Bulletin* 58: 206–209.

G. M. S. and R. S. Wilson. "Notes on the Winter Birds of Attu." *Condor* 48: 83–91.

1947

"David Clark Hilton." *Auk* 64: 179–80.

"Greenland Wheatear in Southern Baffin Island." *Auk* 64: 324–25.

"A Female Cardinal and Her Reflection." *Bird-Banding* 18: 151–54.

"Eye-Color in the Green Jay." *Condor* 49: 196–98.

1948

"Tribulations of a Sparrow Rancher." *Audubon Magazine* 50: 286–95.

"Small Pine Grosbeaks Collected in Tompkins County, New York." *Auk* 65: 125–26.

"White-throated or Bat Falcon in Nuevo Leon, Mexico." *Auk* 65: 603.

"The Curve-billed Thrasher in Oklahoma." *Condor* 50: 40–43.

"The Nest and Eggs of the White-bellied Wren." *Condor* 50: 101–12.

"Comments on *Icterus cucullatus cucullatus* Swainson in the United States." *Condor* 50: 257–58.

"Probable Breeding of the Ruby-crowned Kinglet in the Lower Peninsula of Michigan." *Jack-Pine Warbler* 26: 159–60.

The Juvenal Plumage of the Eastern Warbling Vireo (Vireo gilvus gilvus). Occasional Papers of the Museum of Zoology, University of Michigan, no. 511 [color plate].

"Breeding of Richmond's Swift in Venezuela." *Wilson Bulletin* 60: 189–90.

G. M. S. and W. H. Phelps. *Richmond's Swift in Venezuela*. Occasional Papers of the Museum of Zoology, University of Michigan, no. 505.

1949

"Baby Birds as Models." *Audubon Magazine* 51 (March): 104-108.

"Rose-throated Becard, *Platypsaris aglaiae*, in the Lower Rio Grande Valley of Texas." *Auk* 66: 365-66.

"Validity of the Shorebird Genus *Pseudoscolopax*." *Condor* 51: 259-61.

"Meeting the West on Florida's East Coast." *Florida Naturalist* 22, no. 2: 23–33.

Studies of the Nesting Birds of the Edwin S. George Reserve. Part 1. The Vireos. Miscellaneous Publications of the University of Michigan Museum of Zoology 74: 5-36.

G. M. S. and H. H. Spencer. "Observations at a Nighthawk's Nest." *Bird-Banding* 20: 141–49.

1950

[John Bonner Semple, obituary]. *Auk* 67: 429-30.
"The Voice of *Nyctibius griseus*." *Bird-Banding* 21: 154-55.
"Ruddy Quail-Dove in Tamaulipas." *Condor* 52: 93-94.
"The Southern Limits of the Willet's Continental Breeding Range." *Condor* 52: 135–36.
Review of *Lista de las Aves de Venezuela con su Distribucion*, Parte 2: *Passeriformes*, by W. H. Phelps and W. H. Phelps, Jr. *Wilson Bulletin* 62: 140-41.
"The Crimson-collared Grosbeak." *Wilson Bulletin* 62: 155-56 [color frontispiece facing p. 155].
[Editorial commenting on a paper in *Bird-Banding* about redpolls and the need for specimens.] *Wilson Bulletin* 62: 222.
Review of *British Waders in Their Haunts*, by S. B. Smith. *Wilson Bulletin* 62: 224-25.
G. M. S., R. B. Lea, and E. P. Edwards. "Notes on the Ranges and Breeding Habits of Certain Mexican Birds." *Bird-Banding* 21: 45-59.

1951

Mexican Birds: First Impressions. Norman: University of Oklahoma Press.
"Audubon, Pioneer American Bird Artist." *Audubon Magazine* 53: 31–37.
"Mexico, Land of Colorful Birds." *Audubon Magazine* 53: 382–85+.
"A New Race of Yellow-throated Warbler from Northwestern Florida." *Auk* 68: 27–29 [black-and-white plate of watercolor].
"Birds and an Ant Army in Southern Tamaulipas." *Condor* 53: 16–18.
"Subspecific Status of the Green Jays of Northeastern Mexico and Southern Texas." *Condor* 53: 124–28.
"*Caprimulgus ridgwayi* in Michoacan, Mexico." *Condor* 53: 261–62.
Review of *Grønlands Fugle: The Birds of Greenland. Part 1*, by Finn Salomonsen. *Wilson Bulletin* 63: 55–56.
"The Rufescent Tinamou." *Wilson Bulletin* 63: 67–68 [color plate].
[Editorial on Walt Disney's *Beaver Valley*]. *Wilson Bulletin* 63: 120.
[Editorial on changing scientific names]. *Wilson Bulletin* 63: 210–11.
Review of *Bird Portraits*, by J. C. Harrison. *Wilson Bulletin* 63: 213–14.
[David Clark Hilton, anonymous obituary]. *Wilson Bulletin* 63: 218.
"Dispersal of Mistletoe by Birds." *Wilson Bulletin* 63: 235–37 [color plate].
"*Empidonax albigularis* in Southwestern Tamaulipas." *Wilson Bulletin* 63: 339.
Review of *Grønlands Fugle: The Birds of Greenland. Part 2*, by Finn Salomonsen. *Wilson Bulletin* 63: 350–52.

1952

Review of *The Birds of Newfoundland*, by H. S. Peters and T. D. Burleigh. *Auk* 69: 104–105.

"The Flint-billed Woodpecker." *Wilson Bulletin* 64: 4–7 [color frontispiece facing p. 5].

"Stoddard's Yellow-throated Warbler in Bay County, Florida." *Wilson Bulletin* 64: 49.

"New Birds for the State of Michoacan, Mexico." *Wilson Bulletin* 64: 221–23.

Review of *Grønlands Fugle: The Birds of Greenland. Part 3*, by Finn Salomonsen. *Wilson Bulletin* 64: 124–26.

1953

"Terns Recorded at Lake Texoma, Oklahoma, in Summer of 1951." *Auk* 70: 205–206.

"The Brown-crested Flycatcher in the Florida Keys." *Condor* 55: 274–75.

"The Future of Ornithology in Oklahoma." *Oklahoma Quarterly* 2: 20–22, 30, in *Sooner Magazine* 24(4) [Corrected in pencil in OU Library to become 25(5); this issue of *Oklahoma Quarterly* is within *Sooner Magazine* 24(4) and is paginated continuously with it.].

"Gray Hawk." *Wilson Bulletin* 65: 5–7 [color plate facing p. 5].

"Bronzed Woodpecker." *Wilson Bulletin* 65: 65–67 [color plate facing p. 65].

A. Wetmore and G. M. S. "The Carolina Chickadee in Kansas." *Wilson Bulletin* 65: 277.

1954

"Western Grebe in Oklahoma." *Condor* 56: 229.

"Blackish Crane-Hawk." *Wilson Bulletin* 66: 237–42.

G. M. S. and D. F. Parmelee. "Nesting of the Greenland Wheatear on Baffin Island." *Condor* 56: 295–306.

G. M. S. and D. F. Parmalee. "Nesting of the Snow Bunting on Baffin Island." *Wilson Bulletin* 66: 159–79.

1955

"Glossy Ibis in Oklahoma." *Condor* 57: 119–20.

"Winter Birdlife of the Black Mesa Country." *Oklahoma Quarterly* 4(2): 16–19, 27 [This issue of *Oklahoma Quarterly* is within *Sooner Magazine* 27(5) and is paginated continuously with it, Sutton drawing of the head of Roadrunner is on p. 15, the "cover" of *Oklahoma Quarterly*.].

"Great Curassow." *Wilson Bulletin* 67: 75–77.

"A New Race of Olivaceous Woodcreeper from Mexico." *Wilson Bulletin* 67: 209–11.

G. M. S. and D. F. Parmalee. "Survival Problems of the Water Pipit in Baffin Island." *Arctic* 7: 81–92.

G. M. S. and D. F. Parmalee. "Nesting of the Horned Lark on Baffin Island." *Bird-Banding* 26: 1–18.

G. M. S. and D. F. Parmalee. "The Breeding of the Semipalmated Plover on Baffin Island." *Bird-Banding* 26: 137–47.

G. M. S. and D. F. Parmalee. "The Peregrine Falcon on Baffin Island." *Bird-Banding* 26: 147–52.

G. M. S. and D. F. Parmalee. "Summer Activities of the Lapland Longspur on Baffin Island." *Wilson Bulletin* 67: 110–27.

1956

"The Mockingbird's Song." *Frontiers* 21: 109–10.

G. M. S. and D. F. Parmalee. "On Certain Anatids of Frobischer Bay, Baffin Island." *Arctic* 8: 139–47.

G. M. S. and D. F. Parmalee. "On the Loons of Baffin Island." *Auk* 73: 78–84.

G. M. S. and D. F. Parmalee. "Breeding of the Snowy Owl in Southeastern Baffin Island." *Condor* 58: 273–82.

G. M. S. and D. F. Parmalee. "The Rock Ptarmigan in Southern Baffin Island." *Wilson Bulletin* 68: 52–62.

G. M. S. and D. F. Parmalee. "On Certain Charadriiform Birds of Baffin Island." *Wilson Bulletin* 68: 210–23.

1957

G. M. S. and D. F. Parmalee. "The Purple Sandpiper in Southern Baffin Island." *Condor* 57: 216–20.

1958

"About the Color Plates." Pp. xv–xix in *Georgia Birds*, by T. D. Burleigh. Norman: University of Oklahoma Press.

"Lesser Swallow-tailed or Cayenne Swift." *Auk* 75: 121 [black-and-white plate].

Review of *The Warblers of North America*, by L. Griscom, A. Sprunt, et al. *Auk* 75: 226–27.

1959

"Birds." Pp. 25–26 in *Guide to Roman Nose State Park*, ed. R. D. Fay. Guidebook 9. Norman: Oklahoma Geological Survey.

"The Nesting Fringillids of the Edwin S. George Reserve, Southeastern Michigan (Part I)." *Jack-Pine Warbler* 37: 2–11.

"The Nesting Fringillids of the Edwin S. George Reserve, Southeastern Michigan (Part II)." *Jack-Pine Warbler* 37: 37–50.

"The Nesting Fringillids of the Edwin S. George Reserve, Southeastern Michigan (Part III)." *Jack-Pine Warbler* 37: 77–101.

"The Nesting Fringillids of the Edwin S. George Reserve, Southeastern Michigan (Part IV)." *Jack-Pine Warbler* 37: 127–51.

1960

"Semipalmated Sandpiper and Western Sandpiper in Tamaulipas." *Auk* 77: 83.

"The Nesting Fringillids of the Edwin S. George Reserve, Southeastern Michigan (Part V)." *Jack-Pine Warbler* 38: 2–15.

"The Nesting Fringillids of the Edwin S. George Reserve, Southeastern Michigan (Part VI)." *Jack-Pine Warbler* 38: 46–65.

"The Nesting Fringillids of the Edwin S. George Reserve, Southeastern Michigan, (Part VII)." *Jack-Pine Warbler* 38: 124–39.

Review of *Birds of Anaktuvuk Pass, Kobuk, and Old Crow; a study in Arctic adaptation*, by Laurence Irving. *Science* 132: 802-803.

Review of *Ecology of the Peregrine and Gyrfalcon populations in Alaska*, by Tom J. Cade, editor, *University of California Publications in Zoology* 63(3): 151-290. In *Science* 132: 1832-33.

"Flammulated Owl in Lubbock County, Texas." *Southwestern Naturalist* 5: 173–74.

1961

Iceland Summer: Adventures of a Bird Painter. Norman: University of Oklahoma Press.

"Big Bend country." Pp. 92–100 in *The American Year*, ed. H. H. Collins, Jr. New York: G. P. Putnam's Sons [reprinted from *Birds in the Wilderness*, 1936].

"Caught in a Dust Storm." Pp. 257–68 in *Discovery: Great Moments in the Lives of Outstanding Naturalists*, ed. J. K. Terres. Philadelphia: J. B. Lippincott Company.

"Hudsonian Whimbrel," in entry "Scolopacidae" (75-78). In D. A. Bannerman, *The Birds of the British Isles, Volume 9* Oliver and Boyd, Edinburgh, Scotland.

"Eskimo Curlew," in entry "Scolopacidae" (82-89). In D. A. Bannerman, *The Birds of the British Isles, Volume 9*, Edinburgh, Scotland: Oliver and Boyd.

"Upland Plover," in entry "Scolopacidae" (90-96). In D. A. Bannerman, *The Birds of the British Isles, Volume 9*, Oliver and Boyd, Edinburgh, Scotland.

"American Stint or Least Sandpiper," in entry "Scolopacidae" (272-79). In D. A. Bannerman, *The Birds of the British Isles, Volume 9*, Edinburgh, Scotland: Oliver and Boyd.

"Semipalmated Sandpiper," in entry "Scolopacidae" (295-302). In D. A. Bannerman, *The Birds of the British Isles, Volume 9*, Edinburgh, Scotland: Oliver and Boyd.

"Pectoral Sandpiper," in entry "Scolopacidae" (304-11). In D. A. Bannerman, *The Birds of the British Isles, Volume 9*, Edinburgh, Scotland: Oliver and Boyd.

"Baird's Sandpiper," in entry "Scolopacidae" (315-20). In D. A. Bannerman, *The Birds of the British Isles, Volume 9*, Edinburgh, Scotland: Oliver and Boyd.

"Bonaparte's Sandpiper," in entry "Scolopacidae" (322-26). In D. A. Bannerman, *The Birds of the British Isles, Volume 9*, Edinburgh, Scotland: Oliver and Boyd.

"Stilt Sandpiper," in entry "Scolopacidae" (341-46). In D. A. Bannerman, *The Birds of the British Isles, Volume 9*, Edinburgh, Scotland: Oliver and Boyd.

"Spotted Sandpiper," in entry "Scolopacidae" (24-34). In D. A. Bannerman, *The Birds of the British Isles, Volume 9*, Edinburgh, Scotland: Oliver and Boyd.

"Solitary Sandpiper," in entry "Scolopacidae" (76-84). In D. A. Bannerman, *The Birds of the British Isles, Volume 9*, Edinburgh, Scotland: Oliver and Boyd.

"Semipalmated Plover," in entry "Charadriidae" (163-67). In D. A. Bannerman, *The Birds of the British Isles, Volume 10*, Edinburgh, Scotland: Oliver and Boyd.

Review of *Sea Birds* by Charles Vaucher, translated from the French by James Hogarth. London: Oliver and Boyd. *Science* 133: 1348-49.

"A Painting of Yarrow's Spiny Lizard." *Southwestern Naturalist* 6: 1 [color frontispiece].

1962

"Sabine's Gull," in entry "Laridae" (202-219). In D. A. Bannerman, *The Birds of the British Isles, Volume 11*, Edinburgh, Scotland: Oliver and Boyd.

"Is Bird-Art Art?" *Living Bird* 1: 73–78.

1963

"Birds of Beavers Bend State Park." Pp. 35–37 in *Guide to Beavers Bend State Park*. Guidebook 11. Norman: Oklahoma Geological Survey.

"Interbreeding in the Wild of the Bob-White (*Colinus virginianus*) and Scaled Quail (*Callipepla squamata*) in Stonewall County, Northwestern Texas." *Southwestern Naturalist* 8: 108–11.

"Alexander Wilson's '*Anas valisineria*.' *Wilson Bulletin* 75: 5 [color frontispiece].

"On the Yellow-billed Loon." *Wilson Bulletin* 75: 83–87.

1964

Ecological Checklist of the Birds of Oklahoma. Norman: Stovall Museum of Science and History.

"The Vireos." Pp. 245–53 in A. Wetmore et al., *Song and Garden Birds of North America*. Washington, D.C.: National Geographic Society.

"On Plumages of the Young Lesser Prairie Chicken." *Southwestern Naturalist* 9: 1–5.

1965

"The Black Mesa Country of Oklahoma." Pp. 291–303 in *The Bird Watcher's America*, ed. O. S. Pettingill, Jr. New York: McGraw-Hill Book Company.

"Dust Storm." Pp. 356–64 in *Our Natural World*, ed. H. Borland. Garden City, N.Y.: Doubleday [reprinted from *Discovery: Great Moments in the Lives of Outstanding Naturalists*, 1961].

"Plump Upland Game Birds: Grouse, Ptarmigan, and Prairie Chickens." Pp. 264–77 in A. Wetmore et al., *Water, Prey, and Game Birds of North America*. Washington, D.C.: National Geographic Society.

G. M. S. and G. W. Dickson. "Interbreeding of the Eastern and Western Meadowlarks in Central Oklahoma." *Southwestern Naturalist* 10: 307–10.

1967

Oklahoma Birds: Their Ecology and Distribution, With Comments on the Avifauna of the Southern Great Plains. Norman: University of Oklahoma Press.
"Behavior of the Buff-breasted Sandpiper at the Nest." *Arctic* 20: 2–7.
"Footprint Thieves." *Audubon* 69: 53–57.
Review of *Birds of the Northern Forest*, by J. F. Lansdowne. *Wilson Bulletin* 79: 249–50.

1968

"Young Curve-billed Thrasher Attended by Adult Brown Towhee." *Auk* 85: 127–28.
"The Natal Plumage of the Lesser Prairie Chicken." *Auk* 85: 679.
"Oriole Hybridization in Oklahoma." *Bulletin of the Oklahoma Ornithological Society* 1: 1–7.
"Curve-billed Thrasher in Jackson County, Southwestern Oklahoma." *Bulletin of the Oklahoma Ornithological Society* 1: 19.
"Williamson's Sapsucker in Oklahoma." *Bulletin of the Oklahoma Ornithological Society* 1: 25–26.
"White-rumped Sandpiper [chick]." *Wilson Bulletin* 80: [color plate facing p. 5].
"Sexual Dimorphism in the Hudsonian Godwit." *Wilson Bulletin* 80: 251–52.

1969

"Introduction." Pp. xv–xix in H. L. Stoddard, Sr., *Memoirs of a Naturalist.* Norman: University of Oklahoma Press.
"Harlan's Hawk in Roger Mills County, Oklahoma." *Bulletin of the Oklahoma Ornithological Society* 2: 4.
"A Chuck-will's-widow in Postnuptial Molt." *Bulletin of the Oklahoma Ornithological Society* 2: 9–11.
"Knot in Cimarron County, Oklahoma." *Bulletin of the Oklahoma Ornithological Society* 2: 22.
"The Red Phalarope in Oklahoma." *Bulletin of the Oklahoma Ornithological Society* 2: 26–28.

1970

"Good Day at Black Mesa." *Audubon* 72: 58–67.
"Jenny Lind's Island." *Audubon* 72: 14–35.
"Jaeger Re-identified." *Audubon Field Notes* 24: 653.
"Early Spring and Late Fall Oklahoma Records for the Cassin's Kingbird." *Bulletin of the Oklahoma Ornithological Society* 3: 7–8.
"An Adventure with a Turkey Vulture." *Read* 19, no. 18: 16-21.

1971

High Arctic. New York: Paul S. Eriksson, Inc.

Review of *Birds of the Eastern Forest,* by J. A. Livingston with paintings by James Fenwick Lansdowne. *Auk* 88: 444–45.

"Western Tanager in Cimarron County, Oklahoma, in August." *Bulletin of the Oklahoma Ornithological Society* 4: 8.

"The Black-throated Blue Warbler in the Southwestern United States." *Bulletin of the Oklahoma Ornithological Society* 4: 11–15.

"Fourth Specimen of Sharp-tailed Sparrow from Oklahoma." *Bulletin of the Oklahoma Ornithological Society* 4: 20.

"A New Bird for Oklahoma: Mottled Duck." *Bulletin of the Oklahoma Ornithological Society* 4: 29–31.

"Information Wanted." *Wilson Bulletin* 83: 318.

1972

At a Bend in a Mexican River. New York: Paul S. Eriksson.

"Along Haustec Trails." *Audubon* 74: 68–79 [Title should be "Huastec"; see Sutton letter to Grossman, September 10, 1974, Western History Collection, University of Oklahoma.].

"Tree Swallow in Cimarron County, Oklahoma." *Bulletin of the Oklahoma Ornithological Society* 5: 22.

"Did S. W. Woodhouse Ever See the Black–throated Blue Warbler in Indian Territory?" *Bulletin of the Oklahoma Ornithological Society* 5: 23–24.

"Winter Food of a Central Oklahoma Roadrunner." *Bulletin of the Oklahoma Ornithological Society* 5: 30.

G. M. S. and R. G. Lawrence. "Verdin Collected in Jackson County, Oklahoma." *Bulletin of the Oklahoma Ornithological Society* 5: 32–33.

1973

[Hugh Colman Land, obituary]. *Auk* 90: 964–67.

"Early Nesting of the Cardinal in Central Oklahoma." *Bulletin of the Oklahoma Ornithological Society* 6: 8.

"Mockingbird Eats Flowers." *Bulletin of the Oklahoma Ornithological Society* 6: 16.

"The Belem Tower." *ZooSounds* (Oklahoma Zoological Society) 9, no. 1: 6–7.

"In Defense of Predators." *ZooSounds* (Oklahoma Zoological Society) 9, no. 2: 1.

1974

A Check-List of Oklahoma Birds. Norman: Stovall Museum of Science and History, University of Oklahoma.

"Fuertes Remembered." *Audubon* 76 (November): 58–67.

"An Irruption of Clark's Nutcracker in Oklahoma." *Bulletin of the Oklahoma Ornithological Society* 7: 1–4.

"May an Adult Canyon Wren Become Flightless during Late Summer Molt?" *Bulletin of the Oklahoma Ornithological Society* 7: 15.

"Did This Great Blue Heron Die of Starvation?" *Bulletin of the Oklahoma Ornithological Society* 7: 60–61.

"True to Life." *International Wildlife* 4 (July): 16.

1975

Portraits of Mexican Birds: Fifty Selected Paintings. Norman: University of Oklahoma Press.

"The Footprint Thieves." Pp. 130–34 in *The Pleasure of Birds*, ed. Les Line. Philadelphia: J. B. Lippincott Company [reprinted from *Audubon*, 1967].

"When Does the female Cardinal Start Singing in Spring?" *Bulletin of the Oklahoma Ornithological Society* 8: 7–8.

"Which Subspecies of Vermilion Flycatcher Inhabits Oklahoma?" *Bulletin of the Oklahoma Ornithological Society* 8: 19.

"A Junco Is a Junco Is a Junco." *Nebraska Bird Review* 43: 67–68.

"A Word about the Rancho del Cielo." *ZooSounds* (Oklahoma Zoological Society) 11, no. 5: 6.

1976

"Artist's Preface." Pp. xi–xiii in J. Van Tyne and A. J. Berger, *Fundamentals of Ornithology*. New York: John Wiley & Sons.

"Mexican Masterpieces of George Miksch Sutton: Excerpts from *Portraits of Mexican Birds*." *Audubon* 78: 36–49.

"Pauraque Experiment." *Audubon* 78: 44–45.

"On the Feeding Behavior of the Red Crossbill." *Bulletin of the Oklahoma Ornithological Society* 9: 3–6.

"Cleveland and Oklahoma County Records for the Rock Wren." *Bulletin of the Oklahoma Ornithological Society* 9: 23–24.

"Once More the Amazon." *ZooSounds* (Oklahoma Zoological Society) 12, no. 4: 6–7.

1977

Fifty Common Birds of Oklahoma and the Southern Great Plains. Norman: University of Oklahoma Press.

"Introduction." Pp. 7–8 in T. M. Shortt, *Wild Birds of the Americas*. Boston: Houghton Mifflin Company.

"On Correct Identification." *Bulletin of the Oklahoma Ornithological Society* 10: 28–29.

"How Often Does the Brown Creeper Sing in Oklahoma?" *Bulletin of the Oklahoma Ornithological Society* 10: 33–34.

"The Lesser Prairie Chicken's Inflatable Neck Sacs." *Wilson Bulletin* 89: 521–22.

"A Very Special Bird, the Roadrunner." *ZooSounds* (Oklahoma Zoological Society) 13, no. 3: 4–5.

1978

"Work to Be Done in the Black Mesa Country." *Bulletin of the Oklahoma Ornithological Society* 11: 11–13.

"Wood Duck Nesting in Norman, Oklahoma." *Bulletin of the Oklahoma Ornithological Society* 11: 13–14.

"Ash-throated Flycatcher and Loggerhead Shrike Nesting in Same Tree."
Bulletin of the Oklahoma Ornithological Society 11: 22–23.
"Early Fall Sighting of Townsend's Solitaire." *Bulletin of the Oklahoma
Ornithological Society* 11: 24.
"On Maturation of Thayer's Gull." *Wilson Bulletin* 90: 479–91.

1979

*To a Young Bird Artist: Letters from Louis Agassiz Fuertes to George Miksch
Sutton.* Norman: University of Oklahoma Press.
"On Abrasion of Plumage in the Starling." *Bulletin of the Oklahoma
Ornithological Society* 12: 15.
"Is the American Kestrel Two-Brooded in Oklahoma?" *Bulletin of the
Oklahoma Ornithological Society* 12: 30–31.
"Three Pine Grosbeaks." *Living Bird* 17: 5–6 [color plate].
"A Word about Swainson's Hawk." *ZooSounds* (Oklahoma Zoological
Society) 15 no. 5: 8–9.
G. M. S. and J. D. Tyler. "On the Behavior of American Kestrels Nesting in
Town." *Bulletin of the Oklahoma Ornithological Society* 12: 25–29.

1980

Bird Student. Austin: University of Texas Press.
"Subspecies of Savannah Sparrow Found in Oklahoma." *Bulletin of the
Oklahoma Ornithological Society* 13: 6–8.

1981

"Foreword." Pp. 13–16 in A. Small, *Masters of Decorative Bird Carving.*
Tulsa, Okla.: Winchester Press.
"Do Screech Owls Prey on Bobwhites?" *Bulletin of the Oklahoma
Ornithological Society* 14: 32–33.
"On Aerial and Ground Displays of the World's Snipes." *Wilson Bulletin* 98:
457–77.

1982

J. G. Newell and G. M. S. "The Olivaceous Cormorant in Oklahoma." *Bulletin
of the Oklahoma Ornithological Society* 15: 1–5.
"Pine Warbler in Cleveland County, Oklahoma." *Bulletin of the Oklahoma
Ornithological Society* 15: 32–33.
"Portrait of a Young Cuckoo." *Living Bird Quarterly* 1, no. 1: 16–17.

1983

"On Correct Identification." *American Birds* 37: 230 [reprinted from *Bulletin
of the Oklahoma Ornithological Society* 10 (1977): 28–29].
"A Big Owl Watches the Hand That Portrays It." *Living Bird Quarterly* 2, no.
1: 14–15.

1984

"The Red-bellied Woodpeckers Fail Again." *Bulletin of the Oklahoma Ornithological Society* 17: 1–3.
"Early Nesting of Blue Jay in Oklahoma." *Bulletin of the Oklahoma Ornithological Society* 17: 8.
"Common Grackle Nest in Tree Cavity." *Bulletin of the Oklahoma Ornithological Society* 17: 15–16.
"Singing of Female Northern Cardinal in Winter." *Bulletin of the Oklahoma Ornithological Society* 17: 33.

1985

". . . Forever and Ever, Amen." *Audubon* 87:86–87.
"European Starlings Lining Nest or Roosting Quarters in Fall." *Bulletin of the Oklahoma Ornithological Society* 18: 7–8.
"Eastern Screech-Owl Eats Red Bat." *Bulletin of the Oklahoma Ornithological Society* 18: 22–23.

1986

"Foreword." P. x in Tulsa Audubon Society, *A Guide to Birding in Oklahoma.* Tulsa: Tulsa Audubon Society.
Birds Worth Watching. Norman: University of Oklahoma Press.
"Nests of Western Kingbirds in Pines." *Bulletin of the Oklahoma Ornithological Society* 19: 5–6.
"Dichromatism of the Screech Owl in Central Oklahoma." *Bulletin of the Oklahoma Ornithological Society* 19: 17–20.

1988

"Some Critical Comments about Audubon's Artwork." *Bulletin of the Oklahoma Ornithological Society* 21: 17–18.

1990

"A Big Owl Watches the Hand that Portrays Her." *Bulletin of the Oklahoma Ornithological Society* 23:1-3 [reprinted from *Living Bird Quarterly*, 1983, 2(1): 14-15].

1992

"On Drawing Birds from Life." *Sooner Magazine* 12, new series 3: 8–12.

Works Illustrated by
George Miksch Sutton

The following books and monographs written by other authors are illustrated
entirely or in part by George Miksch Sutton; his contributions are indicated in
parentheses and, though small in some cases, reflect the breadth of his work. In
addition to these, Sutton provided many color plates and black-and-white illustrations for ornithological journals, museum publications, and exhibition cata-
logs. He was generous in allowing his work to be used to further ornithology.

Allen, A. A. *American Bird Biographies*. Ithaca, N.Y.: Comstock Publishing
    Company, 1934. (10 color plates, 10 wash drawings)
———. *The Golden Plover and Other Birds*. Ithaca, N.Y.: Comstock
    Publishing Company, 1939. (7 color plates)
Anonymous. *World Book Encyclopedia*. Chicago, Ill.: World Book, 1941 (sec-
    tion on Birds)
Bailey, H. H. *The Birds of Florida*. Baltimore, Md.: Williams & Wilkins
    Company, 1925. (76 color plates figuring 480+ birds)
Brand, A. R. *More Songs of Wild Birds*. New York: Thomas Nelson and Sons,
    1936. (pen-and-ink drawings from Sutton's *An Introduction to the Birds of
    Pennsylvania* in the book and on phonograph records)
Brandt, H. *Arizona and Its Bird Life*. Cleveland, Ohio: Bird Research
    Foundation, 1951. (2 color plates, 13 pen-and-ink drawings)
Buckelew, A. R., Jr., and G. A. Hall. *The West Virginia Breeding Bird Atlas*.
    Pittsburgh: University of Pittsburgh Press, 1994. (130 pen-and-ink draw-
    ings from Sutton's *An Introduction to the Birds of Pennsylvania*)
Burgess, T. W. *The Burgess Seashore Book for Children*. Boston: Little, Brown,
    and Company, 1929. (4 color plates)
Burt, W. H. *The Resident Birds of Southern Michigan*. Bulletin no. 7.
    Bloomfield Hills, Mich.: Cranbrook Institute of Science, 1936. (23 pen-and-
    ink drawings)
Caire, W., J. D. Tyler, B. P. Glass, and M. A. Mares. 1989. *Mammals of
    Oklahoma*. Norman: University of Oklahoma Press. (1 black-and-white
    plate of a color painting)
de Schauensee, R. M. *The Birds of Colombia*. Wynnewood, Pa.: Livingston
    Publishing Company, 1964. (85 pen-and-ink drawings)
———. *A Guide to the Birds of South America*. Wynnewood, Pa.: Livingston
    Publishing Company, 1970. (22 pen-and-ink sketches, all but one from de
    Schauensee 1964)
Delacour, J., and D. Amadon. *Curassows and Related Birds*. New York:
    American Museum of Natural History, 1973. (4 color plates)
DuPuy, W. A. *Our Bird Friends and Foes*. Philadelphia, Pa.: John C. Winston
    Company, 1925. (1 color plate; 48 pen-and-ink drawings)

Gresham, P. E. *With Wings as Eagles.* Winter Park, Fla.: Anna Publishing, 1980. (dust jacket painting in color)

Hall, George A. *West Virginia Birds: Distribution and Ecology.* Special Publication no. 7. Pittsburgh: Carnegie Museum of Natural History, 1983. (1 color plate, 16 line drawings from Todd 1940).

Hewitt, O. H. *The Wild Turkey and Its Management.* Washington, D.C.: Wildlife Society, 1967. (1 color plate)

Holloway, J. E. *Dictionary of Birds of the United States.* Portland, Ore.: Timber Press, 2003. (23 pen-and-ink drawings, 1 watercolor reproduced in black-and-white, dust jacket watercolor in color)

James Ford Bell Museum of Natural History. *Wildlife Art in America.* Minneapolis: James Ford Bell Museum of Natural History, University of Minnesota, 1994. (1 color plate)

Johnsgard, P. A. *Baby Bird Portraits by George Miksch Sutton.* Norman: University of Oklahoma Press, 1998. (34 color plates)

Norelli, M. R. *Naturally Drawn.* Wausau, Wis.: Leigh Yawkey Woodson Art Museum, 1992. (1 color plate)

Oberholser, H. C. *The Bird Life of Louisiana.* Bulletin no. 28. Baton Rouge: Louisiana Department of Conservation, 1938. (color frontispiece of Ivory-billed Woodpecker)

Pettingill, O. S., Jr. *A Guide to Bird Finding East of the Mississippi.* New York: Oxford University Press, 1951. (73 pen-and-ink drawings)

————. *A Guide to Bird Finding East of the Mississippi.* 2nd ed. New York: Oxford University Press, 1977. (80 pen-and-ink drawings, including 4 created for this edition, and 3 new to this edition from Van Tyne and Berger 1976)

————. *A Guide to Bird Finding West of the Mississippi.* New York: Oxford University Press, 1953. (34 pen-and-ink drawings)

Pettingill, O. S., Jr., and N. R. Whitney, Jr. *Birds of the Black Hills.* Special Publication no. 1. Ithaca, N.Y.: Cornell Laboratory of Ornithology, 1965. (6 pen-and-ink drawings)

Phillips, A., J. Marshall, and G. Monson. *The Birds of Arizona.* Tucson: University of Arizona Press, 1964. (12 color plates)

Pitelka, F. A. "Speciation and Ecologic Distribution in American Jays of the Genus *Aphelocoma.*" *University of California Publications in Zoology* 50, no. 3 (1951): 195–464. (1 color plate)

Roberts, T. S. *The Birds of Minnesota.* Minneapolis: University of Minnesota Press, 1932. (4 color plates)

————. *Bird Portraits in Color.* Minneapolis: University of Minnesota Press, 1934. (4 color plates from Roberts 1932)

Tanner, J. T. *The Ivory-billed Woodpecker.* Research Report no. 1. New York: National Audubon Society, 1942. (color frontispiece same as Oberholser 1938)

Todd, W. E. C. *Birds of Western Pennsylvania.* Pittsburgh: University of Pittsburgh Press, 1940. (117 color plates, 60 pen-and-ink drawings)

————. *Birds of the Labrador Peninsula and Adjacent Areas.* Toronto: University of Toronto Press, 1963. (9 color plates)

Todd, W. E. C., and M. A. Carriker, Jr. *The Birds of the Santa Marta Region of Colombia: A Study in Altitudinal Distribution.* Annals of the Carnegie Museum 14. 1922. 611 pp. (7 color plates)

Vale, R. B. *Wings, Fur and Shot: A Grass-Roots Guide to American Hunting.* Harrisburg, Pa.: Stackpole Sons, 1936. (1 color plate, 33 pen-and-ink drawings)

———. *How to Hunt American Game.* Harrisburg, Pa.: Military Service Publishing Company, 1946. (reprint of Vale 1936 with new title)

———. *How to Hunt American Game.* 5th printing. Harrisburg, Pa.: Stackpole Company, 1954. (reprint of Vale 1936; Sutton cottontail revised)

Van Tyne, J., and A. J. Berger. *Fundamentals of Ornithology.* New York: John Wiley & Sons, 1959; 2nd ed. 1976. (168 pen-and-ink sketches; second edition includes an "artist's preface")

Wallace, G. J., W. P. Nickell, and R. F. Bernard. *Bird Mortality in the Dutch Elm Disease Program in Michigan.* Bulletin no. 41. Bloomfield Hills, Mich.: Cranbrook Institute of Science, 1961. (pen-and-ink drawing of American Robin, cover)

Webb, R. G. *Reptiles of Oklahoma.* Norman: University of Oklahoma Press, 1970. (1 color plate)

Index

This index is primarily to people, places, institutions, events, organizations, journals, and major topics covered in this book. References to birds are placed under the entry "Birds" in systematic order and using (where applicable) the American Ornithologists' Union standardized common names as given in *The A.O.U. Checklist of North American Birds* (Seventh Edition. 1998. Washington, D.C.: American Ornithologists' Union). Mammal and reptile species mentioned are listed alphabetically by common name under the headings "Mammals" and "Reptiles." Most geographic locations, colleges and universities, military bases, museums, and state-wide organizations within the United States are listed alphabetically under entries for each state. Islands on which Sutton worked are listed alphabetically under the entry "Islands." George's honors and awards are listed alphabetically under the entry "Honors." Examples of George's philanthropy are indexed alphabetically under "Philanthropist."

ABBREVIATIONS

CU   Cornell University
KU   University of Kansas
OKC   Oklahoma City
OU   University of Oklahoma
UM   University of Michigan

References to illustrations are set in italic type.

Accident, fire at Stovall Museum, 121–22
Accipiter striatus suttoni (Sharp-shinned Hawk named for Sutton), 80
Alaska, Ladd Field (near Fairbanks, Alaska), 94
Alexander, Charles P., 63
Allen, Arthur A., 53, 66–87, 110, 127
Amadon, Dean, 122
Amazon, 126
American Museum of Natural History, 92, 122
American Ornithologists' Union (AOU): 33, 38, 40, 52, 54, 59, 69, 72, 79, 83, 95–96, 97, 103, 127; George's frustration with, 127–28
Anderson, Eloise, 29, 39, 40–43, 44, 67

Anderson, Mrs. Hartley, 42, 43
Anderson, Ruthanna, 41
Anthony, Chris, 128–29, 140
Anthony, Guy, 140
Arbib, Robert, 26
Art, Sutton comments on: abstract, 158–59; fine, 158 60, illustration, 158–60, 165
Artistic goals, 34
Atlantic Monthly (magazine), 57
Audubon, John James, 52, 85, 140, 152, 159, 160
Audubon Magazine/Audubon, 35, 37, 92, 122, 151, 171, 173
Audubon Screen Tours, 85, 103, 105, 148
Audubon Society of Western Pennsylvania, 28, 31